Immigrant Teachers, American Students

Immigrant Teachers, American Students

Cultural Differences, Cultural Disconnections

Namulundah Florence

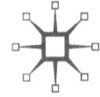

IMMIGRANT TEACHERS, AMERICAN STUDENTS
Copyright © Namulundah Florence, 2011.
Softcover reprint of the hardcover 1st edition 2011 978-0-230-11049-6
All rights reserved.

First published in 2011 by
PALGRAVE MACMILLAN®
in the United States—a division of St. Martin's Press LLC,
175 Fifth Avenue, New York, NY 10010.

Where this book is distributed in the UK, Europe and the rest of the world, this is by Palgrave Macmillan, a division of Macmillan Publishers Limited, registered in England, company number 785998, of Houndmills, Basingstoke, Hampshire RG21 6XS.

Palgrave Macmillan is the global academic imprint of the above companies and has companies and representatives throughout the world.

Palgrave® and Macmillan® are registered trademarks in the United States, the United Kingdom, Europe and other countries.

ISBN 978–1-349-29293-6   ISBN 978-0-230-11630-6 (eBook)
DOI 10.1057/9780230116306

Library of Congress Cataloging-in-Publication Data

Florence, Namulundah, 1958–
    Immigrant teachers, American students : cultural differences, cultural disconnections / Namulundah Florence.
       p. cm.
    Includes bibliographical references.
     1. Multicultural education. 2. Cultural pluralism. 3. Teacher-student relationships. 4. Behavioral assessment. I. Title.

LC1099.F56 2010
371.10086′912—dc22   2010025513

A catalogue record of the book is available from the British Library.

Design by Newgen Imaging Systems (P) Ltd., Chennai, India.

First edition: January 2011

10 9 8 7 6 5 4 3 2 1

To my parents,
Benjamin George Masinde Lyambila (d. 2004)
and Victoria Namaemba Muhindi Lyambila (d. 2007),
to whom I owe much of my cultural capital

Contents

Preface		ix
Chapter 1	Endemic Racial Hierarchy	1
Chapter 2	Comparative Overview of African and U.S. Society	15
Chapter 3	Academic Excellence	75
Chapter 4	Respect	103
Chapter 5	Resources and Relationships	121
Chapter 6	A Window of Time	149
Epilogue		167
Notes		181
References		183
Index		195

Preface

My K–12 teaching experience and ongoing college involvement demonstrate how cultural differences impact classroom interactions. Because of my Kenyan educational background, my classroom expectations appear extremely alien and overly demanding—penalties for missed deadlines, discouraging makeup work, no extra credit, frequently administered in-class writing activities, as well as eliminating bonus points and incompletes. I have felt judged and labeled as the Other, the resident alien because of my expectations. But what constitutes academic accountability? Which is the better approach: set standards based on uniform assessments within a specified duration, which is characteristic of African schools, or take a more flexible approach to educational assessment? The decentralized U.S. system may avoid undesirable uniformity, but this leads to inconsistent policies within and across states (Ravitch, 1995; Ravitch and Viterriti, 2001). While textbooks are relatively uniform with standardized texts for evaluation, students' academic exposure varies across schools and across academic tracks. Consider the proposed K–12 curriculum changes in the state of Arizona to avoid separatist ethnic studies, and in the state of Texas to combat unpatriotic materials. Interactions with colleagues show similar concerns over effective teaching strategies. Indeed, some American colleagues, Black and White, experience comparable challenges regarding students' accountability, respect, and perceptions of intellectual rigor. Phrases like, "It wasn't like this in my school (country)," from immigrant teachers may reflect nostalgic appeals to a bucolic past. Observing schools in the Bronx, Brooklyn, and Manhattan showed differences in classroom etiquette. Teachers' expectations vary and so does the commitment of students to learning. Meanwhuile, national debates on academic achievement focus on the performance of minority students—Black and Latino and some immigrant groups. With increased migrations across the globe, the social history forged from *Immigrant Teachers, American Students: Cultural*

Differences, Cultural Disconnections demonstrates the challenges of foreign-trained teachers to identify strategies for cultural navigation.

Immigrant Teachers, American Students: Cultural Differences, Cultural Disconnections draws upon my experience of teaching in an American urban high school. Ordinary choices and reactions to issues often seemed inappropriate and disconnected from students' expectations in classrooms. Baruti, in response to the questionnaire on differences between the homeland and American norms, captures this ambivalence in her relationship with students: "I am not as casual and friendly with my students the way other faculty members are with their students. There are a few students with whom I engage casually. This could be due to a cultural divide." As to how she deals with this predicament, Baruti admits, "This is difficult.... I try to be friendly but sometimes I don't think it is received as friendliness, maybe more as strangeness." Anecdotes from some African immigrant instructors culled through snowball sampling (referrals from previous questionnaire respondents) as well as existing literature on African instructors depict comparable cultural navigations (Amobi, 2004; DeVita and Armstrong, 1993; Obiakor and Afolayan, 2007; Obiakor and Grant, 2002). The pooled instructors' responses to an emailed questionnaire on perceptions of the United States' and the native country's educational systems raised comparable issues. Observations and interpretations of daily occurrences highlight personal standpoints and ongoing attempts at cultural synthesis (familiar and less familiar norms) as much as understanding the realities of students' lives. Watoya's (a questionnaire respondent) comments capture the cultural straddling inherent in teaching: "While I have a commitment to inculcating values of hard work and sharing knowledge, some students do not understand why they are in school. At college level, many students are not college material but are forced to get a college education. In such cases, a teacher is forced to walk a delicate line so as not to compromise educational standards and a student's future which supposedly is dependent on the diploma." Cultural navigations involve openness to varied conceptions of reality and social expectations even as they challenge personal views to opportunities for change. Students are referred to by their pseudonyms. For purposes of distinction, responses from African immigrant teachers are identified by ethnic names to illustrate the variety in African immigrant experience.

In fall 2005, I designed and taught a one-credit high school elective course, "Breakin' In Breakin' Out: A Cultural Challenge," that explored issues of representation and choice by drawing on mainstream newspaper accounts related to social identity, affiliation, and interaction. Class discussions highlighted the dynamism and heterogeneity of culture to counter conventional conceptions of culture as deterministic and static in debates on the academic achievement gap. In a cited exercise on cultural heroes, students focused on community/national figures to understand the impact of social structures as well as personal choice on perceptions of self, other, and society.

At one session early in the semester I went around the room asking what the students most admired about each of their classmates. After a moment of discomfort, students volunteered responses centered on physique, elegance, and a no-nonsense attitude, with an obvious reverence for those in twelfth grade. That astounded me, considering the school's location on a college campus. The high school shares space with a college; I expected that to raise educational aspirations. Ensuing discussions also helped me understand the students' aspirations; students' choices reflect prevailing socialization patterns and social priorities. Similar to their parents, students embrace group norms in speech and classroom behavior (Glazer, 2001; Harris, 1998; Holmes, 2001; Milner, 2004). Harris (1998), however, focuses on environmental factors: "Parents rear their children the way their friends and neighbors are doing it, not the way their parents did it" (p. 207). The focus on maintaining youthful bodies "through diet, exercise, regular health care, and plastic surgery" among adults shapes children's values (Milner, 2004, p. 165). I never expected twelfth grade to be an exceptional achievement in a developed country like the United States; however, these students did. In later sessions, I discovered that most of the students in the class were the first in their families to get that far in their education.

Situated on a college campus, the urban high school at which I taught elective courses seeks to develop students' respect for each other and their communities, raise academic aspirations, and to provide a strong academic foundation for their transition from high school to college. The school has 565 students in two locations. About 252 are at the eleventh- to twelfth-grade location on a college site. Close to 37 percent of students at the high school qualify for the subsidized lunch program. The high school graduated about 120 students in 2006. Although more than 10 percent qualify for entrance to the accompanying college, the rest choose to go elsewhere.

At the high school, teachers and administrators extend themselves to accommodate students' needs. The atmosphere in the main office is typically relaxed and welcoming to students and faculty alike. Student traffic in the main office is heavy, particularly during class breaks; students socialize among themselves and interact with teachers on a range of issues, not all of which relate to school matters. Every once in a while, I saw a student's head slumped on one of the desks in the main office. The school has since erected a wooden partition with a latched half-door separating the reception area from the administrative staff. A student, who might be ill, could be waiting for a parent or caregiver. Others appeared intent on some undecipherable errand, while some stopped by to pick up lunch from the Styrofoam lunch container that city officials drop off daily. Security guards stationed outside the main office at the entrance of the college building usher the high school students to their respective classes when crowds linger too long or gather at the college entrance. The animated exchanges among high school students separate them from college students, who are more subdued or focused on their destinations. These observations, coupled with personal reflections on daily challenges as a foreign-trained teacher, are the basis of *Immigrant Teachers, American Students: Cultural Differences, Cultural Disconnections.*

CHAPTER 1

Endemic Racial Hierarchy

Various scholars acknowledge the implications of blackness in a world of White privilege (Delpit, 1988, 1995; Kozol, 1991, 1995; McCarthy, 1990; Nieto, 2004; Obiakor and Afolayan, 2007; Obiakor and Gordon, 2003; Obiakor and Grant, 2002; Ogbu, 1992; Tatum, 1997; Traore and Lukens, 2006). Achebe (2009), Appiah (1992), and Morrison (1993) highlight the inextricable link between cultural identities and a nation's literary tradition. Maintaining that authors of American fiction, regardless of race, position readers as White, Morrison notes how prevailing "knowledge" presumes a pervasive whiteness despite the African presence that goes back over 400 years in the United States. It is a phenomenon typical of colonial literature. This construction of whiteness hinges on a Black Other that "provides a way of contemplating chaos and civilization, desire and a mechanism for testing the problem and blessings of freedom" (Morrison, p. 7). Not unlike other former colonies, the United States too has "participated and contributed" to an "invented Africa." The "silence and evasion" of the significance of blackness in historical literary discourse ignores its depiction either as a backdrop to whiteness or as extreme other (Blaut, 1993; Morrison, 1993). Morrison cites Henry James' *What Maisie Knew*, Gertrude Stein's *Three Lives*, Willa Cather's *Sapphira and the Slave Girl*, Mark Twain's *Huckleberry Finn*, Saul Bellow's *Henderson the Rain King*, and Ernest Hemingway's *To Have and Have Not* to illustrate the significance of black characters in tales that center on Whites and whiteness. The slave mistress's character—chastity, diligence, disability, insecurity but also power, womanhood and motherhood cannot be divorced from issues of race. Concepts of whiteness and freedom in the new world are juxtaposed to "blackness *and* enslavement." Blackness embodies the otherness of an American identity. In American writers such as Mark Twain, Melville, Hawthorne:

> Africanism is the vehicle by which the American self knows itself as not enslaved, but free; not repulsive, but desirable; not helpless, but licensed and powerful; not history-less, but historical; not damned, but innocent; not a blind accident of evolution, but a progressive fulfillment of destiny. (Morrison, p. 52)

The denigration of blackness persists in the United States in the twenty-first century, as the incessant disparagement of its first Black president suggests. An anti-Obama rally in Washington, DC (mid-September 2009) featured placards that underscored the historic racial rhetoric. One had a picture of a lion with the caption, "The Zoo has an African lion and the White House has a lyin' African." Another read, "Bury Obamacare with Kennedy." Others read: "We came unarmed (this time)" and "'Cap' Congress and 'Trade' Obama back to Kenya!" Angry talk by the growing Tea Party movement to "take back our country" calls the question of entitlement and history. Who or what is American? The cultural rhetoric can verge on the absurd.

Colonial imperialism in African countries reinforced a similar racial hierarchy in its denigration and dehumanization of the African. Joseph Conrad's *Heart of Darkness* (1899) "portrays Africa as a place where the wandering European may discover the dark impulses and unspeakable appetites he has suppressed and forgotten through ages of civilization may spring back into life in Africa's environment of free and triumphant savagery" (cited in Achebe, pp. 115-6). Defined as and treated like the extreme other, locals internalized the subjugation. Schooled in British-modeled institutions, Achebe (2009) acknowledges the impact of literature on the social consciousness of Africans.

> I did not see myself as an African in those books. I took sides with the white men against the savages. In other words, I went through my first level of schooling thinking I was of the party of the white man in his hair-raising adventures and narrow escapes. The white man was good and reasonable and smart and courageous. The savages arrayed against him were sinister and stupid, never anything higher than cunning. I hated their guts. (Achebe, 2009, p. 118)

Despite the racial bias in books, Achebe (2009) who "never read children's books," acknowledges the need for extending the literary privilege to his children (p. 69). Going beyond realization of the literary gap to action,

Achebe wrote *Chike the River,* which, like bell hooks's *Happy to Be Nappy,* offers a more affirming imagery for Black children. Appiah (1992) is skeptical of such correctives to cultural traditions. While a literal tradition offers validation as a frame of reference, oral African tradition offers definitions that coalesce the complex relationships and counters prevailing cultural issues.

Although conventional standards of race, gender, or class presume cultural homogeneity, reality presents more nuanced categories; for instance, foreigners highlight different aspects of American culture. Mucha (1993) attributes the ignorance of world affairs among most United States citizens to ethnic arrogance: "Americans find themselves in an inferior position because neither history nor necessity has forced them to learn other languages" (Ramos 1993, p. 9). Americans view their culture as the norm and the United States as central to world events. Wafula, a questionnaire respondent, notes this dismissal of anything "un-American" among his students: "I was also amazed at their lack of basic knowledge of the outside world, let alone the intricacies of a working society. What I mean is that there is this attitude of knowing only what they (students) consider necessary to survive in their own environment." While Owolabi (1996) acknowledges the "comprehensiveness of the American education" system, he recognizes a need for "knowledge of other cultures, or even countries" (p. 75). Ramos raises a similar critique: the media report street-corner incidents, but will cover international events only if "directly related to the United States of America. Besides these, only natural disasters, revolutions, and air accidents are covered. The world is too far away" (p. 7).

According to the Eurocentric paradigm, "a human being is assumed to be at his best when *he* is *white, materially* accomplished, achieved through *competitive, independent assertiveness. She* who is *black, poor,* and *submissive* is by definition inferior, abnormal, and/or unintelligent according to this model" (Akbar, 1991, p. 723; cited in Traore and Lukens, 2006, p. 24; Owolabi, 1996). Audre Lorde (cited in Tatum, 1997) extends the mythical U.S. ideal to include thin, young, heterosexual, and Christian. In this racial hierarchy, the African immigrant epitomizes the ultimate other. Owolabi links the reception of immigrants and access to opportunities to the whiteness of one's skin in the United States. In contrast, Borjas (1999) attributes the mobility of second-generation immigrants to the ability and degree of assimilation. He also acknowledges the impact of labor conditions and the demand for social services by different immigrant groups:

> In sum, immigrants originating in developing countries will typically have less human capital for a number of reasons. Workers in developing

countries tend to have less education than their counterparts in the industrialized economies; the less-skilled in the developing countries sometimes have the greatest incentive to migrate to the United States; and human capital acquired in developing economies is harder to transfer to an industrialized setting. (Borjas, 1999, p. 50)

Minnich (2005) recognizes the impact of society's racial, gender, or class hierarchy whereby *"the dominant few defined themselves not merely as the inclusive kind of human but also as the norm and the ideal"* (p. 88, italics in original). Similar flaws are evident in stereotypes of a monolithic Africa and Africans as underdeveloped and living in prehistoric communities, respectively. Falling prey to comparable reductive generalizations, some African immigrants ennoble America with all that is lacking in the mother country—freedom of speech or material access and social mobility while others focus on its parochialism, consumerism, and interracial rhetoric. Ahmad, a questionnaire respondent, lauds the power of speech in the United States' democratic system relative to the system of Sudan, his country of origin. In Sudan, there is "[a]bsolute respect for the teacher from colleagues, students, and the public, but the system is very unjust. On the other hand, in the United States, teachers are always pushing (*sic*) the Union and the government to correct what is wrong and fix flaws either on promotions or employment opportunities." Similarly, Aminata, a questionnaire respondent, commends the respect for teachers in Sierra Leone and adds that United States' "students have too much to eat and to throw away." The cliché of America as the land of plenty ignores the homeless in city streets and shelters as well as the growing number of those living in poverty.

Despite portrayals of blackness as the extreme other from a mythical standard of whiteness, it encompasses a range of contrasts in color, beliefs, and behavior patterns (Appiah, 1992). In a telephone exchange before meeting his United States host, Owolabi (1996) described himself as being of light complexion based on familiar categories in Nigeria, unaware that blackness encompassed a range of skin tones (one-drop rule).[1] In the United States, one in 50 Americans identify themselves as multiracial (Roberts, 2010). Similarly, the association of criminal behavior, unwed teenage mothers, welfare recipients, or substance abusers with Blacks reinforces conventional stereotypes. Conventional stereotypes of Africans and the continent are no less redeeming. Frequent images of blackness, paganism, barbarity, and ignorance emerge in conversations and media portrayals. White and light-skinned or educated and elite Africans appear an aberration. Aarifa's, a questionnaire respondent, experience highlights the arbitrariness of cultural categories; she is treated better than her African-American colleagues because of her speech patterns as the elaborate response depicts:

> One cannot be deemed both Black and African, according to both Black and non-Black students, teachers, and parents—and being treated better than African-American teachers comprises most of my experience as an African immigrant teacher in the United States. Many of my African-American students told me I was not Black because I was from Africa, because I spoke differently than them, and/or because of my hair style or taste in music or clothes was different than theirs or their African-American teachers (many times this was a generational difference that the students conflated as a racial one). I would hold my arm next to my students' arms and show them how our skin color was the same, and then I would reiterate history. It was always a pivotal point when the students recognized that I was Black like them, and then we were able to begin to develop a rapport. For non-Black teachers, students, and parents, they interpreted my difference in diction (which was geographic, predominantly) as racially different, and also told me I was not "really" Black which made them treat me better than African-American teachers. Obviously, this preferential treatment created friction and distrust of me from African-American educators. For many non-Black immigrant students and parents, they saw me as different from African-Americans due to my teaching style, which generally mirrored non-American standards, and they trusted me more than African-American teachers and respected me almost as much as they respected white teachers. White and other non-Black teachers would complain to me about our Black students and defined behavior or performance issues regarding African-American students in racial terms, which disturbed me deeply. In all cases, I had to continually reiterate that I was Black and African, not Black in spite of being African.

There is a pattern to conventional images of what constitutes "American" by both locals as well as foreigners. Disregarding Native Americans and other minority groups, the presumption is that America is essentially made up of White people. Despite the cultural richness of North America's history, conventional portrayals of its people stress the European cultural heritage. Drechsel (1993) highlights the "sociocultural" attempts in the United States to be European; White Americans rarely admit to African elements in their ancestry despite evidence to the contrary, "throughout the South." The resistance reflects fears of (a White) racial dilution from growing ethnic plurality as well as increased migrations and intermarriages. Only recently have Whites been acknowledging African-American relatives as in the cases of the clandestine affair between Thomas Jefferson and Sally Hemings, and the siring by the late Senator Strom Thurmond of a Black daughter, Essie Mae Washington. In contrast, few stories emerge of "I once was Black but now I am White" from Blacks who pass for White.

Black African immigrants feel the brunt of being the extreme other; "It has never been exactly a rousing 'American dream' in the United States for anyone whose skin color is other than white" (Traore and Lukens, 2006, p. xxvii). Kofi's (a questionnaire respondent)students are dismissive of him as a foreigner: "Some make fun of me. Others said I didn't speak English. Few asked me if I was an immigrant. Others asked me to go back to my country. Others mimic (my accent)." Uwah (2002) experienced similar derision of his foreign accent. He expresses anger and shock at available rental spots miraculously pulled off the market when he and his friends showed up to view the premises. Baruti finds her students' receptivity exasperating: "Some students think I don't speak English albeit (*sic*) a language I use at home." She is aware of their skepticism, although students do not raise the issue of accents directly with her. hooks (1995) highlights the impact of the sensational imagery that reinforces "white supremacy...an ideology of difference that says white is always, and in every way, superior to that which is black" (1995, pp. 116-117). Children are socialized into this racial hierarchy (Bateson, 2000; hooks, 2000, 2003).

hooks clarifies that White supremacy does not only favor whiteness per se, as the issue of color-caste hierarchy in Black communities illustrates. Reflecting the historical privileging of house slaves with lighter skin versus darker-skinned and kinky-haired field slaves, some Blacks still prefer one to the other among kin. The norm for female beauty is still "light skin and long straight hair." Paradoxically, it is light-skinned biracial females and dark-skinned males who represent sexual appeal and (coercive) power, respectively. Huntington (2004) contrasts the 1960s slogan of "Black is Beautiful" with the 1990s switch to "Biracial (or multiracial) is Beautiful," reinforced by a 1993 *New York Times* special issue on America's new face. A 1996 Betty Crocker advertisement of a woman with "olive skin and dark hair" replaced the traditional blond model. In 1997, Tiger Woods' image of "Cablinasian" mix (Caucasian, Black, Indian, and Thai) summed up the racial change (p. 307). And yet, contrasting her African-American experience on the margins of White society, hooks (2000) recalls how Black students taunted the minority White students compelled to take the bus as smelly and dirty. She links the association of the underclass with disgrace to an episode in *South Park* in which a student asks the teacher why poor people smell. The teacher professes ignorance in this case. The cultural silence on poverty (we are all middle-class!) ignores its prevalence in developed countries such as the

United States with roughly 40 percent of its population living in poverty. Otherness functions as the alter ego, embodying all that is viewed as undesirable or objectionable in a public/ideal self (Achebe, 2009; Appiah, 1992; Morrison, 1993; Minnich, 2005; Owolabi, 1996). I have heard Blacks as well as students from other racial groups deride each other with the "nigger" label. Sometimes it is used in jest within similar racial groups. In these incidents, perceptions trump reality. Otherness connotes the undesirable in Whites as much as among Blacks. It is rare that the "nigger" word is used to laud an accomplished Black person. Wesonga, a questionnaire respondent, attributes student/teacher tensions to perceptual differences: "Students view things [through] [a] totally different lens and their interpretations are totally different. [He therefore] [c]reates sessions of dialogue [and uses] life examples/their own real life experiences," as a tool for addressing the misperceptions. *Immigrant Teachers, American Students: Cultural Differences, Cultural Disconnections* grapples with conceptions of difference and the impact on classroom interactions.

Who and where are immigrants in the United States? Based on a monthly sample survey of approximately 60, 000 households by the Bureau of Labor Statistics (2010), foreign-born workers include "legally-admitted immigrants, refugees, temporary residents such as students and temporary workers, and undocumented immigrants: Hispanics comprise 50.1 percent and Asians 22.3 percent. In 2009, the group constituted 23.9 million and 15.5 percent of the civilian labor force." According to the 2008 American Community Survey, the top five states with high foreign-born residents were: "California (9,859,027); New York (4,236,768); Texas (3,887,224); Florida (3,391,511); and Illinois (1,782,423)" (Fox, 2010, n.p.). These immigrants constitute a significant percentage of administrators, teachers, and parents of students in the United States school system. Anti-immigrant sentiments can appear haphazard, although economic downturns trigger an increase in nativism.

According to the 2008 American Community Survey, Arizona has 932,518 foreign-born residents, the eighth largest proportion in the United States, comparing different states (Fox, 2010). In late April 2010, Arizona Governor Jan Brewer's Senate Bill 1070, which cracks down on illegal immigrants, sparked national debate. A requirement for candidates for political office supplying birth certificates was rescinded amidst the furor. Meanwhile, under Arizona's House Bill (HB) 2281, the Department of Education instructed "school districts that teachers whose spoken English it deems to be heavily accented or ungrammatical must be removed from classes for students learning English" (Jordan, 2010, p. A3). Would this apply equally to teachers who have a German, Russian, African, Chinese, or Spanish accent? Governor Brewer's HB 2281, signed May 11, 2010, clamps down "on ethnic studies in Tucson schools" because in fostering race consciousness, the classes "promote resentment among races or classes of people." Incompliant schools "risk losing 10 percent of [their] state financing" (Lewin, 2010, p. A13). Opponents to Governor Brewer's anti-immigrant law claim it sanctions racial profiling. Typically, proponents of anti-immigrant laws focus on the drain on the economy:

> The substantial benefits of immigration in terms of economic growth, demographic revitalization, and maintenance of international status and influence may be countered by the costs of higher spending on governmental services, fewer jobs, lower wages, and reduced benefits for native workers, social polarization, cultural conflict, decline in trust and community, and erosion of traditional concepts of national identity. (Huntington, 2004, p. 180)

Rich (2010) roots Arizona's anti-immigrant legislation in America's history of "outbreaks of nativist apoplexy." Acknowledging the complexity and consistency of nativist concerns about cultural diffusion and its impact on nationalism and patriotism, Huntington (2004) views the issue as ubiquitous, as the following litany demonstrates:

> Who are we? Where do we belong? The Japanese agonize over whether their location, history, and culture make them Asian or whether their wealth, democracy, and modernity make them Western. Iran has been described as "a nation in search of an identity," South Africa as engaged in "the search for an identity" and China in a "quest for national identity," while Taiwan was involved in the "dissolution and reconstruction of national identity." Syria and Brazil are each said to face an "identity crisis," Canada "a continuing identity crisis," Turkey a "unique identity crisis" leading to a heated "debate on national identity," and Russia "a profound identity crisis".... The inhabitants of the British Isles have become less sure of their British identity and uncertain as to whether they were primarily a European or a North Atlantic people.... (p. 13)

Political independence and wars as well as security threats spark appeals to national identities which are never uniform or consistent, argues Huntington. From its earliest settlers and subsequent immigrants, the American colony has defined and redefined itself as non-White immigrants changed the pool of its predominantly North European citizenry. At issue has been the racial purity of the "Anglo-Saxon" American even as Indians, Blacks, Asians, Latinos, and recently immigrants from across the globe reconfigured its British-derived institutions, language, laws, customs, and religious practices. Resistance to Catholicism—once viewed as the extreme "autocratic, anti-democratic organization and Catholics as people accustomed to hierarchy and obedience who lacked the moral character required for citizens of a republic" (p. 94)—pales in comparison to the current religious rhetoric directed at Muslims following the September 11, 2001 Twin Tower suicide bombings.

Recent passionate disputes over an Islamic center in New York reflect an endemic religious angst in its populace. Sledge (2010) views the opposition's allegations of desecrating the sacred ground as disingenuous and inaccurate. He insists, "it is not exactly a mosque, nor is it at ground zero" (n.p.). Sporadic rallies have followed with calls to burn the Quran. What about U.S. cultural monuments in Islamic and other countries? Is the United States ready to reject all investments from Islamic-identified financiers? Despite calls for a cohesive cultural history, cultural pluralism plagues the American nation. Inter-group marriages further diffuse any claims of ethnic purity. Horace Kallen's analogy of an American "federation of nationalities" offered a more realistic portrayal: "Men can change their clothes, their politics, their wives, their religions, their philosophies to a greater or lesser extent; they cannot change their grandfathers" (p. 130).

Language of Difference

Blaut's *The Colonizer's Model of the World* (1993) analyzes the Eurocentric ideology of Whites as intelligent, more inventive and innovative, rational, progressive, honorable and courageous and its inherent denigration of non-European peoples and cultures. In explicit and implicit ways, the social hierarchy is taught in schools, and validated by scholarship as well as by the media. Books devote less coverage to issues beyond Europe unless these impinge on the image or policies of European cultural groups. While historians are not inherently prejudiced, "they assert that Europeans invented democracy, science, feudalism, capitalism, the modern nation-state, and so on, they make these assertions because they think that all of this is *fact*." (p. 9; italics in original). Blaut maintains that while "scholarly beliefs are embedded in culture, and are shaped by culture," diminishing the centrality of natural resources and free or cheap labor from colonies in the accumulated writings of generations is "simply the colonizer's model of the world" (p. 10). Missionaries may have loved and respected indigenous converts, but they never equated their cultures with Europe's Christianity. Few entertained the thought of marrying off kins to local converts. That developing countries depend on the First World for economic, technological, and cultural models of upward mobility, reinforces the existing cultural hierarchy that privileges Whiteness among predominantly non-European cultures in Africa. In addition, these explicit forms of cultural dominance and implicit beliefs of White supremacy persist, "unnoticed and uncriticized." African immigrant teachers represent the Other in this racial hierarchy. Their authority in institutions of learning and workplaces is compromised by this reality.

Labeling is endemic to social groups: ennobling some and marginalizing the rest. Further distinctions arise between those who define and those who are impacted by such definitions, as Achebe (2009) illustrates in analyzing Joseph Conrad's *Heart of Darkness*. Depending on the reception of immigrants in host countries, some teachers are dismissed on sight while others get a free pass (Li and Becket, 2006; Martin, 2007; Minnich, 2005; Morrison, 1993; Uwah, 2000; Walkerdine, 1990). Imperialism, through language, literature, capital, and weaponry, created a racial hierarchy that scientific progress as well as globalization both reflect and reinforce. In media propaganda or international investments, players rarely change places: a dominant industrialized world pit against developing nations. As social structures, schools embody these hierarchies to create insiders and outsiders. Even teachers who disavow the categories are embedded in ideologies that shape social interactions. Who has never felt an outsider at some point? Individual students label others and are labeled in turn: some for the better—although this is not always the case. Stepping into a classroom of students with dismissive glances, students with belligerent attitudes, or students who are turned off school, teachers look for a sign, anything, to connect, even if it's just to get through the next five minutes. Even the ritual salutation feels like a groping in the dark. The feeling is not exclusive to immigrants. Most teachers have experienced alienation in school settings; frequently, one chooses what feels right rather than the (culturally) familiar. Appiah (1992) insists that history is never definitive; people can and do change. Cultural exchanges expose unexamined perceptions of the Other.

As cultural outsiders, immigrants identify structures of meanings that insiders consider routine, "and provide other ways of understanding how American behavior is culturally constructed" (DeVita and Armstrong, 1993, p. xv). Drawing on field notes and reconstructed conversations, the analysis of my experience teaching high school and college students depicts a process of cultural navigation. Studies in identity politics including multiculturalism, Black studies, feminist or critical pedagogy acknowledge the significance of primary backgrounds on self-conceptions (Delpit, 1995, 1998; Gay, 2000; Heath, 1983; Giroux, 2005, 2008; Harris G, 1997; Harris J, 1998; hooks, 2003; hooks and mesa-bains, 2006; Ladson-Billings, 1995a, 1995b, 2001; Lawrence-Lightfoot, 1999; Li and Becket, 2006; McCarthy et al., 2005; McWhorter, 2001; Morrison, 1993; Nieto, 2004; Ogbu, 1992; Rogoff et al., 2003; Willis, 1981). Acknowledging the age-old dualistic contrast between quantitative and qualitative research methodologies, Goodson and Sikes (2001) advocate the use of life history methods in studying "topics related to schools, schooling, and education" (p. xii). Generalizable claims from quantified studies offer a framework for understanding groups of people or processes. However, given the dynamism of cultures and countries, as much as the intricacies of the teaching/learning process, particularistic findings in cultural studies—in this case, African immigrant teachers and American students—appear inadequate and limited. Another limitation to nonquantifiable studies is the changing nature of tales as data sources. That respondents' tales vary depending on interviewer and timing of interview may compromise the legitimacy of claims. However, the very choice of story and its construction are significant as a tool of investigation. Life histories explore narrative choices and their import for an individual's perceptions and lived choices. Why tell this story now? Herein lies the value of methodologies that capture the complexities of human interactions, perceptions, and cultural definitions: "Assumptions of linearity of chronological timelines and storylines are challenged in favour of more multiple disrupted notions of subjectivity" (Goodson and Sikes, 2001, p. 15). Indeed, Appiah (1992) maintains that oral traditions capture the complexity of relationships and social process in a more comprehensive manner. In day-to-day conversations, people tend to narrate a story rather than to dissect scientifically the pros and cons of choices or their positions in life. It is these stories that researchers tease out in order to explore "possible influences, explanations, interpretations and alternatives, silences and significances" (p. 1). Consider responses people give to questions like: Who are you? Why did you do it? In addition, it is in these day-to-day negotiations within a particular context that individuals exhibit their value structures—hopes, fears, and aspirations. Responses to a questionnaire on differences between the motherland and American norms among African immigrants allow readers to glimpse the definitions, negotiations, and aspirations of African immigrant teachers on foreign soil. The benefit goes beyond naming people's experiences to offering a framework for understanding an outsider's experience, whether the alienation is based on national boundaries, racial categories, gender classifications, or religious identifications, to name a few. Goodson and Sikes recognize the importance of life histories in broadening "our practical strategy for personal and professional development" (p. 4). Stories have a tendency to elicit reactions from an audience. While presenting "subjective perceptions" of reality, life histories also compel onlookers into reflective stances toward such individuals and their assessments. *Immigrant Teachers, American Students: Cultural*

Differences, Cultural Disconnections, offers a window for understanding the perspectives of African instructors in U.S. schools.

Socialization equips one with skills of perception, recognition, and articulation (Jacobs, 1995). Rogoff et al.'s (2003, 176-80) theory of "learning through intent participation" captures people's unconscious embrace of society's value structure through observation, listening, and participation in rituals. Other scholars (Brandes, 1980; Gonzalez et al., 2005; Kanga, 2004; Minnich, 2005; Nasong'o and Ayot, 2007; Walkerdine, 1990) reiterate this impact of daily interactions on identity construction. Stuart Hall's (1996) work on representations demonstrates the power and potency of cultural images. However, as Giroux (2005, 2008), hooks (2008), and Martin (2007) argue, cultural crossings pertain to immigrants no less than natives: "Diversity is native to every household and countryside" (Bateson, 2000, p. 13). Bateson (2000) focuses on generation transitions, what she terms "an immigrant from the past" (p. 4). Cross-generational interactions involve tremendous adaptations. Men no less than women "face new discontinuities in their own lives" (Bateson, 2000, p. 94; Martin, 2007). Focusing on social class, Ira Shor (1996) terms students' voluntary apartheid (isolating themselves) in college settings a "Siberian syndrome" against the political and intellectual disempowerment that constitutes foreign territory. On the other hand, Ogulnick (2000) highlights cultural differences between provincial and urban residents as well as between Blacks in White racial groups. Analyzing the evolution of America's national identity, Huntington (2004) highlights the perpetual relocation of Americans: "Between March 1999 and March 2000, 43 million Americans changed their residence" (p. 50). In this light, identities can be "enabling and exclusionary" (p. 6). Whether among native-born or immigrant teacher-student interactions, schools compel border-crossing in teachers as well as students (Giroux, 2005). The process involves exchanging the familiar and ordinary for spaces of "multiple cultures, languages, literacies, histories, sexualities, and identities" (p. 2).

Although I taught high school in Kenya, teaching in the United States has been unique because of differences in academic accountability and classroom etiquette. The experience shattered my expectations of a shared cultural heritage with urban minority students. African immigrants appeal to a "common ancestry" with Blacks and hold to hopes of a "common future," despite mutual suspicions between these two groups (Aman, 2002, p. xvii). I could identify with the 96 percent Black student body at the high school, given the minority identity as an African from a former colony that privileged White (colonial) interests in official communication and school curriculum. In contrast, Bateson (2000) exposes this fallacy of a solidarity based on skin color, language, accent or even education: "Likeness does not mean liking"

(p. 88). Visiting Ghana, the African-American Celeste feels "so Western, so American, so lonely" in the country of her ancestors. Aman (2002) attributes tensions between Blacks to resentment; African Blacks benefit from the African-American struggle against racism in the United States. And yet, members of both groups face similar "frustration and isolation" on campuses from White conservative politicians and ideologues who view self-confident Blacks as "uppity." In general, Blacks are stereotyped in U.S. society as welfare recipients and blamed for decaying neighborhoods and also not credited for success, academic or otherwise (Aman, 2002; Morrison, 1993; Traore and Lukens, 2006). Meanwhile Whites can reinforce the divisions between Blacks by lauding one group at the expense of the other. The rhetoric includes claims of superior intelligence among immigrant Blacks compared to American Blacks (Daniels, 2004; Duster, 2009). Borjas (1999) disputes Daniels' (2004) claim that first-generation immigrants from developing countries are hindered by language skills and a lack of transferable job skills: less-skilled workers in these countries are motivated to migrate. Overall, African immigrants and African-Americans share the experience of marginality.

African immigrants straddle a tortuous middle. While they may feel somehow superior to African-Americans, the feeling is tentative, since the United States is foreign territory to them, as well. African-Americans and African immigrants share the bond of skin-color, making them, in some ways, fellow victims, setting both against more generously-portrayed groups in the American racial/ethnic hierarchy, many of these groups favored by a looming ideal of Whites and whiteness. As a result, African immigrant teachers feel an ambivalence, part of no group other than their own, which shapes their receptivity to the host country and its classroom practices, an ambivalence heightened by their students' haphazard and unpredictable receptions of all teachers, immigrant and local, alike.

CHAPTER 2

Comparative Overview of African and U.S. Society

Scholars and policymakers agree on the need to improve academic achievement among racially and economically disadvantaged students but debate the process of attaining this goal (Apple, 1996, 2006, 2008; Ravitch, 1995; Ravitch and Viteritti, 2001). Similar concerns arise in accommodating the needs of immigrants or English-language learners, given ongoing migrations and cross-border permeability (Nieto, 2004). The reliance on tests to measure students' academic improvement limits a teacher's flexibility in meeting the needs of a culturally diverse student body (Apple, 1996, 2006, 2008). As a corrective measure, advocates of a multicultural approach underscore the impact of "cultural understanding, cross-cultural competencies and cultural empowerment" to address school failure, presuming a link between social biases and the economic mobility and cultural pride of minorities (Foster, 1997; Gay, 2000; Ladson-Billings, 1995a, 1995b; McCarthy, 1990, 1993; Nieto, 2004). They ascribe minority students' alienation and poor academic performance to structural biases. Borjas (1999) attributes academic success and economic mobility in immigrants to assimilation. In contrast, Ravitch (1995; Ravitch and Viteritti, 2001) focuses on the role of national standards in fostering academic success.

The complexity of improving academic performance, creating culturally inclusive curricula and pedagogy, or empowering historically marginalized groups raises issues of priorities, role expectations, and strategies for navigating classroom ecologies. Advocates of a culturally relevant pedagogy focus on the dynamics between privileged White teachers in predominantly underprivileged minority urban schools. They ignore the shock foreign teachers experience learning to teach in American schools despite an increase in foreign-born teachers in the United States (American Federation of Teachers, 2009; DeVita and Armstrong, 1993; Martin, 2007; Obiakor and Afolayan, 2007; Obiakor and Grant, 2002). A report by the American Federation of Teachers (2009), estimates 19,000 foreign teachers with temporary U.S. visas in 2007, with more than 3 million in American public schools (Dillon, 2009). Specifically, African immigrants number over 1 million and Africans account for one in three foreign-born blacks in the United States according to the 2010 Census. Besides professional demands, immigrant teachers grapple with new structures of meaning in social interactions, however ambiguous the process or arbitrary the reception in host countries (American Federation of Teachers, 2009; Borjas, 1999; DeVita and Armstrong, 1993). They encounter different social norms, school policies, curricula and instruction strategies, and all the while having to decipher native accents. Ahmad modifies mathematics lesson plans to integrate teaching materials and technological resources in the United States: "At home you teach [concepts] the traditional way and you keep doing it until the students master it and they feel very happy doing it. Over here, students do not tolerate the long procedures and they quickly give up and get the calculator to solve the problem." His effort to accommodate students' learning styles has not eliminated their focus on accents: "Some students ask me to explain a procedure more than twice because they do not understand my accent, some of them ask me to repeat certain words on purpose like the word I will never forget [parallel]." While an immigrant's cultural adaptation varies depending on country of origin, class, race and gender, a longer stay eases the individual's sense of alienation. For instance, Ahmad avoids discussions of his ethnicity given his obviously Muslim-sounding name. On occasion, particular incidents jar a teacher's perception of self and surroundings (Borjas, 1999; Obiakor and Grant, 2002; Owolabi, 1996). Indeed, most immigrants claim the sense of alienation never abates wholly (DeVita and Armstrong, 1993; Owolabi, 1996); what Kim (1993) calls "a half-hearted spectator" role. For African immigrant teachers the cold weather feels brutal compared to the warm temperatures to which many are accustomed (Obiakor and Gordon, 2003; Owolabi, 1996).

Often, differences in social and academic expectations between teachers and students, whether immigrant or native, create misperceptions and can involve frustrating negotiations for teachers as well as students. Within schools, demonstrable achievements (test scores and attendance records) provide a sense of ease and confidence in the individual's ability to excel. Successful students feel a sense of belonging that prepares them for academic challenges: they view school as a necessary hurdle rather than something to be resisted (Ogbu, 1992). In contrast, Lane, Wheby, and Cooley (2006) attribute the success of high school students to the ability to control their tempers in conflict situations with peers and adults, to comply with school rules, to heed classroom instructions, as well as to adapt to classroom activities. School policies and schedules help students negotiate these social and academic milestones. For teachers, course objectives, scheduled class meetings, and assignments provide frameworks for establishing priorities or maintaining order. Critical theorists (Apple, 1996, 2006, 2008; Giroux, 1988; Shor, 1996) deride this neoconservative view of schooling, privileging elitist conceptions of knowledge that are divorced from the struggle of everyday existence. In this view of schooling, failure translates to poor grades and an undesirable character. Tensions often arise from inaccurate expectations and perceptions of school structures. In terms of respect, my students and I operated from different conceptions of civility, a state that created endless tensions. When teacher and student expectations conflict with the demands of their roles in classrooms it feels like a tightrope run at best, a trap door at worst.

While *Immigrant Teachers, American Students: Cultural Differences, Cultural Disconnections* explores the impact of teacher/student backgrounds, it also questions the presumption of cultural groups as homogenous. In addition to the looming impact of structural inequalities, attributing classroom practices to cultural differences ignores individual choices within and across cultural groups. Specifically, what is the American school culture? How distinct is a minority culture? Consider how, "Minority members who have close expressive relationships with those of other races and ethnic groups or who are too preoccupied with conforming to the norms of the dominant group are often seen as disloyal, as denying their macro identity" (Milner, 2004, p. 124). For elites such as Colin Powell, class trumps racial identity. Powell claims people see him as Black, "but they also see a secretary of state, a retired four-star general, the leader of America's military in a short, victorious war, and, if they are internationally oriented, the principal proponent in the Bush administrations of multilateralism in American foreign policy" (Huntington, 2004, p. 309). Among Black students, accusations of "acting White," implies a denial of slavery's "collective memory and societal politics" (Luken and Traore, 2006; Ogbu, 1992). Wesonga's urban minority students disengage from schooling claiming it is a "White" thing. However, associating Blacks with academic underachievement ignores historical attempts among Blacks for an education (Bateson, 2000). Duster (2009) shows significant literacy achievements among African Americans: "Nearly 400,000 Blacks—about 10 percent of those in the South—possessed some degree of literacy in 1865. Not all were free Blacks. During the 1930s, of the nearly

3,500 former slaves... five percent had become literate before emancipation (p. 101). On the other hand, how significant are racial identities among the youth? Adolescents show greater preference for freedom of expression, dress, behavior, and easy grades as opposed to a teacher's focus on subject matter, working conditions, and related professional issues (Milner, 2004; Ravitch, 1995). Harris (1998) insists that peer relations override parental or even racial categories in explaining youth behavior.

Despite the presumption that cultural groups are homogenous, teachers' expectations vary and so does the commitment of students to learning. Although youth culture is distinct (Bateson, 2000; Harris, 1998; Lawrence-Lightfoot, 1999; Milner, 2004), studies underscore the impact of racism on cultural identities (Delpit, 1995; McWhorter, 2001; Morrison, 1993; Tatum, 1997). But then, the idea of a Black culture among proponents of culturally relevant pedagogy is debatable given the impact of time and location on cultural identities (Appiah, 1992; Bateson, 2000; Ogulnick, 2000; McCarthy, 1990, 1993; Shor, 1996). Cultural debates often amount to "divisive rhetoric" rather than concrete contrasts (Bhabha, 1996; Grossberg, 1996; Hall, 1996). Culture wars include a fair amount of caricature, focusing on extremes to undermine opponents. Bateson (2000) decries the "crude oversimplification of the color line in non-English speaking countries and within the African-American community itself" (p. 9). The color line divides even as it unites members (Appiah, 1992; hooks, 2003). First, the concept of an "integral, originary and unified identity" implies an impractical uniformity within groups (Hall, 1996). While a cultural identity—Kenyan as opposed to American—implies particular beliefs and behavior patterns, the concept is always contextual rather than definitive. One can distinguish the ideal from lived reality as, for instance, the "national" identity of the United States relative to the reality of differences within and among cultural identities (Bhabha, 1996). Even at the individual level, identity is rarely consistent: people make choices that either reflect or defy expected cultural patterns of behavior. For instance, society contrasts blackness to whiteness although the concept of blackness encompasses a range of experiences not all of which individual members embrace (Appiah, 1992).

Badillo (2006) and McWhorter (2001) exemplify the disassociation from conventional Hispanic and Black "anti-intellectual" identity, respectively. Cultural identities are further complicated for immigrant teachers who exhibit a more hybrid culture that reflects what James Clifford (1986, 1997) terms multi-local attachments: elements of the old country relative to acquired beliefs and patterns of behavior (Achebe, 2009; McCarthy et al., 2005; Said, 1993). Educated in systems that mirror Western rather than indigenous structures, many African immigrant teachers embraced colonial structures for social mobility's sake. My boarding school experience involved living with students from different ethnic groups and social classes, abiding by school rules and regulations as well as the insistence by teachers that we communicate only in English. Abiding by school policies was a necessary evil; the adoption of "foreign/Imperial" ways of being, feeling, and thinking in a language divorced from one's primary experiences was the order of the day (Achebe, 2009; Appiah, 1992). Borjas (1999) maintains that the process of cultural adaptation is natural. His studies link social mobility to an immigrant's ability to assimilate dominant cultural values (Alba and Nee, 2003). Achebe (2009), like many Africans, defines himself as "multiethnic, multilingual, multireligious, (and from a) somewhat chaotic colonial situation" (p. 39). International travel opens one's eyes to the unfamiliar even as it compels one into a re-assessment of familiar habits and beliefs. Students in the United States increasingly interact with non-Western peoples and cultures; locals no less than immigrants navigate new terrains daily.

Concepts of "newness" presume a past or previous. For Africans, devoid of a concrete past, the fluidity of adjusting to newness defines an ever tentative identity—pre-migratory, pre-sedentary lifestyles, pre-colonial, pre-Western education, pre-urban, pre-global. Always adapting, always seeking a cultural anchor, immigrant teachers confront new challenges despite the regular need to find stability. As Werbner and Ranger's (1996) work illustrates, for postcolonial Africans, there is an absence of clear delineation of ends or even beginnings. Appiah's (1991, cited in Thornton, 1996) analysis of a postcolonial identity is illusory; one merely substitutes one authority for the next. For Africans, there is the authority of ethnic elders, politically appointed chiefs, the police, presidents and ultimately comparable structures in host countries.

Resident Aliens

Resident aliens straddle two cultures, compelled to forge loyalties to the homeland and host country. For African immigrants, the cultural synthesis reaches back to the colonial era, when many embraced a Western-style education, even as home cultures demanded allegiance to indigenous norms. Du Bois' sense of "double consciousness" captures the African immigrant's tentativeness in social interactions. Raised and schooled in cultures that stress social obligations over individual interests, African immigrants wonder how and where to draw lines between enforcing classroom discipline and accommodating students' interests. The resulting cultural disconnections are ambiguous and create unexpected apprehension, complicating the teaching/learning process. American students may consider African names undecipherable, while

American stereotypes of a backward African continent, reinforced by media portrayals of wars, poverty, corruption, and illiteracy, may highlight disparities between students and teachers:

> It is common practice for foreign teachers to use Western names or to westernize their names for easier communication with their colleagues and students who usually have difficulties pronouncing non-Western, particularly African, names. I once took my students to the Arizona state legislature for an educational tour and was the first one to sign in the visitors' book. When our host proposed a motion on the floor for us to be recognized and our names to be entered into record, she could not read my name, and after laboring for a minute or so, just asked us to stand up to be recognized! My students blamed me for causing them to lose this golden opportunity to have their names in an official government record. On the way back to campus they christened me "Wally O'Connor!" (Watoya, a questionnaire respondent).

A sense of foreignness is often compounded by the accents of Africans who speak versions of English that reflect their countries of origin, not America. Seeking familiar names for seemingly undecipherable foreign terms is a ubiquitous practice. During the colonial era, locals in Bungoma, my home district in Kenya translated foreign names and terminology to familiar phrases and sounds: Fourti for Ford, Arnota for Arnold, Torofu for Rudolf, and Chilande for Grant, to name a few.

Most African immigrant teachers grapple with cultural changes, given a pervasive sense of otherness due to race, language, or class differences. For instance, the cultural stereotypes of wealthy (superior) Europeans, studious Asians, primitive Africans, and belligerent Muslims persist. In addition, recent immigrant groups fall prey to cultural hazing from groups who arrived before them. The traditional focus on dominant White biases against minorities often obscures these complexities among groups. Schools presume relative uniformity in the transmission of curricula while advocating civility in social interactions, despite the diversity in teacher/student experiences and expectations of each other. Similarities in terminology in subject areas often ignore significant differences in conception and application of academic standards across cultures. Take the process of multiplying two sets of numbers, both of which have more than two digits. Some immigrant teachers learned to multiply numbers from right to left. Students familiar with the practice of multiplying numbers from left to right experience frustration and find the line-up of numbers for addition rather confusing. And yet, students' academic success hinges on teacher-student relationships and understanding. The sense of alienation in African immigrants arises from differences in educational training and socialization, the uniqueness of names, race/ethnic characteristics, and differences in language and accents in a predominantly White society. Often, multiculturalism debates focus on diversity among students to the exclusion of teachers' experiences.

Though empowered by the title of teacher and its responsibilities, teachers are still tentative about their identities and those of students. The U.S. Department of Education specifies learning standards for different subjects and grades—mathematics, physical education and health, social studies, and language arts (Ravitch, 1995). In Kenya, the Ministry of Education supplies a four-volume secondary education syllabus for specific subject areas including languages, math, sciences, humanities, and practical subjects. Little mention is made of the complexities of implementation, particularly the human element, in either system.

How does one reconcile academic concessions such as bonus points and make-up work with accountability, given disparities in application even within one school? Many immigrants consider it a luxury that students "are told in advance the topics that might be on the examination, and they are given sample questions, so that they know the level of difficulty for which to prepare" (Ravitch, 1995, p. 18). Further, in the United States educational system, students of similar grade levels have different learning experiences: specifically, differences among honors, regular, and special education or ESL (English as a Second Language) students. Enshrined as school electives, the practice of tracking separates working class from privileged students; subordinated groups fall prey to "a trivial pedagogical fashion" of basic skills, filling out worksheets, and industrial arts with little exposure to college-entry subjects and critical analysis (Giroux, 1988; Ravitch, 1995). These differences in education access exist within and across schools. In contrast, Kenyan schools hold students to uniform standards particularly at the eighth and twelfth grade levels, which are the transitions to high school and college, respectively. Schools assign examination index numbers for candidates (eighth grade and fourth form) according to performance on end-year tests. However, except for differences among schools and regions, or between public and private institutions, regarding access to school supplies and teachers, students in various (ability tracked) sections and disciplines (Arts or Sciences) of a class grade are taught by the same teachers. Students' performance on qualifying examinations determines their eligibility to the next academic rung in a highly competitive educational system. In contrast, immigrant teachers commend the apparent flexibility in U.S. schools but wrestle with the seeming laxity of endless choices when students change schools or drop classes rather than persevere through demanding options.

Differences in role expectations and social interactions pose further challenges for immigrant teachers. Familiar words and behavior suddenly acquire new meaning. What constitutes appropriate teacher/student interactions? Whereas a student's quiet demeanor shows respect for authority or class forum, speaking out of turn or making demands reflects a lack of respect in Kenyan cultures. Most African communities consider avoiding eye contact a sign of deference, while in the U.S. culture, the gesture is regarded as shifty (Nieto, 2004); or what Owolabi (1996) terms a sign of intimidation. At a more basic level, accustomed to European-style spelling of English words, African immigrants discover differences in basic terms such as colour for color or lorry for truck. What about the confusion over parentheses and brackets in mathematics, or periods instead of full stops and zeds over zees as the last letter of the alphabet, in writing. When is English, English? The Portuguese Ramos (1993) captures a common bewilderment among foreign speakers of English, including Africans, over the usage of the term "nice." It is nice to meet people, who can be nice to you in doing something nice. That someone has a family is a nice thing. Oh, and a day can also be nice. Then there are what Stefan (2000) terms the long words such as "forhereortogo" that can be undecipherable to English language learners. Further, teachers from former French colonies are compelled to teach in relatively unfamiliar language patterns; academic literacy differs significantly from rhetoric competence. A foreign-trained teacher from former English-speaking colonies may communicate fluently in English, but still have difficulty explaining academic terms to students accustomed to a particular dialect.

Oliveira et al.'s (2009) study on "Students' Attitudes Toward Foreign-Born and Domestic Instructors" links academic literacy and rhetorical competency. A teacher is "good" if they can speak standard English. Indeed, students preferred domestic instructors, rating them higher on communication. However, "if students regularly engage multiple cultural schemas, as well as foreign accents and languages, they may no longer rate domestic instructors much above their foreign-born counterparts in communication" (p. 122). Oliveira et al. attribute students' preferences for domestic instructors to a cultural familiarity. In Ahmad's case, the focus on accents derails the academic agenda. The word "parallel" occurs frequently enough in mathematics lessons to cause Ahmad angst. Ahmad is frustrated by his students' focus on accents, particularly their teasing him about not pronouncing the word "properly":

> I deal with the issue of accents very professionally and patiently. I tell students that talking with an accent is not a defect; it's a privilege which means that you speak more than one language and if you can speak more than one language with no accent it is a plus, but if you don't it is not a minus.

Although the process of cultural crossings differs among immigrants, each recalls the apprehension of second-guessing oneself over choices that previously appeared straightforward. On the other hand, language proficiency is a window to cultural inclusion for many foreigners (Appiah, 1992). Phrases such as, "Oh, you speak English!" in host countries appear as gestures of inclusion to an elite club of humanity. On the continent an individual's facility with the imperial language is a sign of sophistication.

Small incidents, little miscues, heighten an immigrant's sense of alienation. An incident feels right but not the reaction of participants; familiar structures of meaning are violated with the culprits apparently unaware of causing displeasure to the other. A "good morning" is ignored or met with a grunt in contrast to the formal acknowledgment of teachers in hierarchically structured schools typical of African education systems. Sometimes my urgings to students to refocus on an activity or uphold some routine seatwork such as a writing activity would be met with, "Whatever!" It was unclear what the student's reaction to my intervention was. In social interactions, discussions generally draw upon acronyms such as CUNY, BC, GWB; UCLA; terms such as "the City," Bush, W.; DiMaggio, Jon-Benet Ramsey; in short, the cultural context that immigrants lack. It took me over 13 years of residence in the United States to realize that my spelling of "judgement" differed from standard U.S. spelling. Thirteen years! How could I have missed the difference in spelling? What went through my students' minds to see the "misspelled" term (if they noticed it)? For immigrants, these cultural missteps highlight the "agonizing realization that one must endure matters of functional and cultural literacy, emotional and psychological fulfillments, and family obligations" (Obiakor and Afolayan, 2007, p. 265). Amobi (2004) depicts migrations as a crossing of "geographical, political, linguistic and several time-zone borders" (p. 167). Despite differences in country of origin, phrases such as "Only in America!" from immigrants capture the sense of perpetual wonder at unique American norms; a country that offers the good, the bad and the ugly (Obiakor and Grant, 2002; Owolabi, 1996). Both Ahmad and Baruti capture the ambivalence of African immigrants toward their host country. More mellow in her assessment, Baruti describes her teaching experience in the United States as "positive and negative." She refrains from expounding on the terms. Ahmad is more explicit: "My teaching experience at my current school is a mixed feeling of joy and anguish." Overall, African immigrant instructors experience destabilization in cultural identity in host countries, intent on settling yet reminded daily of disparities between the familiar and the new.

Post-Colonial Graduates

While *Immigrant Teachers, American Students: Cultural Differences, Cultural Disconnections* focuses on an African immigrant teacher from Kenya, discussions with other African immigrant teachers highlight similarities in socialization patterns and expectations of students. Regional disparities in educational systems within and across the continent reflect differences in economics, communications networks, and missionary activities. Overall, national and missionary-run schools offer a similar curriculum and have been publicly funded for the most part. More significant differences exist across regions; national schools are still better funded, mostly from endowments, and they attract high-caliber teachers and command greater resources—computer and foreign language facilities. In term of competitiveness, national schools are ranked highest relative to provincial and district schools in terms of endowment. Some private schools also reflect a similar competitive advantage. Kabarak High School is coveted more than Kimaeti or Napara Secondary Schools in my neighborhood. The former is better equipped. It is owned by the former President Arap Moi and is therefore a private school. In general, urban-center private schools in Kenya are better equipped than public schools.

The experiences of sampled African immigrants who grew up in post-colonial British and French regimes reflect the impact of colonial policies and practices on existing education systems. However, imperial policies and practices, including those regarding education, were never coherent or consistent. The very process of assimilation or integration into an imperial system presumed a superiority in that system. In both French and British systems, formal education was promoted as redeeming and civilizing the native (Achebe, 2009; Blaut, 1993). However, it was from the very elite that colonial administrations feared rebellion and political instability. The systems of education were elitist, focusing on talented minority students or those from the upper class, with curricula mirroring that of the colonial administration, even the textbooks. Both French and British systems had a hierarchical structure with elementary, secondary, and post secondary education, with a few entrants to university or study-abroad programs. Contrasting inhibitive from attractive elements in the Sierra Leone education system, Aminata, a questionnaire respondent, notes: "Elementary school is free but college education is not free." Of course, fewer students qualify for the free college education. The pyramid-type structure has masses in elementary school with students streamed and selected for the top rungs. In Kenya, the secular system operated alongside missionary-run schools with both receiving government aid. Indeed, all public secondary schools are funded by the government regardless of whether they are sponsored by churches or not. In addition, all public schools offer the same curriculum, although questions arise about the level of uniformity.

Recent wrangles over primary and secondary school curricula between the Ministry of Education and the Kenya Publishers Association expose the fragility of public policy. The confusion reflects an overlap in responsibilities for designing and assessing official curricula, a process which determines students' performance in a highly competitive education system. If, as the Kenya Institute of Education (KIE) alleges, there is inaccuracy of content in some circulated texts, how then does the Ministry implement its policies, curricula and syllabi considering that formal assessments are based on school textbook materials. On the other hand, as the publishers note, the Ministry neither has the time nor resources to design and distribute textbooks (Siringi, 2010).

Much like Britain, Kenya, a former colony, has a system of education which is centralized, with a national curriculum and examinations. Because of the high stakes in Kenyan national tests, schools and candidates take these seriously; test results determine students' admission to the next academic rung and entry to elite schools as well as employment prospects. The examinations are administered at the end of primary school and secondary school and each academic year at the tertiary levels. O'Brien (1996) notes how education determines a student's access or the lack thereof to political power in Mali and Senegal. Indeed, school dropouts have limited if any prospects of independence in adulthood. In Kenya, growing family sizes and pressures on available resources heighten the stakes of national examinations. Concerns about "teaching to the test" in the United States would fall on deaf ears in Kenya, given its inherent high-stakes testing culture. These assessments shape what and how students learn in different grades. There is an inbuilt clarity of student expectations in the syllabus as dictated by national examinations. In Kenya, teachers are celebrated and vilified for their students' performance on national examinations; it is rare that parents complain about a teacher's lack of sensitivity to students' needs, particularly in schools that consistently post high grade points. Ethnic rhetoric applies to education access rather than multiculturalism in curricula and pedagogy. In early 2010, the Kenyan government reinstituted a quota admission system to high-performing schools to address regional/tribal disparities. Marginalized groups welcomed the move but critics cited declining standards in their opposition to the bill. It has always been the tradition for national schools to draw students from across the country. Every provincial school is required to take a certain quota of students from every district in the province. Despite the policy, some schools consistently post better grades. It is these schools for which parents clamor.

As in historical studies on colonial education by Clignet and Foster (1964), recent works by Davis and Kalu-Nwiwu (2001) as well as Genova (2004) note similarities in policy and practice despite varied imperial goals in French and British colonies. Both colonial systems unified otherwise disparate groups separated by language, custom and traditions (Achebe, 2009). The French system was more assimilationist in approach; the administration imported teachers from France and later, due to a shortage of teachers, trained a local cadre that taught across French-speaking countries including Guinea, Côte d'Ivoire, Niger, Senegal, Algeria, and Dahomey (now Benin). French was taught right from the early years of schooling. Even Marxist states in Africa such as Angola, Mozambique, and Guinea-Bissau adopted colonial languages (Achebe, 2009). In the system's selectivity, teachers groomed children of chiefs and powerful families or talented students. While the process of assimilation built on the French revolution's motto of "equality, fraternity and liberty" to anyone French, it also dismissed existing African cultures by omission. Further, the shortage of personnel and reliance on indigenous representatives led to a great deal of variation in law and administration. Overall, in fashioning economic and political structures "in their own image, [Colonists] successfully established the means by which many of those they conquered understood themselves" (Gottschalk and Greenberg, 2008, p. 29). In literary collections, Europeans portrayed and interpreted indigenous beliefs and practices based on familiar norms in the mother countries. Dom Henrique, the son of the Mweni-Congo, studied Portuguese and was later appointed by the Pope in Rome as a bishop of his country. Chinua Achebe (2009), the British-Protected Child, acknowledges the uniqueness of his exposure to Western education. Although orphaned at a young age, Achebe's father was raised by a maternal uncle who had land to house English Evangelicals. He was "an early convert and a good student" in an Anglican Mission school. His mother was a graduate of St. Monica's Girls' School, the first of its kind in Igboland. Their house, he notes, "was a modern affair: mud walls and corrugated iron roof" (p. 26). His elder brother John was a primary-school teacher. He provided room and board for the younger Achebe to attend the Government College, Umuahia. One of his professors, James Welch, was "head of religious broadcasting at the British Broadcasting Corporation (BBC) in London, chaplain to the king, and principal of a theological college" (p. 22). Later, Achebe arrived at the BBC staff school in London courtesy of his former professor Welch. The pattern of a privileged few has been evident across the African continent.

Kenya's first president, Jomo Kenyatta, first visited the United Kingdom as a lobbyist for the Gikuyu Central Association but later settled to study and raise a family before returning to Kenya in 1946. With Professor

Bronislaw Malinowski's support Kenyatta undertook advanced studies in England without the requisite academic credentials of Barack Obama Sr.'s cohorts who studied in the United States following independence. Professor Malinoski was extremely famous for the ethnographic method that anthropologists use in the field. Upon his return, Kenyatta married into the prominent Mbui Koinange family but lost his wife at childbirth. Few locals claim this pattern of privilege.

The British model of indirect rule implied an acknowledgment of indigenous structures and customs—to some extent.It was also cheaper and provoked less resistance, although African appointees only operated locally and always served as lower cadres relative to Europeans and Indians. Although few, the authority of Whites was apparent in the administration, in the church, and in commerce. In Nigeria, senior positions in the civil service were called "European posts" (Achebe, 2009, p. 31). Missionaries such as Albert Schweitzer acknowledged Africans as brothers, albeit *junior* brothers (p. 80). In schools students like Achebe read books for English boys such as *Treasure Island, Tom Brown's School Days, Oliver Twist, The Prisoner of Zenda, David Copperfield*: "They were not about us or people like us, but they were exciting stories" (p. 21). But there were limits to assimilation. African teachers, however educated, reported to a European. The Ivorian Dr. James Kwegyir Aggrey returned from studies in America to serve "not as principal, which he deserved, but as an assistant to a nice but colorless English cleric" (p. 29). That was colonial rule in daily practice. In retrospect Achebe can understand the pervasiveness denigration of blackness:

> The frankness of those days was nowhere better demonstrated than in an editorial by *The Times* of London expressing outrage at the decision of Durham University to affiliate with Fourah Bay College in West Africa. *The Times* asked Durham quite pointedly if it might consider affiliating with the zoo! (p. 62)

Language: Continental scholars fall primarily between two camps, however false the dichotomy: those who deride affiliation to the West and the rest. The masses of people focus on survival in often economically and politically oppressive regimes; in these environments facility in colonial languages such as English, French, or Portuguese enhances an individual's economic mobility. In often simplistic either/or debates on language policy, Achebe recounts ongoing efforts by colonists and indigenous leaders to integrate foreign languages in local schools. Africa's first independent president, the Ghanian Kwame Nkrumah, expressed concern about the "divisive impact of a mother tongue" in a multilingual regime. Colonial languages persist on the continent because of local demand as much as imperial imposition and propaganda.

Reflecting a language debate that rages on in former British colonies such as Kenya, historical policies of promoting indigenous languages in early primary school have impeded the integration but also the economic development of rural areas relative to urban centers such as Nairobi, Mombasa, Kisumu and Nakuru. In Kenya, children learned in their mother tongue and only later grappled with the official languages and medium of instruction in English and Swahili. National examinations still are primarily in English except for the Kiswahili test. The existing demand for Western formal education illustrates the impact of assimilationist policies in the British system. European languages were a gateway to the growing industrial and political structures; these distinguished the elite from the majority *wananchi,* citizens, in Kenya. Outstanding students such as U.S. President Barack Obama's father earned scholarships to study in the United States, a program organized by a government minister, Tom Mboya. Oginga Odinga, the first vice president, coordinated the program for students bound for the Soviet Bloc. His son Raila Odinga studied in East Germany. Other groups of potential elites headed to South Africa, as did the former government minister Masinde Muliro. Subsequently, with the advent of Western political and economic systems in the region, educated elites replaced traditional ethnic authority figures (chiefs). In Nigeria, Islamic schools existed in the North among the Hausa-Fulani alongside Christian enclaves in the Southeast and Southwest of the country. In Kenya, a three-tier education emerged that catered to an elitist White settler community on top; the Indian population was on the middle rung, and indigenous Africans were relegated to the bottom in terms of resource allocation and social mobility.

The aversion to integrating indigenous languages and practices into formal schools stems from Kenya's colonial history. In designing an education system suited to the populace, a 1949 Committee led by L.J. Beecher reviewed its relevance in scope, content and methodology. A key proposal was the need for mother-tongue instruction for children unfamiliar with English, the official language in school curricula. The policy was endorsed by UNESCO in 1953 and the Ominde Commission under a politically independent Kenya in 1964. Instructing children in their primary language builds on previous experience, reducing their alienation in schools. By contrast, African leaders viewed this as another policy that reinforced an emerging tiered system with Whites at the top, Indian immigrants next in rank and indigenous Kenyans at the bottom of the hierarchy. However laudable, instructing children in local languages reduced their competitiveness in an English/Kiswahili-dominated public sphere. That school instruction and the national examinations employ

English as the medium undermines the legitimacy of maintaining local languages in official transactions; after all, schools prepare children for participation in the nation's economy rather than for neighborhood pursuits. In addition, increased family relocations and ethnic intermarriages complicate a community's choice of instruction medium. A host of constituencies including parents, students, and politicians are focused on grade rankings more than the ethnic inclusivity of schools. Well-performing schools appeal to an unbiased criterion of grades (meritocracy) in justifying existing ethnic compositions. It can be a self-serving rallying cry to maintain the status quo. Duster's (2009) study shows the strong resistance to anti-discriminatory use of affirmative action in the United States, India and South Africa: "Elites in every society are understandably threatened by insurgent and populist calls for social change because such changes constitute a potential redistribution of wealth and privilege that have been assumed as established rights and entitlements" (p. 109). The rallying cry centers around individual meritocracy. For fair competition on nationally administered examinations, students in poorly equipped schools or marginalized regions expect perquisites evident in privileged schools. Fluency in English (along with motivation and intelligence, no doubt) guarantees academic success and subsequent economic mobility. Kenya's debate on language policy mirrors similar ambivalence in the United States over bilingual education.

Respect: Regardless of national origin, African immigrant teachers stress formality in teacher-student relationships. In Africa, a teacher's status within the school carried over to the community. In Kenya, students no less than acquaintances used the term *mwalimu* (teacher in Kiswahili) in addressing them. Reflecting existing gender, age, and class hierarchies, anybody with some authority and national (city slicker) or international exposure (been-to) was respected and admired by the community. Teachers often favored students who were bright and respectful, or those whose parents had status within the community such as a fellow teacher, business owner, the local district commissioner, local councilor, or pastor. Having a vehicle elevated one's status within the community. The owner enjoyed a special seat at religious functions as well. Although prevalent within playgrounds or during out-of-school interactions, student-on-student violence is quickly checked by the presence of an adult. What is common and an accepted practice is teacher discipline of students. Wesonga, a questionnaire respondent, recalls teachers' commitment to students' learning in the Kenyan school he attended. The most attractive aspect of Kenyan schools is:

> The fact that teachers never gave up on us. In spite of all the hardships encountered [in the United States], I try to show my students that I am

not giving up on them. [I p]ersist in what I do—teach. [In addition, t]he respect that teachers got [reflected] Their dedication and pride that result from teaching. [They i]nspire the young people into [the] teaching profession. I am a teacher today because of the inspiration from my teachers at school as well as in family.

Standards and Classroom Etiquette: My colleagues tease me about academic rigor. "She will work you," some colleagues tell students to my face. It sounds like an accusation and aberration. Isn't that what we are about, I wonder? Take the issue of deadlines which either motivate or paralyze students. Even as educators deride the sweep of business models in school practices, deadlines and benchmarks focus students' effort. At each semester's end, some students question the practicality of deadlines and seek concessions in the form of make-up work, incompletes or extensions for assignment submissions. My high school students resisted writing a piece at each class despite their awareness of class requirements at the beginning of the semester. The complaints subsided, particularly by mid-semester, as the tasks became a ritual. Challenging students to complete assignments within a specified time or expressing surprise at a lack of diligence with "You didn't do the work!?"; "Sharon, not again!"; or an outright, "But what does that have to do with the topic?" brought forth charges of sarcasm and thoughtlessness from students. In contrast, my bafflement comes from the experience of direct confrontations with teachers in Kenya, for infractions, gaps of knowledge, or perceived flaws in character. Boarding schools operate like military boot camps. These injunctions are familiar to many African immigrant teachers: "Get back to your desk and behave! Stop chattering and do your work! Where do you think you are going? Grow up!" In addition, Kenyan schools rely heavily on in-class written assessments to measure students' academic performance. This practice is changing with the introduction of parallel programs at the university level, probably due to increased demands on facilities and faculty. Within programs such as medical sciences, engineering, architecture, and veterinary medicine, both regular and parallel students take classes together. In other programs, all parallel students take the same number of units, sit examinations moderated by external examiners, and have to pass all the required units before qualifying for graduation. However appropriate or practical the assessment form, the absence of "open-book" examinations compels students to memorize and regurgitate facts to demonstrate competency in a field. Wesonga laments the impact of changing times on perceptions of schools and relationships in the United States:

> Teachers were very highly regarded people. Even though not very well paid, but it was so rewarding to be a teacher. Every person I knew wanted

to be a teacher. Today, teachers are not viewed by society as pillars that support future generations. None of the kids I teach wants to be a teacher. Not even my own children want to be teachers. Today, students are not seen as being as enthusiastic as in the old days. The impression they give is that if they had a choice, they would not come to school. They view education as trying to be "white," something that is not acceptable to most minority kids. That attitude makes a big difference between the old and the new school.

The Canadian expatriate Fast (2000) arrives at similar conclusions, having taught mathematics in a rural Zimbabwe school. Youngsters rarely question an adult's proclamation and learning focuses on the memorization and regurgitation of facts in an extremely competitive system of education. Students' grades are based on their performance on in-class timed tests. What matters to students are the "red check marks, or 'ticks' " in exercise books that teachers use to assess academic progress. Kofi, a questionnaire respondent, highlights the pressure for academic excellence in Ghana; without the policy of social promotion, and because of the priority of respect for authority figures, "children listen as teachers teach. (There is) absolutely no vulgar language in class." Never? Herein lies the danger of thinking in absolutes.

Throughout Kenya, examination candidates including Standards Eight and Form Four, sit for what are known as "district mocks." Some districts also have district examinations for Standard Seven pupils to pre-select promising examination candidates. To avoid lowering the primary school's score or undermining the image, primary school headmasters in schools such as Napara Roman Catholic (RC) administer regional exams to promote a selective group of seventh graders to eighth grade, candidates for national examination. (Well-performing schools draw more students and also attract high-performing students.). Each year, eighth graders take national exams that determine their eligibility to even fewer high schools across the country but less so in rural areas. Institutions from primary to higher education broadcast students' academic performance in rank order; sometimes, heads of schools display students' results on the office wall to the pride of some and chagrin of many. Kenya's pyramid style education system (masses of students in primary schools, fewer in high schools, and even fewer qualifying for university or college), sacrifices masses to poverty, illiteracy, and unemployment. In an economy with high unemployment rates even among university graduates, high school dropouts face a dim future. From primary school, teachers push students to excel, aware of the hurdles many face ahead—finances, opportunities in "good" schools, and employment prospects. Delpit's (1995) call for minority students in the United States to become familiar with the dominant culture's structure, for political and economic survival, reflects similar sentiments. Schooling is a priority for teachers and students even in Liberian and Sierra Leonean refugee camps (Traore and Lukens, 2006). Girikaze, a questionnaire respondent, notes a similar reverence for education in her country of birth:

> In Burundi, education is a privilege, not a right. [Many] children who have the potential to do well simply cannot do it due to poverty. That is really inhibitive. Another inhibitive factor is lack of teaching materials, again due to poverty. In Burundi, schools rely on hand-me-down books which usually present information in very old-fashioned ways. So the students are not prepared to compete successfully in the global market. Finally, education is seriously affected by lack of qualified teachers. Qualified teachers (like you and me) ironically are drawn to look for better-paying jobs. Very few parents can afford to put their children in private or prestigious schools. Private schools are too expensive, whereas prestigious government-subsidized schools are highly competitive. Recently another inhibitive factor has affected most African schools. It is the war. Education has been terribly affected by the war in many countries.

Wafula focuses on limitations in the Kenya education system:

> The liberal nature of the U.S. education system is attractive. What I mean is that unlike Kenya, students here can study anything they choose. During my student days in Kenya, the emphasis was on specialization which encouraged a narrow view of field of study. It was almost an equivalent of pre-ordination of sorts. You could only be good in Math and not in creative art or any other discipline. I recall a friend of mine in Kamusinga [high school] who was made to repeat his class after his father found out that he was not doing Math, Physics, Chemistry. Such would have placed him on a path to Medical school and so on. It was refreshing to find out that the US system allowed/encouraged interdisciplinary education. As a liberal student I was able to learn computer science etc. The emphasis on specialization in the Kenyan education system does not allow a wider perspective of academia.

Kenya's 8-4-4 system, instituted in the late 1980s, no longer separates students between the sciences and humanities, as was Wafula's experience. However, even in the current system, Wafula's disheartened friend would require Biology units to qualify for a medical degree. The MPC (math, physics and chemistry) combination, as it was popularly known, was for engineering and architecture students. Indeed, Kenya's re-design of the primary school curriculum was to address the very obstacles Wafula encountered in his schooling. In contrast to the structural dilemmas raised by Wafula, Aarifa links income and gender disparities to education access in Ethiopia:

> What is attractive about the system of education in my country of birth is that it has the exact same educational standards for children regardless of ethnicity and class, unlike the United States. What is inhibitive about the system is that many poor children cannot afford the cost of pencils and papers, cannot attend regularly due to poverty, and that girls are treated differently than boys, still. What my country displays in regard to respect for authority is also an indication of how deeply rooted in tradition and custom it is, which makes issues of gender equality difficult, such as class equality in the United States.

Examinations: Kenyan newspapers boast record sales at the beginning of the year following the release of national examination results, particularly at the Standard 8 level, a high school gatekeeping entry. Newspapers provide statistical breakdowns of top ranked students and schools by district with names of the top candidates listed. Newspapers typically display the top candidate in national examinations on the front page, with an accompanying feature story. Schools compete in recruiting students with top marks. Students are normally placed in individual schools by the Ministry of Education. Some head teachers have exploited parents during the second selection process after those on initial lists fail to show up. Currently, heads of schools receive government-generated computer lists of Form One admissions although they have some leeway to replace no-shows. In addition, heads of schools are courted by parents for students' placements in high-performing schools. Students who fail to secure places in coveted schools settle for second- and third-rate secondary (high) schools that tend to be privately owned and relatively expensive. It is a stigma for a student to be left back at any grade level or to be relegated to less competitive schools. The competitive school system has bred its own woes (Otieno and Kangoro, 2007).

In 2007, the Kenya National Examination Council nullified the results of more than 40,000 students due to "malpractice and compilation errors." At the secondary level, masses fall prey to fraudsters peddling a set of examination copies at prices from Kshs 6,000–15,000 ($80–200). The cutthroat competition for admission to high-performing schools is compounded by disparities in the quality of education across the country. In the past, examination cheats sneaked in textbooks, cheat sheets or copied each other's work, sometimes relying on impersonations of registered students. Current technological advances offer more options. Students receive mobile-phone and email tips on questions and answers before and during examinations (Otieno and Kangoro, 2007). Examination cheating dogs Kenya's high-stakes testing culture.

In September 2008, a month prior to the scheduled national examinations in Kenya, America's BBC newscast and *The Standard* as well as the *Nation*, newspapers cautioned against examination cheating. Masinde Muliro University of Science and Technology in Western Kenya had expelled 10 students over examination irregularities. Following university investigations, culprits are typically suspended, ordered to repeat the academic year or expelled. While examination cheating reflects a faulty education system whereby a candidate's destiny is determined by a couple of hours' work, the focus has been on culprits and penalties. As of 2010, Kenya's Ministry of Education requires primary school examination candidates to produce birth certificates for registration, having issued 800,000 birth certificates between January and April. The practice should reduce fraud whereby students, parents and schools enlist ghostwriters to ensure a child's pass on national examinations. The fallout has been a scramble for birth certificates in a land where only a few elites or those born in hospitals have birth records. Fewer still celebrate birthdays. Admittedly, many parents simply fail to apply for birth certificates even after registering births with village headmen or local provincial administrators. The failure has nothing to do with literacy. An upcoming proposed bill requiring birth certificates for National Identification Cards will compel more Kenyans to get birth certificates.

In contrast, Girikaze paints a more rosy picture of the Burundi system of education.

> The one thing I treasure about the assessment system in my country is the practice of make up exams (although I never sat for one). Students who have failed up to a certain number of courses are given the opportunity to take a make up exam in each of the subjects, provided that they have a passing average in the overall (50%). I like this option better than the summer school here, where students just go to school to be babysat.

Immigrants experience some cultural shock when confronted with the "real" news about their country. Limits to communications networks explain the ignorance of residents about "national" news—whether good or bad. While natural and political disasters threaten to overwhelm Africans— "war, genocide, military and civilian dictatorships, corruption, collapsed economies, poverty, disease, and every ill attendant upon political and social chaos...local news cannot report these events without unleashing serious and even deadly consequences" (Achebe, 2009, p. 93). Typically, foreign media exposes government corruption in many African countries whereas local whistleblowers are ostracized, jailed or silenced. The availability of television and cell phones has widened many people's knowledge base. There is growing national outrage over allegations of examination cheating although resolutions tend to be limited to implicated persons and regions. The immigrant can have a rude awakening when such formerly undisclosed issues in his or her country of birth are revealed. The awareness could also liberate immigrants from being "prisoners of the past." Reality is not always what one is told or sees. There must be Americans who, adamant about their country's benevolence and political transparency, experience shock at its image abroad. While the realization creates a sense of betrayed trust, the individual also learns that perception and reality are not always the same. In addition, personal and local practices differ significantly across regions.

<u>Resources:</u> Napara R.C., my rural neighborhood primary school, is bursting at the seams with pupils. In contrast to the United States, where learners at any acadaemic level are students, Kenya reserves the term students for post-primary candidates. Before high school, the term "pupils" suffices. (I use "students" to encompass all learners—primary and beyond). Teachers rarely use the word "overcrowding" to describe classrooms; conversations among teachers and students identify the few with potential who can be groomed to break out of the masses. Standard One and Two comprise about 150 students each, sitting on benches, worn out from over 20 years of use, which can seat about 15 students packed like sardines at any one time. The rest sit lotus style on the dust floor. There should be two teachers to each class although I have only observed one teacher at any one time. Even government-aided schools such as Napara R.C. work in dilapidated facilities; they experience shortages of supplies and a lack of qualified teachers. Despite central government financial packages to districts, the only enclosed space with windows and a lockable door is the headteacher's main office. Decades after the school's establishment, all the classrooms have gaping spaces awaiting fittings of windows and doors. But there has been improvement; students learn in enclosed spaces rather than under the shade of some big tree in the school compound. A new block of classrooms from the Community Development Fund (CDF) awaits completion.

Cries of "foul play" are exposing the fallacy of Kenya's free primary education program. To date, financial woes—a loss of Kshs 103 million, due to government graft—has not sat well with international donors. Head teachers from my home district, Bungoma, rely on parental contributions to purchase "books and chalk." Meanwhile, parents of pupils at Embu Urban Primary School help school "by providing food." Although each student is allocated about Kshs 10,265 ($146), this is rarely distributed. In Meru Central Kuppet the secretary general, Julius Mbijiwe, claims only 10 out of 200 schools in the area received any money. Those who did only received about Kshs 1,065 ($15) per pupil (Siringi, 2010, "School Heads," (n.p.).

At the tertiary level, government universities and colleges have introduced parallel programs to accommodate excess demand. Despite the association of parallel and evening programs with the wealthy, the picture is more complex. Students in parallel programs attend classes in the evenings and on Saturdays when the facilities are not in use by regular or day-time students. In the past, these facilities were underutilized. On the other hand, registrations for parallel university and evening classes include students straight from secondary school as well as paid workers desirous of advancing themselves. Private universities with facilities of education run similar programs across the country. In the highly competitive educational system, there is limited room at the top of the academic rung. Further, an employee can accumulate degress with few prospects of advance.

Students in our neighborhood have limited contact with foreigners. There is the occasional encounter with some White doctor or priest, or with Indian businessmen and their families. Somali families in the town keep their distance from local residents. Locals work the gardens of these minority elites, clean their houses, wash and rear their children for a salary. In 2008, I was shocked to learn a cousin had never traveled to Bungoma town. It is only about 15 kilometers away from the homestead. She may never have boarded a bus or other form of public transportation. Like my cousin, few of the students at Napara have "outside" exposure. Yet they are aware of the privilege they lack. Theirs is a world of unlimited chores, particularly for females; Sunday service; and, on rare occasions, a visit to kinsfolk. In boarding schools, students carry out general cleaning and maintenance themselves, responsibilities typically assigned to custodial crews in U.S. schools. They cut the grass, pick up trash, and mop floors, and maintain cleanliness in bathrooms. Schools contract workers to prepare meals.

In Kenyan boarding schools, the popular (well-off?) students received frequent family visits and stocked up on snacks. The rest of us looked on with envy. How to explain why one's parents rarely visited or, when they did, brought so few snacks? I sensed a similar angst in the urban high school groups I taught. The recent institution of parental visits in Kenya's primary and secondary schools, particularly girls' boarding schools, borders on a ritual. With a line of cars parked nearby, parents laden with snacks for their children huddle at school gates long before the visiting hour strikes. Mwololo

(2010) calls the charade, "The Big Show-Off that is School Visiting Day." Affluent parents arrive dressed for show and off load portable furniture to pitch small tents in the relegated visiting area. With a mini gas cooker and cylinder, the visitors proceed to cook an assortment of dishes, whose enticing food smells impress and annoy the less endowed parents and students alike. During the visit, music blares from loudspeakers in packed cars. Not surprisingly, schools like Thika High School, Ithanga Secondary School in Thika and St. Mary's Yala have scrapped the practice while Baricho Boys in Kirinyaga and Aquinas High school in Nairobi opt for a day off or have prize giving ceremonies. At Nairobi's Precious Blood High School and Muindi Mbingu Secondary School in Machakos, principals advocate moderation to avoid reinforcing class hierarchies in schools. Meanwhile students talk endlessly of whose parents are lavish as opposed to those on the fringes, whose parents rarely come or bring little to boast of. While "notions of unlimited growth and expansion work" benefits the rich economically, this myth of plenitude keeps the "have-nots from utilizing their limited material resources in the most life-enhancing and productive ways" (hooks, 2000, p. 76). hooks' critique was aimed at more affluent students in the United States.

The large class sizes in my local primary school further limit any hopes for teacher accommodation of students' special needs, intellectual or emotional. In 2008, the headmaster made a point of introducing to me the only primary school student with special needs, in her case mental retardation. Her inclusion appeared to be a major achievement although little else had been done for her. When I have shared my experiences of schooling in Kenya with students in the United States both at the high school and college level, some admit to similar pressures in their country of origin. Most however are shocked at the rigidity of the Kenyan school system and the material lack. "I would transfer to another school," someone calls out. "Where to," I ask the person, "without the financial resources to join a less structured private school?" It is a harsh reminder of the plight of students in other countries as opposed to the abundance in America. The resigned response of "Oooh," from students illustrates an appreciation of the opportunities many take for granted. This is new cultural territory for them.

According to the *World Fact Book* (2009) Kenya's Gross Domestic Product (GDP) was $63.52 billion with a population of about 39 million and a growth rate of 3 percent in 2009. Its gross enrollment percentage ratio of students at the primary level was 94.9 percent; secondary level was at 31.7 percent and the tertiary level at 5.1 percent. About 7 percent of the GDP is spent on education at all levels of schooling. In government subsidies such as the Free Primary Education Program (FPE), government graft has cost Kshs. 103 million, funds designated to supplement tuition, purchase of supplies, and custodial services such as a watchman's pay. Clifford (2010) bemoans a similar trend of lengthier school supply lists in the United States due budgetary cuts. Parents purchase the usual writing materials as well as cleaning supplies such as liquid soap, paper towels, and disinfectant sprays for preschoolers and older students alike. In Kenya, parents shoulder fees for remedial classes and lunches. The price of a secondary education defies logic, given the economic state of towns such as Bungoma. Even district schools such as St. Cecilia's Girls Misikhu charge Form Ones Kshs 27,000 ($386) per year. Girls admitted to boarding schools face a mandatory shopping list of Kshs 22,000 ($315) upon enrollment. Required supplies include a mattress and bedding, school uniform, sanitary napkins, geometry sets, the Bible, petticoats and socks, and so forth. Students cannot enroll for classes before producing the required accessories. It is common to see students in uniforms on public transportation during the semester or, in the case of day scholars, during class time. For debt collection, schools typically send students home at the end of each month when paid workers receive their salaries.

Notwithstanding differences in household income or consumption by percentage share (lowest 10 percent with 2 percent and highest 10 percent with 37 percent, according to 2000 estimates), Kenya's unemployment rate is around 50 percent and about 50 percent of the population lives below the poverty line. Parental investment in children's education borders on religiosity. Families sell ancestral lands and family herds; they borrow from loan sharks at exorbitant interest rates to cover tuition. This has always been the case, for example, when parents raise funds to educate children in India and, more recently, Europe and the United States. Meanwhile, Kenya's president earns a gross salary of US $615,000, more than the American president ($400,000), and the British prime minister (pounds sterling 187,000). The presidents, vice president's and prime minister's salaries as well as other ministers and members of Parliament (MPs) are covered by the Parliamentary Service Commission (PSC), a body chaired by the speaker of the National Assembly and comprised of other members of Parliament. The Kenyan vice president earns more than the U.S. secretary of state and its attorney general. Indeed, some wealthy Kenyans live lifestyles many Americans only dream about (Kamotho, 2008):

> It sounds unfair for 20 million poor Kenyans to receive $50 of welfare per year while MPs laugh all the way to the bank with $180,000. In other words, an MP will earn an equivalent of what 3,600 poor Kenyans will earn from government assistance.... Although Kenya has been stuck at 147th position in the UNDP HD index for the past 4 years and is ranked 92nd on the human poverty index, 52% of its population live below the poverty line of $2 income per day. Although 74% of Kenyans are literate,

43% do not have access to clean water and 20% of the children are malnourished. (Okumu, 2010, p. 30)

Relationships: Extracurricular clubs offer students a venue for bonding with classmates beyond regional or ethnic loyalty. Sporting events (athletics, football, netball, rugby, tennis), and music competitions at the school, district, provincial, and national levels draw students and teachers together. National holidays such as Independence and Christmas center on celebrations across the country. Achebe (2009) writes about celebrating Empire Day and Queen Victoria's birthday in the colonial era. Recently, Kenyan schools have instituted prayer days for candidates of national examinations whereby parents are invited to school and classes are cancelled for the event. Within schools, students from urban centers have cliques that reflect their cosmopolitan exposure or Kiswahili/English linguistic facility. Fundamentalist in the reading of Scripture, born-again Christian converts stay true to narrow definitions of religion—etiquette, prayer, quiet demeanor. In his study on premarital sexuality and modern identity in Southeastern Nigeria, Smith (2000) expresses surprise at parental reservations toward youths who were too modern as much as toward "born-again" Christians who "openly flaunt their religious conversions and...proselytize even among their parents and elders" (p. 116).

In a special issue on sexuality and generational identities in Sub-Saharan Africa, *Africa Today* illustrated its complexity with particular reference to disparities in beliefs and practices. Though frequent, boy/girl relationships tended to be clandestine. Boys claimed to have girlfriends from as many good schools as possible and letter writing took up most of the time allocated to evening study. Parents expected sons to have and even entertain girlfriends but clamped down on daughters for fear of pregnancies and the dreaded stigma of promiscuity, school expulsion, and loss of educational opportunity, if not the accompanying responsibilities of childrearing. Sexual activity among youth is condemned by parents and also by peers in most communities. Parental apprehension toward cross-gender associations among youth also reflects material limitations in many African communities. Social dating requires finances and space that few youth possess. Siblings share sleeping quarters and families auction livestock to cover tuition. High unemployment rates among university graduates deflect hopes of immediate education benefits that would afford youth spending monies. In addition, daughters face ostracism following unwanted pregnancies.

Both Wafula and Smith (2000) in his Nigerian study acknowledge the exploitation of vulnerable female students by male teachers and administrators. National outrage grew in the latter part of 2009 against teachers who impregnate students, as media accounts demonstrate (Siringi, 2009; Mukele,

2009, Oriang, 2009). A report by Kenya's Teachers Service Commission (TSC) found that between 2003–2007, 12,660 girls had been sexually abused by teachers and yet only 633 of these faced charges (Siringi, 2009). The Teachers Service Commission (TSC) dismissed more than 500 teachers "implicated with impregnating girls in primary schools" (Ndurya, 2010). It is the girls that pay the price. Sometimes parents are swayed by sexual predators not to pursue charges in exchange for token reparations. When proven guilty, sexual offenders are summarily sacked. In one incident, a male teacher was fired long after the girl had got married to someone else.

For African immigrants, America epitomizes excesses in human liberties but also the promise of re-inventing oneself. To many foreigners the United States is "the land of quick successes...the cradle of democracy...an unrestrained jungle of competition; and, finally, as the model to follow" (Ramos, 1993, p. 2.):

> The American educational system is very good, given that it is open to everybody. I like the fact that the opportunities for an education are endless in the United States. I have heard stories of people who came from Africa with basic high school education (no O or A levels) and who excelled in good colleges. Actually, I have met a girl from Zimbabwe who came with no formal education at all, attended some adult education classes, took the GED and landed in Brooklyn College. In the United States, anybody who is motivated to learn can learn. Eligibility for financial aid is a true blessing. Honestly, I like the tests (shhhhh). There is nothing wrong about the test. (Girikaze)

Aarifa, a questionnaire respondent, like Yetunde, commends the United States education system but also acknowledges its inhibitive aspects:

> The most attractive and inhibitive aspect of the system of education in the United States is it is public and a socialized system. Unfortunately, this socialized system also reflects the capitalist nature of the United States, and districts that are comprised of wealthier families generally receive more funds or preferential treatment which determines the quality of education their children receive. This is inhibitive since the public assumes that since [sic] education is free and available to all, that the system is not flawed and that it treats all children and families, regardless of race and class, similarly. I do not believe this is so, and think that the educational system in the United States is segregated, classist, and racist. (Aarifa)

While Girikaze emphasizes the opportunities to immigrants, Yetunde focuses on the resources within schools: "The most attractive part of the educational system in the United States is the abundance of educational resources (books, libraries, funding for research, information technology that can be used for educational purposes, journals, good physical plant/facilities, etc). The least attractive is the high cost of education, particularly in the 'elite' institutions at all levels." Similarly Wafula commends the U.S. education system for its resources as opposed to that of his country of birth: "In Kenya, libraries are very poorly stocked. One could blame it on the institutions for not encouraging lecturers to do research and publish materials that would in turn become resources in the libraries. There seems to be non/little incentive for educators to publish original research." The situation has changed tremendously in the last decade. University libraries even have e-journal access. On the other hand, some lecturers in Kenya are content with moonlighting (sideline teaching jobs), devoting limited time toward research. Funds for university research also dried up during President's Moi's last years in office although lecturers from the biological sciences consistently publish more than colleagues in the humanities and social sciences. Wafula also complains about the commercialization in the United States, and its impact on public education, particularly at the college level:

> What I find inhibitive is the business nature of education in the United States. Education is a commodity and is traded via tools such as student loans etc. Education should be a right and not a privilege. If you happen to be from an economically disadvantaged family, you are less likely to have a higher education since the cost is so prohibitive. Other associated costs such as books make education very expensive. There is almost what seems like a plot to make education a preserve of the rich. In Kenya, I did not have to buy expensive books semester after semester. One history book lasted an entire course. In the United States, books are semester based and very expensive. I recall the Chair reminding us to make students buy books. I have seen students struggle because they can't afford class texts. Even with well established libraries, class texts are rarely in the libraries. The publishing industry is preying on the students and parents. Every other day, publishing companies display their wares in colleges urging professors and decision makers to use this book or that book.

In contrast to the material disparities within schools and colleges, *Immigrant Teachers, American Students: Cultural Differences, Cultural Disconnections* highlights the cultural mishaps of African immigrant teachers, the often inexplicit expectations in social interactions. The issue goes beyond the level of competence African immigrant teachers exhibit. Classroom diversity, reflected in differing perceptions and behavior patterns, makes emotional discomfort inevitable in classrooms as my experience and similar exchanges during the semester demonstrate.

Hitting the Ground Running

After a confrontation a student, Paula, charged me with insensitivity, a label that shocked me. I had urged her to integrate more sources in her Internet research project on Che Guevara. Paula had the required six-paragraph essay (with two to three sentences for each paragraph rather than the recommended four-plus sentences per paragraph) and resisted having to do more work. She stormed out of class after threatening to drop the class. Paula returned toward the end of class. She reiterated her earlier charges: I was rude, the sarcastic comments I made were uncalled for, and my glance was disrespectful. My bafflement must have been obvious.

> *I don't like the way you look at me*, Paula announced.
> *What?* I was truly bewildered. I make a point of speaking directly to students, eye-to-eye.
> *You treat us like inferiors.*
> *How?*
> *You people always look down upon us*, she continued, refocusing the charges.
> *Who are you and what am I?*
> *You English people look down upon us Americans.*
> *What? I am not English.*
> *Yes, you are.*
> *How would you know?* I asked, baffled by her certainty.
> *You think I am dumb? I can tell,* she insisted, drawing out her sentences with evident petulance.
> *But I am not English*, I tried to explain to her.
> *You are,* she insisted.
> *I am American like you.*
> *But you grew up in England.*
> *No!*
> *Well you went to school there.*
> *No*, I reiterated. It was a battle of wits. The rest of the class had by now left, leaving the two of us to face off in private.

Sometime into the discussion, Paula's voice appeared to mellow enough for me to counter her charges of insensitivity. The flaw in her earlier stereotype of me as English may have deflated her vehement charges. She then accused me of imposing unrealistic standards; a charge I could counter with reference to class requirements and my one-on-one support during writing assignments. Later in the exchange, I stressed the importance of an open mind. I reminded Paula of the books I read and which I brought along to share with the class. I was learning Spanish, which took time and energy. Surprisingly, Paula tolerated my lengthy speech. She seemed to listen to what I was saying. "There is always more to learn, a humbling process for most of us," I told her before excusing myself to rush off to an on-campus lecture that afternoon. Teaching involves developing relationships with students despite inevitable misunderstandings; teachers expect to return to classes the next day, and they expect better days!

In that class, most of the students walked around and worked in cliques. Paula's aloofness was surprising given the level of interaction among a 252-student body of 11–12th graders. She had joined the class late and was among the minority four of 14 twelfth graders who rarely sat with or interacted with the rest of the class unless I directed them to do so during a class activity. When Paula openly accused me of disrespect in class, none of the others spoke out to support her. On the other hand, this recounting of the incident omits Paula's sense of self, the unvoiced expectations of me, and her frustration at my failure to accommodate her needs. Both teachers and students respond to the behavior and verbal expressions of the other, all of which individuals interpret from the lens of previous experiences and beliefs. The experience is not unique to foreign-trained teachers (Bateson, 2000; Benton, 2009; Lake, 2009; Shor, 1996).

The tension with Paula is typical of student/teacher power negotiations in class settings. In this case, the tension illustrates differences in role expectations and interactions. Paula completed her required six-paragraph essay, however skimpy; I wanted her to do more, to provide an excellent rather than an adequate piece. I was the insensitive "Other" perhaps, relative to other teachers. Raised to be assertive by standing her ground and demanding her rights, Paula talked back, charged me with inappropriate behavior and threatened to drop the class. Her dismissal of my suggestions to integrate more research sources in her analysis of Che Guevara surprised me. In Kenya, students bask in the attention offered by a teacher for one-on-one consultations to improve the quality of a task, given large class sizes and limited curriculum materials. Increasingly, parents fork out extra funds for tuition over and above government-dictated school fee structures. Some children have formal instruction (with extra tuition) all year. It is considered a privilege. Understandably, teachers pay more attention to children whose parents extend themselves to accommodate teacher interests. Contrasting the Nigerian to the U.S. education system, Yetunde notes how:

> Teachers have more authority and are afforded more formal respect in my country than in America. Standards are higher. Grading is harsher than here in the United States. There is less discussion and more lecturing. There is more of an assumption that the professor is passing on valuable information than obtains in the United States.

Paula probably viewed my suggestions to integrate more research as an undue demand or critique of her work or of her as a person. In a later class on parental influence, Paula informed the class how her mother would not dare enter her bedroom to chastise Paula on tardiness. If true, another woman's critique could not have been anything but an affront to her sense of self. On the other hand, there are elements in the African-American traditions of collective childrearing (Bateson, 2000). Notwithstanding lower living standards, African students are more mature despite the difficulties encountered daily, claims Ahmad. Ahmad attributes differences in teacher-student relationships to socialization and, also, educational access. Without libraries and related school support facilities, African students rely heavily on the goodwill and expertise of individual teachers:

> [In Sudan,] a teacher is very much appreciated and it is easier to transmit facts. With regard to students differences I adapt myself from absolutely obedient students to students who question everything with no boundaries or borders.... USA students have access to any piece of material that the teacher needs to teach and there is no excuse for students not to learn. It is no secret the resources are very limited for students in Sudan.

Obiakor and Gordon (2003) attribute such mishaps to cultural disconnects, while other scholars root these issues in maturity or the lack thereof, in adolescents' testing boundaries with teachers (Harris R, 1998; Lightfoot-Lawrence, 1999; McFarland, 2004; Milner, 2004). Whether the issue is cultural misconceptions or adolescent rejection of authority, such incidents create tensions that detract from the focus on factual transmission and classroom decorum with respectful exchanges:

> The biggest inhibitive aspect of American education is the non-reinforcement of teacher respect and classroom discipline. It is not fair that students who want to learn and teachers who want to teach cannot do it just because some unmotivated students decide to disturb the class. (Girikaze)

Since shared values between parties offer a common language and a sense of mutuality, the cultural disconnect between immigrant and American students reflects its absence. At times, the affinity between groups reflects the value placed on education rather than a shared racial, gender, or class identity (Bateson, 2000; Harris, 1998; Hemmings, 2003; Lane, Wheby, and Cooley, 2006). Diligent students appreciate teachers who consistently hold them to high standards regardless of the sacrifices involved, a trait Traore and Lukens (2006) note among African-born immigrant students in the United States. But who is the cultural outsider? The sense of tentativeness is not exclusive to foreign-trained teachers; however, discussions on teacher alienation in school settings center on differences in names, race or ethnic characteristics, and language, specifically with regard to accent.

Citing Oscar Handlin's (1951) *The Uprooted,* Jane Roland Martin illustrates similarities between traditionally defined immigrants and those who make cultural transitions or physical relocations, including emotional and physical experiences. Students who move into a different class, gender, or racial environment (re)negotiate identity in unfamiliar settings. In each case, individuals experience alienation and the consequences of moving into unaccustomed environments and adapting unfamiliar habits. Each undergoes tremendous challenges in forging a new identity, new relationships in environments that are often "harsh and hostile." Torn from familiar customs, even simple acts of existence involve a weighing of alternatives. Some use the analogy of a new birth, learning a new language, getting accustomed to new foods, new ways of dressing, and acquiring or understanding prevailing speech patterns. For newcomers in a new social milieu, regional relocations, residence in a new country or in the case of females, entering male-dominated careers such as politics, law or engineering amounts to cross-cultural movement. In the United States, and in other predominantly European societies, Blacks undergo similar trials with academic and economic success. Viewed as different and a liability, men of non-European origins and most women rarely enjoy "active cultural citizenry here." For them, cultural crossings involve a tightrope existence of "living in and between two cultures" (Martin, 2002). Both Baruti and Ahmad attribute their frustrations in the United States' system to being viewed as the other.

Students' receptivity to different ethnic groups plays a significant role in the classroom atmosphere, according to Baruti: "If I weren't Black, I think I would be received differently." Ahmad's response is even more poignant: "I am hesitant to say anything about the role ethnicity plays in teaching for fear of the repercussions, but it has set me back and denied me very many opportunities." As the discussion demonstrates, the cultural outsider label can be a perceptual location or one imposed by others. Regardless of the basis, teachers, local and foreign-trained, navigate classifications that foster or hinder the teaching/

learning process. Baruti "ignores" the friction in student/teacher, male/female relationships but admits that, "Some white males are very difficult to deal with. I often think they are scared of me as they try to avoid me." On the other hand, Ahmad intervenes when necessary: "In the United States, relations between male and female are open due to their studying together, but in Sudan schools are separated by gender due to conservative Islamic tradition laws.... I try to keep an eye on relationships that arise between males and females and not to let these interrupt the education process." Aminata utilizes parent/teacher conferences to address classroom misunderstandings. Even in one's country of birth, individuals make choices about when to intervene in school-related issues, whether academic or relational. It is often a question of priorities. One chooses which mountain to die on! As Achebe (2009) notes: "When the Igbo (Nigeria) encounter human conflict, their impulse is not to determine who is right but quickly to restore harmony" (p. 6). He insists that while this often means avoiding direct confrontations or particular issues, it is never an act of cowardice but of strategy.

While Baruti ignores emotional issues regarding relationships including "rudeness," she relies on laid-down expectations to handle conflict. Baruti attributes teacher-student tensions to students' inflated expectations: "Most students have low academic output and expect high grades. The experience is typically: below output = low grade," and adds that classroom interactions between American and South African students are similar "except rudeness stemming from [students' unrealistic expectations)]." Her refuge is the almighty syllabus: "I have a rubric for every graded assignment in my syllabus. This has helped a lot!" On the other hand, the multiple locations offer an opportunity for negotiation of personal and social transformations. Ahmad is resigned to the inevitability of change: "In Sudan, a teacher is very much appreciated and it is easier to deliver content material. With regard to students' differences I have to adapt myself from dealing with absolutely obedient students to students who question everything with no boundaries or borders."

People extend themselves daily in adapting to the unexpected. We apologize for breaches. We ask for clarity in the event of confusing claims. We initiate conversations with strangers. We adopt mannerisms and speech patterns not of our primary cultural groups. We negotiate for compromise on a range of issues. Humans have the capacity to change. Indeed, change is inevitable, whether gradual or immediate, conscious or otherwise.

Names

What is in a name? During introductions, I readily volunteer the response, "You can call me Florence." It is my name although the primary aim is to avoid endless questions of how to pronounce my African name, Namulundah, what it means (does Smith mean anything?) and, "Could you say it again?" requests. Mufwene is even dismissive of genuine attempts by non-Africans at pronouncing the names. The few Americans who call immigrants by their foreign names do so because it is "musical" or as a show of achievement in contrast to those who avoid trying to pronounce such names; although the initial interest or repetitions do not guarantee the name's recall (Mufwene, 1993; Owolabi, 1996). Some immigrants face a similar handicap with "American" names. Ahmed (a pseudonym), a student in one of my college classes, lamented his inability to recall names, including mine, Florence. "[People in the United States] don't look like their names," he added with all seriousness. At the time, I doubled over with laughter. "People [in Guinea] look like their names. But Smith...?" he concluded. It wasn't until a month later that his apt observation dawned on me. In the United States, other than skin color and accents, the African name readily identifies a foreigner.

African names are central to a person's identity (Appiah, 1992; Traore and Lukens, 2006): "Traditional naming ceremonies in African societies are significant events because the naming of an individual derives from meaningful identification of a particular relationship, characteristic, or predestination for the development of one's personality" (Traore and Lukens, 2006, p. 11). My own sub-ethnic group, the Bukusu, name children after deceased family members as a form of rebirth; some claim that children turn out with similar characteristics. There is the belief that children "select" the name: acting agitated until they are called by the right ancestral name. In Kenya, names such as Ouko, Kamau, Namaemba, Nyamboto, Kipchoge, Kalungu, Ahmed, or Mwachofi locate a person's birthplace and typically, the ethnic group. People's names are significant indicators of their cultural identity much like Rodriguez or Vladimir as opposed to names like George, Vanessa or Derrick. Locals within countries readily identify distinctions within sub-groups: the shape of cheekbones, hair, skin tone, or accent with an official language. In the United States, the ability of friends and colleagues to distinguish a New York from a New Jersey or Boston accent never ceases to amaze me.

When a person's name isolates, few clamor for the negative attention (Traore and Lukens, 2006). Kenya's post-election violence raised ethnic tensions to the fore although university students always had ethnic/regional associations that unified students through established networks. Invisibility offers a sense of relief; it reduces teasing. In some cases, refugees who escaped war-torn countries such as Rwanda, Guinea, Liberia, Ivory Coast, and Sierra Leone, or recently Kenya, resist publicizing their names, aware of the implications of belonging to any one tribe: "The tribal conflicts seem to be a problem for them even here" (p. 40). Achebe (2009) acknowledges the importance of being known by name in a foreign land. He is excited at being recognized by a taxi driver in New York's bustling city. On the other hand, Nuruddin Farrah, the Somali writer, had once "narrowly escaped death at the hands of agents from his homeland" by denying his identity upon confrontation (p. 76). For some immigrant students, invisibility serves other functions. As a student, the Kenyan professor Mukuria (2003) marked his assignments with serial numbers rather than his name "for fear of repercussions resulting from grading bias" (p. 56). Some professors were surprised to discover that he performed well on tests, which he claims might have been a different case had they been aware of the student's identity beforehand. To avoid unnecessary attention, foreigners such as myself use European sounding names that are familiar to people in the United States.

In the late nineteenth century, early Christian missionaries infiltrated the African continent, introducing a new religion coupled with Western administrative and educational structures (Appiah, 1992). Religion divided villages between "the people of the church and the people of the world" (Achebe, 2009, p. 12). Converts to the faith severed ethnic links either out of disdain or a show of loyalty and took on Christian/European names such as Mary, Beatrice, Charles, Crispus, Robin, Makerious, Victoria, and Benjamin, that symbolized a new identity. Some Kenyans are now reclaiming the dignity of ethnic names. Across the African continent parents often give children European (Christian) first names such as Zipporah, Bonaventure or Pius and Moses followed by African names; for instance, Martha Nangoka. Yet it is common to find people with last names such as Classpeter, Wilson, Wilberforce, Robertson and Ison among the Fanti in Ghana's central region. Similarly, residents of Nigeria's Delta region have last names such as Goodwill, Johnson, Benson, Clark, etc. In contrast, names such as Simiyu Wandibba or Wafula Okumu bypass Christian names despite the individuals' religious affiliation. The media currently portrays Africans, initially accused of irreligiosity as potential converts from paganism and barbarity, as profoundly religious; the developing world has turned out to be the nexus of Christianity as opposed to the dwindling numbers of practicing believers in developed countries. Whether names provide easy classification of cultural insiders and outsiders, to some, these signifiers embody a reality that empowers or disempowers teachers and students. Indeed, popular students and teachers often acquire nicknames that proffer insider status. A colleague at the College calls me Nami!

Regarding names, African Americans wrestle with issues similar to those of African immigrants. Luo (2009) illustrates the lingering racism in U.S. employment practices despite "decades of progress...culminating in President Obama's election." Black graduates, even those from respected colleges, cite covert racism during interviews: They told "subtler stories, referring to surprised looks and offhand comments, interviews that fell apart almost as soon as they began, and the sudden loss of interest from companies after meetings" (A1). Mr. Barry Jabbar Sykes of Morehouse College uses the initial "J" to avoid associations with Blackness at interviews, at least the entry stage. Barry sounds Irish. John R. Williams omitted his membership in the University of Chicago African-American Students Association on his resume, for similar reasons. The interviewed Black applicants insist on the importance of names in getting job interviews, if not the job itself. Applicants with Black-sounding names such as Lakisha and Jamal receive 50 percent fewer call-backs than those with names such as Emily and Greg. Luo cites another study in the academic *Journal of Social Problems* which "found that white males receive substantially more job leads for high-level supervisory positions than women and members of minorities." (p. A1)

Race and Ethnicity

Colonial images of an Africa "rooted in the ancestors and committed to the co-existing harmony with the world, the environment, and with every other living creature" (Traore and Lukens, 2006, p. 44) contrasts with the "cutthroat world of corporate greed and insatiability found in America" (p. xvi). Cultural comparisons can be just as simplistic and stereotyping as the case of ahistorical depictions of Africans. Molefi Kete Asante attributes Africa's image as "uniformly backward, primitive, or dangerous" to U.S. propaganda (Traore and Lukens, 2006, p. x; Obiakor and Afolayan, 2007; Obiakor and Grant, 2002; Owolabi, 1996). Movies such as "Roots," "Amistad," "Shaka Zulu," as well as those featuring Tarzan, or *Survivor*-type reality TV programs, and National Geographic imagery, "contribute to the stereotypes of Africa(n)—jungle, desert and living among the animals" (p. 16). This negative imagery of Africanness creates a chasm between Africa and American society (Dodoo, 1997; Obiakor and Gordon, 2003). Reflecting xenophobic stereotypes, Americans denigrate and associate the continent with slavery, natural disasters, civil wars, and recently the HIV/AIDS pandemic. Despite the African view of American culture as alien, Lukens and Traore (2006) admit that graduates "educated from overseas in the colonial countries were considered for higher-level positions…in some instances in the recent past this would include Ministers or even Heads of State" (p. 45). Practically all the first African presidents trained overseas, including more recent heads of state: Julius Nyerere (Tanzania), Kwame Nkrumah (Ghana), Jomo Kenyatta (Kenya), the medical doctor Kamuzu Banda (Malawi medical doctor), Houphouët-Boigny (Côte d'Ivoire), Ahmed Ben Bella (Algeria) and Ellen Johnson Sirleaf (Liberia). Kenya's President Mwai Kibaki was trained in the United Kingdom while Prime Minister Raila Odinga studied in East Germany.

The historical and static image of primitive Africans and a left-back continent reflect Tarzan-like movie propaganda (Appiah, 1992; Obiakor and Grant, 2003; Owolabi, 1996; Traore and Lukens, 2006). At one session, the high school class discussed Appiah's (2006) *New York Times* feature story on cultural contamination in Ghana, his country of birth. Reflecting a static view of African history, students appeared shocked at the cosmopolitan elements—cell phones, elaborate clothing, some of it Western, in an open-air market. Alex, who rarely spoke in class, broke out into a laugh. "What is it?" I asked. "They have cell phones," he called out, still gazing at pictures of local people in traditional attire talking into cell phones. Owolabi (1996) too recalls the looks of "amazement and surprise" to his claim of daily telephone conversations with family in Nigeria. Decrying campaigns by cultural purists calling for authentic local elements, Appiah (2006) illustrates the inevitability of cultural exchanges. Already reflecting cultural pluralism, Kumasi comprises English, German, Chinese, Syrian, Lebanese, Burkinabè and Ivorian ancestry. Appiah (1992) should know for he was born to a Ghanaian and English mother. His sisters are married to a Norwegian, a Nigerian and a fellow Ghanaian: their children's hair ranges from his black father's to the Viking ancestors' color, a reflection of their accents. This is cultural pluralism at the doorstep. Ghanaians are as familiar with the football player Renaldo, Coca Cola or Guinness as they are with the local Star and Club beer brands. Indigenous communities, however, are selective with international cultural adaptations. Appiah acknowledges the weariness of even cosmopolitan Ghanaians with early romances among youth and public displays of intimacy as much as resistance to the spread of nursing homes. The aversion to the "crass consumerism of modern Western society" and its global influence contrasts with the lure of foreign products. Similarly, Muslims chafe at the immodesty reflected in swimming pools that permit "women to swim almost naked with strange men."

Monolithic conceptions of Africa ignore differences among African immigrants, as well as the continent's varied economic and political systems. Analogous to the presumed cultural homogeneity within the United States, African immigrants differ in "racial, ethnic, linguistic, family, and class backgrounds" (Obiakor and Afolayan, 2007; Obiakor and Grant, 2002). Similar to the American populace, Africans range in color—black, white, Arab, non-black; with about 70 percent being black (Obiakor and Afolayan, 2007). Aarifa's acquaintances mistake her for being Spanish rather than Ethiopian-African. For some Africans, part of the cultural shock comes from the sudden labels as " 'black,' 'colored,' or minority members, terms that rarely formed part of their self-identity" (Traore and Lukens, 2006, p. 92; Owolabi, 1996). The Ethiopian professor Abebe's

(2003) experience captures this paradox. He felt pressured to disassociate himself from his war-torn country with its dictators, yet was alienated because of his foreign birth. "It is quite perplexing to a Black person from Africa when he or she is considered neither Caucasian nor Black!" (p. 21). Aarifa offers a context for the skepticism between African-born immigrants and African Americans:

> American students think African-born immigrants aren't exposed to similar levels of racism or difficulty. Moreover, African-born immigrants do not understand or empathize with the pressures of American society pushed onto students here. Both sides view each other as aliens and without frank conversation, the divide remains. Once I allowed American students and teachers to discuss their misconceptions with me and I was able to address each one with facts, then the divide lessened and I was able to be much more effective within the classroom and in my personal interactions with students and parents. I was also at an advantage since I was educated here.

African immigrants of former colonies share some experiences with marginalized Blacks in the United States based on relations of "established structures of power" that privilege or marginalize particular groups or individuals (Grossberg, 1996; Freire, 2000). Appiah (1992) disputes claims of a solidarity based on "a shared common ecology... a common historical experience or a common threat from imperial Europe, but because they belong to this one race," a perception held by self and others. The arbitrariness in racial distinctions in no way undermines its currency (p. 5). Yet, as Yetunde notes, the shared racial marginality has failed to unify the two groups. Noting that American students presume an intellectual incompetence in African immigrant teachers upon initial contact, she adds:

> Colleagues are more difficult in the sense that most African-Americans do not embrace me as one of their own and often act in ways that exclude me from their social and associational agglomerations while white Americans either largely seem to desire to maintain the privileges offered by their white skin or act as though I am the exception to the rule when it comes to Black people. It is a very strange experience. I do not feel at home and often long for the ability to go back to my home country where I feel a sense of belonging.

Paradoxically, U.S. racial categories lump continental Blacks and African Americans together.

Social interactions blur the implied cultural distinctions within and across groups in nation-states (Appiah, 1992; Bhabha, 1996; Bateson, 2000). For instance, solidarity based on class or gender may supersede race/ethnic alliances. My high school students bonded along gender lines in a class with more females than males. Overall, habitual patterns of behavior offer personal anchors for day-to-day choices. People fall back on what is familiar whether in their perspective or their ultimate decisions. Cultural identities such as Black, no less than White, are neither uniform nor static as the difficulties between me and the mostly Caribbean students I taught in high school demonstrated. A shared race/ethnic cultural identity between African-born Blacks and African Americans has failed to eliminate mutual suspicions between the two groups (Aman, 2002; Obiakor and Gordon, 2003; Tatum, 1997):

> [There is] the assumption that Africans are more ignorant and poorer than Americans and should want to stay in America forever and ought to be grateful to the United States for taking them in. Africans sometimes look down on African-Americans and Africans of Caribbean descent because they have the erroneous belief that they are better than these other Black people and have better work ethics and demonstrable achievement. The other groups also have similar beliefs. This causes strained relationships. Vis-à-vis white Americans, there seems to be some kind of adoration at the achievement and a desire to emulate what's perceived as their "progressive" and "successful" behavior. There seems to me to be more socializing between Africans and white Americans than with people of African descent in the United States. (Yetunde)

Mutual suspicions create mistrust or put-downs and also heighten the quarrels over derogatory labels. The jockeying for position among minorities, including immigrants, over political representation, labor, immigration, education, and cultural rights, inadvertently reinforces a White norm; after all, who defines the "model minority"? (hooks and mesa-bains, 2006). African-American faculty view African immigrants as too conciliatory, a trait valued by "those White folks." African immigrants do not assert their rights and are reputed to take jobs away from African Americans (Uwah, 2003).

Comparing African-born immigrants to African Americans in view of their value of education is a classic example of conventional cultural rhetoric. Wafula captures this African faith in education: "For me education was my meal ticket. Working hard was the only option for me and my siblings. There was a weaning process along the road to academic excellence. I was tested with national exams every step of the way. I remember vividly the sleepless nights before such national exams." Africans view education as the key to upward mobility while some African Americans regard it as a "White" thing (hooks and mesa-bains, 2006; Maathai, 2007; McWhorter, 2001; Ogbu, 1992). Insisting on basic writing proficiency in assignments appears to reinforce a White norm and dismiss minority linguistic patterns, something advocates of culturally relevant pedagogy recommend (Uwah, 2003). Kincheloe and Weil (2001) argue quite cogently against the mythical belief in established standards for reforming education in the United States. The presumption of a national debate and academic standards ignores the fact that few elites with the "power to decide," design and mandate these ideals on a largely disempowered populace. Differences within the populace in perspective and visions are sacrificed for sanitized version of history and civic goals. Generalizations about minority under performance ignore a history of African Americans' academic achievements as well as resistance to school among African born immigrants. Aarifa acknowledges the impact of differing living standards between Africans and Americans on educational pursuits:

> The majority of children in my home country cannot afford basic school supplies such as paper and pencil and work to get the money to purchase those items. Also, education is not free and many children of parents who are part of the servant class do not live near their parents and are raised by extended family. They are expected to perform at the level of children who do have material privileges and they relish the opportunities for education.

Watoya makes a similar claim with regards to Kenyan students: "Students in my country are highly motivated to learn and excel in their studies. However, there is little incentive for teachers due to low remunerations and poor facilities." Aarifa attributes the embrace of education among African-born immigrants to expediency rather than priorities. Africans who immigrate to the United States are already products of selection, due to finances and physical distance, and this skews such comparisons. Ignoring the rationale for differences in educational priorities undermines the cultural solidarity between immigrants and African-American Blacks. Most Africans have financial responsibilities for less well-off relatives that shape their choices (Owolabi, 1996).

Fellow minorities question Professor Abebe's (2003) understanding and commitment to minority interests because of his foreign origins. In Professor Gwalla-Ogisi's (2003) case, "a delegation of students approached both the Chair and Dean to register their concern" that a South African professor lacked "the knowledge base and experience that was relevant to them" (p. 27). Social interactions reflect similar contentions among Blacks regardless of age. On one subway ride, a couple of Black youth sat around me. Not soon after, they began singing *Kumbaya* and pointing at me. It wasn't until years later that I discovered the song's association with Africa. The vilification is mutual. African parents warn children against associating with African Americans to avoid the negative stereotypes of Black youth. Although no less complimentary, the image of African students as "ignorant, stinking, and mostly naked, uncivilized, live in jungles, eat raw animals, have no cars or TV," does not contrast any more favorably than the image of African-American students as "lazy, rude, welfare dependent, disrespectful, and ignorant" (Luken and Traore, 2006, p. 130; Obiakor and Gordon, 2003). At Largo High School in Maryland, the Nigerian Ms. Ihekweme recalls how "kids at school taunted her, making fun of her accent and her hair, which she couldn't afford to get professionally done" (Fogg, 2009, B14). For Traore and Lukens (2006) inter-minority tensions "represent an example of those at the bottom of the hierarchical ladder of esteem finding someone under them that they can look down upon, or an example of the oppressed acting like oppressors when given the chance" (p. xxiv). The mutual suspicion, whether obvious or unconscious, influences classroom interactions between the groups (Luken and Traore, 2006; Obiakor and Gordon, 2003). These cross-cultural tensions detract from a teacher's focus on course content or fostering interactive activities as Wafula and Girikaze acknowledge:

> African immigrants are viewed suspiciously by their African-American counterparts. It is as if there is unspoken competition over unseen resources which the African-Americans feel "owed" to them. There is obvious disdain in most cases between the two. (Wafula)

Girikaze, a questionnaire respondent, distinguishes her reception as an African immigrant teacher by African Americans and by foreign-born students to her, another prophet dismissed within purportedly familiar cultural groups:

> My teaching experience as a female African immigrant has been particularly difficult due to my French-speaking background. American-born students, black and white, show no enthusiasm whatsoever about my teaching. They have difficulty accepting the fact that an African-born individual can be knowledgeable in the field of language and literacy education. To the contrary, foreign-born students are eager to get into my class. They appreciate the amount I spend reading and responding to their work and are willing to dedicate as much time as needed on the improvement of their projects.

Dingane attributes the strained relations between African Americans and African-born immigrants to ignorance although he is one-sided in apportioning blame: "American students have limited knowledge of African cultures, histories and religions; hence, there are fewer social interactions between the two groups." Girikaze's comments illustrate the precarious solidarity among Blacks. One would expect American-born students to be more supportive of African-born faculty given the relatively common origins. Behind the disappointment of African-born faculty is the nostalgic appeal to an unqualified bond among Blacks. Achebe (2009) focuses on the historical context of this Black-on-Black aggravation. He calls for Black solidarity. Achebe draws on his meeting with James Baldwin to illustrate the need for solidarity between continental Africans and African Americans:

> They must work together to uncover their story, whose truth has been buried so deeply in mischief and prejudice that a whole army of archaeologists will now be needed to unearth it. We must be that army on both sides of the Atlantic. The grievance against Africa sometimes encountered among African-Americans must be critically examined…the intention to separate us must be confounded if we are to succeed. (pp. 66–67)

Migrations, mass media and relocations within nation-states undermine community and ethnic bonds and the impact on identities (Bateson, 2000; Ogulnick, 2000; Stefan, 2000). Further, adages of collective responsibility for children's welfare within African villages ignore the price involved.[1] Traditional communities stifle dissent and ostracize mavericks to foster social cohesion (Maathai, 2007; Mori, 1997). Structured regimens in Kenyan schools and workplaces dispute clichés of "African time" where deadlines are but a formality. (I have since heard similar charges against African Americans and Hispanics.) Talking back creates angst in African-born students and elicits apprehensive signals in the audience; it is a sign of poor upbringing. Watoya finds the jostling for authority between teachers and students rather disconcerting. He commends the U.S. system of education for the "Opportunities to develop professionally and the educational facilities. On the other hand, students have too much freedom and are encouraged to undermine teachers." Many American students demand their "rights" with little mention of social obligations, as David's dismissal of the role of police later demonstrates. However, comparisons across cultures involve static assessments that ignore variations in cultural expressions and allegiance to cultural identities (Appiah, 1992).

Within African countries, the focus on negative "foreign" cultural influences on indigenous practices to explain disruptions in social norms overlooks an inevitable process of living organisms. In the post-independence era, nostalgia for the "good old days" among ethnic loyalists contrasts sharply with the openness to modern frames of reference and relative improvements in economic standards evident among most Kenyans. According to Mazrui (1972) such polemic approaches to cultural or historical debates ennoble the hospitality of traditional villages with romantic luster while eulogizing the African genius for collective life. Given the existing polarization of cultural debates, an affirmation of African culture amounts to a backhanded denigration of European cultures. But is it? Neither the Western-style education immigrants receive or physical distancing conceals syncretism or severs the African from the cultural bond (Appiah, 1992).

In contrast to African immigrant instructors in developed nations, Western expatriates in former colonies such as Kenya and Zimbabwe are bolstered by association with their country of origin. As a minority lacking in indigenous communication nuances, some expatriate teachers treat indigenous groups as homogenous rather than as individuals with differing fears, hopes and aspirations. These teachers operate in schools that rely on colonial languages and systems with school texts written by indigenous or foreign scholars in languages (English or French) to which the teachers are accustomed. Ensconced in Western look-alike administrative systems, expatriates work with indigenous students who are financially, economically and politically dependent on developed countries. On the continent, African teachers of literature deliver a Eurocentric curriculum to students for whom an imperial system is the standard. For African students, the American culture is "by some objective standard, superior." In contrast, American (Literature) teachers deliberate over a curriculum that is depicted as the standard but also one reflective of their primary identity; the American student in relativistic rhetoric "acknowledges the value of African culture" to Africans but the American culture assumes an aura of normality and superiority (Appiah, 1992, p. 69). For Africans, prevailing literary traditions reinforce the myth of Western legitimacy as Achebe's (2009) educational experience illustrates. Margaret Mead's daughter Bateson (2000) admits the affection and privilege this status endows even when she has been in the minority in Israel and Iran. In Africa expatriates are surrounded by indigenous people who admire and envy what they stand for. The Canadian expatriate Fast (2000) is surprised by the reverence for the printed word among Zimbabwean students; they even doubt his exposure of obvious misprints and calculation errors in test review papers. Fast was shocked at students' glossing over an examiner's error in defining a problem on an exam sheet. It went unchallenged.

Paradoxically, Peace Corps volunteers, 91 percent "white and middle class males," are perturbed by classroom challenges in the United States, their own country, relative to their experiences in foreign countries such as Kenya, Zaire, Cameroon, Mexico and Western Samoa (Siegel, 1996):

> In those countries, teachers lecture to as many as 70 students in a class and write voluminous notes on the board or even on the walls. Students dutifully copy the notes as they prepare for the highly competitive English- or French-style exams. But such an approach does not work in American classrooms.... [Despite] the lack of books, blackboards, or even heat or hot water in their foreign postings, many Peace Corps volunteers admit working with foreign students, an elite, groups "who made it to the secondary level... these were often [students] with social status. Motivation was not a problem and they usually showed deference to the teacher. (n.p.)

Academic excellence determines a student's mobility in these settings. How can experts (or adults) be wrong? Although rare, open dissent among students and adults (parliamentarians, political activists) reflects ongoing cultural changes.

The Model Minority

Within the United States, the Chinese epitomize the ambivalent truce in cultural bridging despite obvious differences with mainstream Americans. Although Chinese-Americans are touted as the "model minority," the label "emphasizes their collective experience," ignoring a history of institutionalized exclusion (Li and Beckett, 2006: Miscevic, 2000; Tatum, 1997). The Chinese arrived in the United States at the same time as the Irish and prior to the Southern and Eastern Europeans but remained largely invisible. In the mid-1800s, they replaced Black workers following the Emancipation Proclamation in the late-1800s, confronting White hostility for flooding the labor market. Besides pervasive wage inequities relative to locals, legislatures in California, Oregon, Montana, Nevada and Idaho enacted a tax against Chinese workers. Media portrayed the Chinese as "quiet, peaceable, patient, industrious, and economical" (Miscevic, 2000, p. 69; Tatum, 1997), but also as "backward, defiled, infidel, bloodthirsty, gangsters, gamblers, and pimps" (p. 89). Overall, "As people of color, the Chinese were automatically seen as inferior, unassimilable aliens" (p. 83). Following the Pearl Harbor bombing, China and the United States became allies against a common enemy, Japan, a measure supported by President Franklin D. Roosevelt's executive order calling for "an end to racial discrimination" (p. 143). The Korean War in the mid-1900s revived United States belligerence against the Chinese. Since the mid-1960s the success of upper-middle class professionals from Taiwan, Hong Kong and mainland China in business and education surpasses the White community's achievements. Alongside the Chinese model, minority roles are those "employed as waiters, dishwashers, and in other service occupations in hotels and restaurants" (p. 194).

In *Strangers of the Academy: Asian Women Scholars in Higher Education* Li and Beckett (2006) depict the interlocking academic, cultural and linguistic challenges facing Asian American female scholars. Despite differences in gender, class, family income, employment and English language proficiency, stereotypes of Asian Americans range from the "yellow peril" submissive to the model educated and successful minority label. (The labels underscore the power of Whites in serving as power brokers.) American students are more likely to challenge the expertise and authority of Asian female immigrants, in linking their professional performance to the teacher's skin color. Meanwhile, Chinese immigrant teachers grapple with the "ambivalence, contradictions, and paradox" of differing norms and practices in the mother country and their resident culture. The process of seeking a balance between the two often boils down to Asian immigrant teachers masking their frustrations to avoid emotional conflict. This insider-outsider identity compels individuals into ongoing cross-cultural negotiations for a balance in social interactions: fulfilling professional obligations, and self-definition. Increasingly, success among Asian groups is attributed to their "cultural heritage," and its value for education as opposed to African-American students. The value of education among other immigrant groups shows the flaw in cultural identities; the commitment to education extends across all ethnic/racial groups.

Fogg's (2009) feature story of Chuma Nwanguma, a Nigerian immigrant in Largo, Maryland, is a classic example of an African's faith in education. The family arrived in the United States five years ago seeking "the best education for their five children." Mr. Mwanguma gave up secure employment as an assistant bank manager and the wife her teaching career. Similar aspirations have always been evident within African-American communities (Bateson, 2000; hooks, 2003; hooks and mesa-bains, 2006). Bateson attributes the fall-back on prejudice toward immigrants "to an intellectual and emotional avoidance of grappling with difference" (pp. 13–14). Gottschalk and Greenberg (2008) as well as Sledge (2010) extend the critique to America's receptivity or the lack therof to Islamic issues. While McWhorter (2001) chides African Americans for their disdain of education, his own academic career, and that of many other "successful" Blacks undermine his claims, a point hooks (2003) and Tatum (1997) highlight.

In contrast to the touted cliché of Asians as the model minority, Black immigrants surpass native-born Blacks and Whites as well as immigrant populations in educational attainment. This fact disputes conventional stereotypes of Blacks as intellectually inferior to Whites across the globe. It is difficult to estimate with precision the number of African immigrants in the United States, particularly Black, as opposed to Whites whose parents claim the continent as their place of origin. The *Journal of Blacks in Higher Education* puts the figure at 75 percent who are in fact African Black in the United Kingdom and the United States. The Census does not distinguish Black from White Africans. Studies of African students in both countries find that African immigrants comprise the "most highly educated" group relative to native-born Whites and Blacks as well as immigrant populations:

> Despite lower levels of education, Asian immigrants to the U.S. had a median household income that was 37 percent higher than the household income of African immigrants.... Despite the fact that African immigrants are nearly as likely as white Americans to hold a college degree, the median household income of African immigrants was 36 percent below the median household income of white Americans. These income statistics may reflect a continuing degree of employment discrimination against people with a black skin. (*Journal of Blacks in Higher Education*, Winter 26: pp. 60–61)

According to the U.S. Census Bureau, compared with other Americans, Nigerian immigrants are relatively better educated (Okome, forthcoming). Nigerians were part of the first wave of Africans to be brought to the Americas as indentured servants and, later, slaves, to work as coerced labor in the institutionalized slavery that became the norm in the New World. (http://en.wikipedia.org/wiki/File:Williamsburg_VA_slave_notice_1766.jpg). The second wave occurred after the Second World War, from 1945–1965, followed by a third wave from the political turmoil during the Biafran wars with an Igbo refugee flow into the United States. Subsequent waves of Nigerian immigrants have reflected both push and pull factors. For instance, in the 1990s, many Nigerians came to the United States as either recipients of the Diversity Lottery or as health care professionals. According to the U.S. Census Bureau, there were 91,499 Nigerians in the United States in the 1990s, and 164,691 in 2000, a figure representing 0.1 percent of the total U.S. population and an 80 percent increase from the previous decade (http://www.census.gov/prod/2004pubs/c2kbr-35.pdf). Analyses by several scholars confirm this (Butcher 1994; Dodoo 1997; Takyi 2002; Logan and Deane 2003). As Amadu Jacky Kaba shows, the 1990 Census indicates that:

> of 158.9 million people in the United States aged 25 and over, 20.3 percent had bachelor's degree or higher and 7.2 percent had graduate degree

or higher. For 52,388 Nigerians aged 25 and over, 52.9 percent had bachelor's degree or higher and 26.3 percent had graduate degree or higher. The 52.9 percent of Nigerians with bachelor's degree or higher were second only to another African group, Egyptians, with 60.4 percent. The 26.3 percent of Nigerians with graduate degree or higher was the highest rate among all 68 ancestry groups listed.... The above statistics show that Nigerians in the United States are at the top of the ladder in 1990 in educational attainment. Their average rate in bachelor's degree attainment was 36.6 percentage points higher than the national average and doubled and tripled many of the dominant groups in the country in 1990. Their average rate in graduate degree attainment in 1990 was 19.1 percentage points higher than the national average and more than doubled many of the dominant ethnic groups in the country. (http://www.westafricareview.com/issue11/kaba.html)

Leslie Casimir (2007) also draws upon the United States Census Bureau's 2006 American Community Survey to show that 37 percent of Nigerians in the United States had bachelor's degrees, 17 percent had master's degrees, and 4 percent had doctoral degrees ("In America, data show Nigerians are the most educated immigrants."). (http://naijanet.com/news/source/2008/may/27/1000.html, accessed 11/9/2009).

Asked to explain the academic success among Nigerian immigrants, Yetunde warns against the danger of reduction in analyzing social issues or advocating corrective measures while highlighting the group's diligence. Immigrants are never a representative sample in terms of ambition or achievements.

> Highly educated Nigerians are a statistical minority when one considers the home country's total population. However...I think what one observes among Nigerians in the United States can be attributed first to the self selection that informs the decision to emigrate—the highly educated and skilled choose to go, and these are the people one finds here. Also, it's a question of opportunities—the U.S. wants highly educated and skilled people and those people have an easier time of getting integrated into the United States because they can more easily get jobs, sometimes after getting more education and training. Finally, and I think this answers your question: most Nigerians want their children to get ahead in life. The lesson learned from contact with the West is that the knowledge possessed by the West enabled it to conquer and dominate Nigerians. There has since then been a deliberate, systematic, concerted effort to garner the knowledge, and through this, catch up

as well as surpass the West. This desire was much stronger during the nationalist era—the 1900s to the 1950s. There is a sentiment also in most Nigerian ethnic groups that one's children must surpass oneself in accomplishment, educational attainment and other measures of success. The nationalist generation produced children who want to surpass their parents. To use myself as an example, I am one of the children of the nationalist generation. So, I went to Columbia for my Ph.D., and my husband has a Ph.D. from New York University. My sisters (and my late brother) are also highly accomplished educationally, in our case, because that was the only option, as far as our parents were concerned—they saw our education as the only legacy they could give us and made sure they sent us to the best schools, and required the best academic performance from us. I grew up with a sense that the sky is the limit and there's nothing I cannot accomplish, plus no other human being is superior to me. Naturally, my children want to surpass me, although unlike my parents, I don't push them. My older son went to Princeton for his BSE (Bachelor of Science in Engineering). He doesn't want to go into an academic career, so, he's going to the University of Pennsylvania's Wharton School of Business, and he wants to become a big name in business. His junior brother—my younger son wants to do better than his big brother, not by anyone insisting that he must but just by seeing his family as role models. I think Nigerian parents also invest a lot of time, money and energy into facilitating their children's success. Many Nigerians for example, pay their children's school fees. Many of them also push their kids to excel.

According to Amadu Jacky Kaba, African immigrants in the United States, including Nigerians, may be highly educated, but they are poorly paid compared with other groups with similar levels of education (Okome, forthcoming). The Bureau of Labor Statistics (2009) report depicts the discrepancy in remuneration of foreign-born workers relative to native workers. In 2009, foreign-born workers earned $602 to $761 weekly pay earned by native-borns. While earnings by foreign-borns increase with education, native-born workers earn more regardless of educational level. Many obtain advanced degrees in their youth, driven by immigration mandates requiring credits to maintain an F-1 student visa as much as by prospects of a longer stay. Employment when acquired has its price. Many accept low wages as a gateway to career progression. The more assertive Nigerians tone down complaints to avoid compromising sponsors for the coveted green card. Youth and inexperience also account for low wages (Butcher 1994: 267–268). In addition, race, skin color and skin tone and the prejudicial behavior that darker skin still evokes mean that Nigerian immigrants may earn less than lighter-skinned Africans from Northern and Southern Africa.

Scholars attribute the disparity between earning power and education to race and skin tone (Dodoo, 1997 and Takyi 2002; Keith and Herring, 1991; Breland 1998). Other factores are lack of social capital, that is, limited networks in well-paying fields (Reitz and Sklar, 1997), and unfamiliarity with U.S. structures (Moore and Foster, 2002; Bucher, 1994). Contrasting Black and White immigrants from the African continent, Dodoo and Takyi (2006) argue that wage disparities cannot be entirely attributed to social capital or length of residence in the United States. White privilege continues to influence access to resources in the United States. Thus, being predominantly black-skinned, Nigerian immigrants' earnings may well be negatively impacted by enduring vestiges of discrimination toward darker-skinned people in the United States (Dodoo and Takyi, 2006, pp. 168–188).

Paradoxically, in host countries, questions of one's African identity come across as "a penalty" or "responsibility" both of which are tags of disability (Appiah, 1992, p. 74). There are two levels of cultural outsider status for African-born immigrants seen against dominant Whites and minority Blacks. The label "foreigners" pits African-born immigrants against locals, yet their assimilation into mainstream education and labor systems gives them an advantage relative to conventional stereotypes of African Americans. Embedded in social structures—media and popular culture—that reinforce social hierarchies, Blacks fall prey to self-denigrating attitudes and behaviors coupled with in-group jostling for positions, either of which reinforces a racial hierarchy of white supremacy (hooks, 1994, 2003). Despite the cultural diversity in schools and evidence of academic success, Blacks represent the Other given the group's conventional association with academic underachievement (McWhorter, 2001). Appiah's (1992) corrective to cultural labels is more explicit: despite the impact of tradition(s) on cultural identity, what emerges in each case is a matter of choice. This rationale reflects the dynamism of cultural conceptions and also the variability within cultural groups. The ambivalence of cultural identities for Africans centers around creating a public role, in a world that demeans or denies their presence.

Language/Accents

Foreign-trained teachers adopt new strategies as they immerse themselves in the literature and education processes familiar to students (Mori, 1997). Economic mobility compels immigrants to "discard the attributes, habits, and characteristics that can hamper the success of making it in the American economy, and pick up the ones that enhance their chances"

(Borjas, 1999, p. 32). Language is one aspect that separates cultural insiders and outsiders in schools (Appiah, 1992). In my early years, I relied heavily on lip reading to understand people's speech. Although I speak English, what I heard in the United States sounded foreign to my unaccustomed ears. I smiled to cover my apprehension and the fear of saying or doing something inappropriate. Owolabi (1996) experienced similar frustrations in trying to decipher his classmates' as well as the instructor's accents. Overall, while scholars highlight the significance of a shared cultural heritage between teachers and students, studies underscore the role of committed teachers regardless of cultural identity (Wood, 1992, 2005; Delpit, 1988; Heath, 1983; hooks, 2003; Ladson-Billings, 2001; Foster, 1997; Nieto, 2004).

In the high school class I taught, it perturbed students that I was dark-skinned, not sophisticated in lifestyle but spoke standard English. I had an accent. The voiced comment: "She is a professor," or "She speaks English," made rounds in the class on the first day. In subsequent meetings, students referred to me with the common "Miss" or proceeded with a request devoid of any title. Paula's insistence on my non-African upbringing reflects similar questions. No doubt, based on their previous contact with continental Africans, students wondered about my claims of a Kenyan upbringing. My accounts of working on the ancestral farm—weeding and planting, carrying loads on my head—met with skepticism, reflecting a conventional association of country life with parochial characteristics relative to those in cosmopolitan cities. Accents, no less than English proficiency, distinguish insiders from outsiders in the United States. The Disney film Lion King uses "ethnically identifiable voices... Spanish Cheech Marin and the Black slang of Whoopi Goldberg clearly mark the undesirable hyenas racially... and the evil lion (is) darker in shade than the good lions" (Morrison, 1993, p. 48). Wafula's experience illustrates the conventional links between accents and intellectual ability:

> I have been teaching at a Community College which is predominantly African-American. There is what I consider an attitude regarding accent. The white students become more intellectually curious about your country of origin while there is aloofness on the part of the African-American students. I have also noticed that it took longer to gain intellectual confidence from both groups. It was as if my accent meant "intellectual inferiority" until I demonstrated the opposite. I also found it helpful to lay out my resume and experiences on the very first day of class as if to demonstrate that my accent had nothing to do with my intellectual acumen.

Sometimes students made an issue of something I said with exchanges swelling around me about what I meant interjected with elaborate clarifications from fellow classmates. I used the word "habit" in one context. "What?" one called out. Some laughed while others scoffed at classmates that the term caused such confusion. Ahmad encounters similar reactions for to his pronunciation of the word, "parallel." Like Ahmad, my professional reaction continues to be one of tolerance; personal frustrations with conventional linguistic usage and accents make me more accommodating of diverse speech patterns in class settings. There were days when I teased students back, with a "You have an accent too!" illustrating that differences exist even among American students. Reflective of previous responses to my "linguistic" transgressions, the incident ended with, "She says it differently." Like Wafula, Girikaze captures the frustration of dealing with negative stereotypes while reiterating the pressure to assert personal credentials:

> Occasionally I can see students asking each other, "What did she say?" I make sure that I let my students know on the first day of classes on, that I am a multilingual person, and that my exposure to French, Kirundi, and British English discourses will affect the way I express myself. At times, I simply utter French words, when I feel that an English term will not be able to translate my thought adequately. You get to the point when you become immune to criticism.

Obiakor and Gordon (2003) cite similar linguistic frustrations experienced by professors from Nigeria, Mali, Kenya, Egypt, Liberia, Ethiopia, etc. Wesonga is concerned about the impact of "accent" perceptions on the teaching/learning process: "The accent and modes of expression are a barrier to the delivery of content/subject material to students. Based on the age of students that I personally deal with, it is tough to get them to focus. For the most part, they pay more attention to the accent, pronunciation of words…instead of listening to the subject matter. And that is a problem that one has to overcome."

Bateson (2002), Ogulnick (2000), and Tatum (1997) link identities to sociological, historical and political factors. Learning a new language is transformative (Ogulnick, 2000). For some the experience amounts to a "loss of a prior self" (p. 1). The process of moving into unfamiliar territory "creates a sense of dislocation.…A person may feel uncomfortable at best and humiliated at worst, due to chauvinism built into cultural and linguistic boundaries" (p. 3). Stripped of the ability to communicate in one's primary language undermines an individual's sense of security and pride. For native-born Africans, the sense of dislocation is heightened in acquiring a new language and confronting accusations of an undecipherable accent: "In other words, language learning entails a process of fitting into one's place in society, or rather one's imposed place (p. 170). On the African continent, elites educated in Colonial literary traditions—English or French—look to these as markers of class. Official languages such as Kiswahili take a backseat to foreign Western languages. The reverence for English is inextricably tied to the European link (the faith is Europe and Europe is the faith!), and by extension "civilization and progress" (Appiah, 1992). Ethnic enclaves hamper individual efforts at developing fluency in a host country's official language: "In sum, the larger and more geographically segregated the ethnic group becomes, the less likely that persons in that group will become proficient in the English language, and the less likely that the group will be fully integrated into American economic life" (Borjas, 1999, p. 34). Huntington (2004) concedes the impact of immigrant "diversity and dispersion" in the assimilation process, but identifies other factors. Immigrants from countries considered compatible and similar to U.S. culture tend to assimilate more easily. Consider the Irish and Cubans in the United States. However, while Asians and Japanese were once considered ultimate extremes culturally in America, these groups are increasingly celebrated as model citizens, embodying the prized Protestant work ethic once presumed unique to Anglo-Saxons. In addition, wars increase host country receptivity to immigrants who bolster forces. The integration of immigrant populations and their unique allegiances begs the question of national identity and a core American culture. African immigrants settling in Michigan, New York, Salt Lake City, Texas or Miami, and so forth, assimilate to different cultures depending on the neighborhood.

A Kenyan professor points to a double standard with regard to accents: "I suppose if it had been a German or a Dutch person with limited American English language skills, no such complaints would have been raised irrespective of how unintelligible his or her English was" (Mukuria, 2003, p. 60). Since cultural identities overlap to reinforce or ameliorate marginality in the United States, a European foreign accent is considered chic while "Hispanic" speech patterns or Ebonics are ridiculed (hooks and mesa-bains, 2006). Owolabi (1996) concurs with hooks and mesa-bains on the preferential treatment for European and Asian immigrants in restaurant busing while Africans are confined to backdoor errands such as dishwashing because of the accent. Kofi's frustrations are familiar to most African-American teachers, particularly those with noticeably "un-American" accents. After Uwah lost a job offer, the department chair commended him for "a rich background but regretted that my accent got in the way" (Uwah, 2003). Uwah did not pronounce the word "tree" the American way (p. 66). Ahmad is teased by students for fumbling over the word "parallel." The dismissal of nonstandard English extends to the speech patterns of other non-White groups. While Li and Beckett (2006) point to similar frustrations among teachers with accents from India or China, Owolabi (1996) insists there are double standards in managements' tolerance of foreigners from India and Thailand relative to his own negative experience as an African immigrant at a restaurant in Columbia, South Carolina. And yet, despite complaints about the inconvenience of listening to foreign accents, most urban teachers eventually work with students who are culturally and linguistically diverse (Obiakor, 2003). In classrooms, some students are ridiculed for having an accent. Similar challenges arise in the corporate world; workers and supervisors are compelled to live with difference.

Immigrants such as myself try to communicate and understand a new language: English, in this case. The idioms and cultural nuances come much later, sometimes never. In most cases, the frequent charges of, "You have an accent," identify one as the outsider. Sometimes the pronouncement feels like a gavel dropping rather than the piquing of curiosity, or in my case, commendation for some achievement. A graduate student requested exemption from a general education class I taught, attributing it to my undecipherable accent. She had pleaded for an over tally (to be registered beyond the required class limit) the previous semester. The issue of accents never arose when she finally had to take the class. She, however, negotiated for make-up work, extra credit, and a decent grade for the greater part of the semester. Uwah (2002) distinguishes the reception of foreigners with an accent that is not British; they are viewed as ignorant. Indeed, foreign accents elicit questions about one's country of origin (Dodoo, 1997).

> No matter how well they may have mastered the English language, however, or how many other languages they may speak fluently, from their first encounters with American peers having a noticeable accent puts the African students [and teachers] in a "less than" category, a position of inferiority and suspicious difference. (Traore and Lukens, 2006, p. 2)

The significance of language in social status is not unique to the United States, according to Jane Roland Martin (2007); education "changes the way we humans walk, talk, dress, behave, view the world, and live our lives" (p. 1). Simplistic conceptions of racial inequality in the United States attribute disparities in school performance to an inability in minority students to "speak standard" or "correct" English; society attributes school failure to individual flaws (Arnot, 2006). By implication, social inequalities can be "overcome if everyone learns to talk, act, and think in a good, normal middle-class fashion" (Carlson, 2006, p. 107). Kenya's ethnic rhetoric, preoccupation with economic disparities and political tensions, overlooks affiliations of class reflecting school attendance, particularly accents and residential addresses. Overall, concerns about accents in social interactions prevail across the globe.

In their work on Islamophobia, Gottschalk and Greenberg (2008) discuss the emergence of norms within communities and how these serve to justify bias against an identified other even as the concept reinforces the superiority of an in-group. The in-group considers itself as speaking "normally" while others "have accents." For instance, a central Connecticut resident argued that "only people in the middle of the state had no accent: people on one side sounded like Rhode Islanders and on another like Massachusetts residents." While national media creates and reinforces a nationally accented norm that transcends regional accents, the choice "makes Southern or New England or Texan accents sound like, well, accents. [Regional accents are highlighted to depict some flaw]: the redneck Southerner, the prim New Englander, or the garrulous Texan" (p. 91). The African immigrant with an "indecipherable" accent stands out as the extreme other.

Aminata asserts that "students have never had problems with my accent." For Wafula, accents are a marker of insider/outsider status: "Speaking with an accent is an extra burden as one will constantly have to explain where they come from and why they are here. [It is] very uncomfortable." A foreigner's facility in English determines students' receptivity to them: "When you do not speak the English language as an American, they close their ears to what you are saying" (Bashir, a questionnaire respondent). Dingane claims that students use accents as an excuse to avoid academic accountability: "Students who perform well in my classes never complain about my accent but some of the students who perform badly use my accent as an excuse. I haven't had any complaints regarding my mastery of English or modes of expressions in class." Owolabi (1996) also maintains that Americans use the excuse of accents not to engage an issue or a particular person.

As a student, Professor Amobi (2004) recalls the shock of realizing that "others had difficulty understanding my thoughtfully crafted spoken English" (p. 170). She sought invisibility to avoid negative attention in classrooms: "pained by quizzical looks" each time she opened her mouth to speak. Fellow graduate students excluded her from teams for fear of being held back in group projects. As a professor, Amobi confronts the same quizzical looks, but this time from students, particularly early in the semester: "Students tend to see and hear my otherness, define me by it, before recognizing my humanity and intellect" (p. 176).

Paradoxically, a Black person's (foreign) accent absolves them of the conventional U.S. prejudice against African Americans (Dodoo, 1997; Traore and Lukens, 2006). While some immigrants work to "lose" their accent in order to assimilate earnestly, adopting conventional American accents, other immigrants court invisibility to avoid highlighting their linguistic inadequacy. Tatum (1997) notes how "first-generation Black immigrants from the Caribbean tend to emphasize their national origins and ethnic identities, distancing themselves from U.S. Blacks, due in part to their belief that West Indians are viewed more positively by Whites than those American Blacks whose family roots include the experience of U.S. slavery" (pp. 70–71). The choice of words can also distinguish African immigrants from locals in a community. Most African immigrant teachers complain about the frequent usage of curse words in class settings; a few adopt conventional speech patterns (What's up? I am good! and the use of expletives) for cultural insider status. African Americans face similar challenges in mainstream schooling.

In "Fluctuations of Social Capital in an Urban Neighborhood," Grant (2001) illustrates the impact of social networks on the academic success of teenagers. There is Beppy, who cares only for making money. He is typical of a group who may have "no one holding these kids accountable, expecting them to work hard or to measure up to any ideals" (p. 110). They dismiss teachers and cops "as part of the opposition. To be seen cooperating or being compliant with either diminishes one's respect on the street" (p. 110). Beppy claims to be self-reliant, not even taking advice from his mother. In contrast, the academically successful African-American TJ attended a parochial high school and had a mother who monitored his school progress daily. Glazer (2001) and Holmes (2001) acknowledge the centrality of parents in students' academic success; they influence youth "not just at conception but continuously through childhood and adolescence" (Holmes, 2001, p. 207). Ravitch (1995) extends the social network: "peers, colleges, employers, the community, and the media, each in their own way, send a message to students about the kind of behavior and performance that is expected of them" (p. 97). Although few parents can assist their children with schoolwork at my neighborhood primary school in Kenya, many urge them to succeed, making comparisons to academically successful neighbors and relatives. Aminata attributes her success in teaching to the "great rapport [she has] with colleagues and parents." Indeed, it is to parents she turns when students act out of line in class. But, argues Apple (1996), focusing on "parental involvement in economically depressed and racially segregated areas—misses the depth of the problem and what may be necessary for lasting transformations" (p. 106).

In the United States, what perturbs African immigrants is the use of curse words. At one of the class sessions, a student admitted to her parent's lack of control over her choices. Paula claimed her mother chided her about missing school but could not mandate her class attendance. "The b—— (expletive) (the mother) dare not enter into my room," Paula informed the class one day, rather casually, much as one would announce the delivery of a newspaper. There are limits to transgressions. Paula's admission to having called her mother the "b——" word drew shock and ire from her classmates. "My mother would kill me!" Lisa shot back. The unanimous gasps at the breach were instructive. For once, I was in the majority; there are limits to free speech after all. I wonder if students in the United States curse as frequently at home as they do in school. One minute they are cussing each other out. The next, there they sit all cuddly and conspiratorially. The occasional camaraderie in class was a welcome reprieve. I covered more material with greater ease. At other times getting the paragraph out of students felt like pulling teeth. Wafula acknowledges both the fulfilling and frustrating aspects of his American residence:

> Very fulfilling at a personal level but difficult when it came to adjusting to the America educational system—such ranged from what I considered rude (use of profanity among students, rampant phone use and disregard for basic instructions) and what I considered unacceptable attitudes toward scholarship in general to the silliest of excuses for not completing basic tasks. Students tend to be more keen on their rights than putting effort in scholarship.

Most recently, the term "issue" is taking on new connotations. I recall my earlier bafflement with the conventional use of "attitude." "X has an attitude" is a familiar phrase; it is damning. I would wait for clarification, the accompanying adjective. It never came. Increasingly, the term "issue" appears to absolve students of all improprieties; it excuses tardiness, late or un-submitted assignments, class absences, lack of or limited class participation, below-average performance and emotional outbursts. Students attribute these and more to, "I have issues." When I have asked for clarification, the response inevitably was, "I cannot talk about it!" Students used to partial/extra credit, make-up work, and incompletes pose further challenges. Where to draw the line? To many African immigrants, concerns for emotional and economic survival overshadow such issues until specific incidents compel a redress. Baruti's choice of avoiding conflict by a militant focus on syllabi is not unique. Ahmad too, limits his interactions with students to avoid what Kofi terms, charges of misconduct against male teachers in the

United States. When countless relatives back home depend on the African immigrant's salary, job loss entails greater risk. Refugees have no mother country to return to if deported for real or trumped up charges. Aminata admits the challenge of "going to school part time and working to support my schooling." It helps to be disciplined, she adds. However, reflective of differences within the group, African immigrants from financially stable backgrounds and assertive cultures (respondents from West and Southern Africa) deride the apologetic demeanor of fellow immigrants with a dismissive, "I am good. I am smart. Too bad, if the (Americans) can't deal with it!"

Language plays a central role in cultural definitions and practices; it is a tool used by both insiders and outsiders: "For intellectuals everywhere are now caught up—whether as volunteers, draftees or resisters—in a struggle for the articulation of their respective nations, and everywhere, it seems language and literature are central to that articulation" (Appiah, 1992, p. 56). But there is a danger of characterizing people and harboring parochial expectations due to cultural anchors: familiar structures of meaning. The insecurity lures people into a pathological characterization of difference as a threat. Beneath the impulse to rank people, events, or ideals, lie appeals to what is familiar as the norm. Cross-cultural exchanges compel a reassessment of taken-for-granted norms and practices. At best, conversations about cultural priorities raise awareness of the differences in social interactions between foreigners and U.S. students. The discussion demonstrates the limitations of cultural conceptions and practices despite the essentialist racial rhetoric embodied in stereotypes of African immigrants and African Americans. Although destabilizing, the process broadens perspectives while acknowledging the inevitability of difference. On the other hand, the extension of global communication networks fosters homogeneity beyond national borders in beliefs, lifestyles and language.

Take the case of France. While over 200 million speak French worldwide only 65 million are actually French. More than 50 percent of French speakers are African. Other speakers of French include Haitians, Canadians, and immigrants from Southeast Asia and the Caribbean who have settled in France. In *French Melancholy,* Eric Zemmour (himself a settler from Spain) of *Le Figaro* attributes the "end of French political power to the end of French," to growing French immigrants as much as diplomats who would rather speak English. At the fortieth anniversary of the International Organization of the Francophonie celebrating French globally, French President Nicolas Sarkozy too chimed in, similarly, concerned about the erosion of French. Just as there are concerns about the spread of Spanish in U.S. schools, France worries about losing its linguistic integrity and cultural uniqueness. In reality, French is just one among several languages spoken in France and other French-speaking countries. As the French political scientist Didier Billion, who is interested in French culture, acknowledges: "A multipolar world has emerged...40 years ago the French language was a way to maintain influence in the former colonies, and now French people are going to have to learn to think about francophone culture differently, because having a common language doesn't assure you a common political or cultural point of view" (Zemmour, 2010, p. SR 21).

Teachers need to facilitate discussions regarding the appropriate use of language. Immigrant teachers can initiate such talks by sharing their frustrations at the frequent use of profanity or confusion over the use of unfamiliar terms and gestures. A specially designed exercise can help students identify specific incidents or questionable speech patterns that shocked their sensibilities. Acknowledging these frustrations publicly allows teachers and students to establish appropriate classroom codes of conduct. At the least, broaching the subject raises consciousness about differences in sensibilities and social expectations among teachers and students. Absent such forums, parties retreat to essentialist perceptions of cultural groups.

Students who view a teacher as a cultural other, act out in resistance to them; collaboration between the two takes time and energy. African immigrant teachers educated in Western-style systems embody this quandary but for one difference: the imperial other, as the experience of expatriates and Peace Corp teachers illustrates, represents superiority and therefore desirability. For African immigrant teachers, the process of cultural assimilation is an imperative, embracing the best in a "superior" culturally dominating Other. These African immigrant teachers have developed "an essentially comparative perspective" in cross-cultural engagements (Appiah, 1992, p. 92). The ensuing cultural negotiation creates new definitions but also concessions of incompatible primary elements. What they face in urban schools are students who for the most part view the cultural exchange as dispensable—the United States is superior and English a global language. For both, cultural bridging involves an engagement of the other as of equal value. However, as authority figures, teachers initiate cultural bridging and create forums for cross-cultural exchanges. As Wesonga points out with regard to accents in his advice to teachers: It "[r]equires one to slow down/ take the slow pace approach to teaching. Otherwise the kids will not understand what you are trying to put across. Lots of patience is needed. Repetition—you have to keep repeating yourself over and over again."

The need to address challenges faced by immigrant teachers in U.S. schools reflects global trends to accommodate population diversity because of increased migration and relocations within national borders. According to the American Federation of Teachers (2009), the United States granted temporary teaching visas to about 19,000 immigrants in 2007, a number that continues to increase due to shortages in "hard-to-staff inner-city or very rural schools teaching the hard-to-fill disciplines of math, science and special education" (p. 7). The difficulty of accessing and disaggregating data on immigrant teachers suggests actual numbers may be higher. The recruitment of international teachers follows a similar trend in nursing within the past 50 years. Importing healthcare workers from developing countries subsidizes industrialized nations by about $500 million per year according to Schrecker et al. (cited in the American Federation of Teachers, 2009). Overall, global trends in migrations and relocation bring immigrants into schools, the labor force, and the wider society. About 33 international recruitment firms work with U.S. schools. For example, Avenida International Consultants serves Baltimore schools; Visiting International Faculty services mostly the Southeast; and the Teachers Placement Group (TPG) in New York draws teachers from India. In 2004, Omni Consortium, Multicultural Professionals and Multicultural Education Consultants faced charges of exploitation in recruiting teachers for Texas from the Philippines. There were only 100 openings upon arrival for the 273 recruits. Overall, the American Federation of Teachers highlights "abuses ranging from visa fraud to substandard housing to inequitable distribution of benefits" in the recruitment of overseas-trained teachers (p. 7). The introduction of an already trained staff for limited benefits is a temporary solution to an endemic problem in recruiting and retaining domestic educators for hard-to-staff troubled inner-city schools. In this light, offshoring includes both the export of American jobs overseas as much as the recruitment of foreign workers for jobs in the United States. Indeed, national ambiguity toward foreigners as competitive labor and a drain on resources or an expert corps influence cross-cultural interactions, specifically, teacher-student relations.

Within schools, academic success will require the acknowledgement and accommodation of challenges faced by students as much as teachers. Socialized differently, the resultant disparities in teacher/student expectations of each other complicate the teaching/learning process. The American Federation of Teachers (2009) notes the culture shock of overseas-trained teachers in American schools whereby "students do not stand up when their teachers enter the room, parents regularly challenge teachers' authority and there are metal detectors in many schools" (p. 19). The concerns of Filipino teachers working in Baltimore about American students sum up sentiments in the discussion of African immigrant teachers: "Back home it's so different. It's all obedience and respect. Here students are, um, very direct and bold.... They get free lunches, and yet you hear them complain.... They're loud.... They are intimidating." In addition, the American Federation of Teachers (2009) recognizes these "migrant teachers also have little context for dynamics such as parental relations and grading standards in the American school system" (p. 27). Watoya captures this predicament: "I was brought up holding teachers with highest respect as people helping me to achieve my life goals. American students do not understand this. Maybe they have many other avenues for getting knowledge and life skills and teachers are seen as merely inconveniences in their lives. American students sometimes want to treat teachers as equals."

Differences also emerge among students and teachers from similar racial backgrounds. Erik Eckholm and Katie Zezima (2010) reported an unfortunate incident at South Hadley High School in Massachusetts, in which the 15-year-old Irish-born newcomer Phoebe Prince hanged herself from a stairwell in January 2010. Ms. Prince had endured consistent taunting and physical threats by classmates with little intervention from school officials. The American Federation of Teachers cites the suicide of two Filipino teachers working in Baltimore within two years. Although rare, at least unpublicized, such cases highlight the dangers of bigotry as much as the emotional toll on immigrants in an increasingly global world. Teacher Education programs can design forums to redress these challenges and offer mentoring to alleviate the cultural shock of overseas trained teachers.

Based on a seminal work on ethnocentric bias by G.W. Allport, de Oliveira et al. (2009) administered a questionnaire to 128 students in an Introductory Psychology course in a Midwest private college to compare students' attitudes toward foreign-born and domestic instructors. Notwithstanding the impact of age, exposure to diverse cultures through study-abroad programs, individual personalities and stereotypes shape students' receptivity to foreign-born instructors. Overall, students with limited exposure to foreigners preferred domestic instructors. That students attracted to study-abroad programs prefer foreign-born instructors reflects a similar dualistic pattern. Multiple regressions "showed positive effects for student agreeableness, conscientiousness, and interest in study abroad" (p. 122).

According to de Oliveira et al., stereotypes influenced students' receptivity to foreigners. Most significant was students' rating of domestic instructors as superior in communication. The American Federation of Teachers' study (2010) acknowledged the tendency among American students "to get distracted and confused by unfamiliar accents, which can serve as an impediment to teaching and learning" (p. 20). Both studies noted the association of English proficiency in immigrant teachers to competence. As a precaution, American students rely on teaching assistants after class, "request printed handouts and record lectures," unnecessary measures if foreign-born instructors do not fit the stereotype (Oliveira et al., 2009), p. 122). Students' preference for domestic instructors and motivation to study under this group reflected an ethnocentric bias: "In a fairly homogenous setting, having a foreign-born instructor is unusual, and novelty tends to breed uncertainty and anxiety, whereas familiarity breeds security and fondness" (p. 120).

Immigrant populations in U.S. schools and colleges show little sign of abating in an increasingly global world where "foreign-born authority figures are ever more common" (Oliveira et al., p. 122). That the United States seeks, as do other nations, to attract competent workers and their families underscores the need for education programs that acknowledge and address issues of cultural pluralism in curricula and pedagogical styles. If national stereotypes account for students' receptivity toward instructors, schools require forums for acknowledging and addressing such factors.

Oliveira et al. advocate study-abroad programs to counter ethnocentric bias in culturally homogenous groups. The dualistic pattern in students' preference for domestic or foreign-born instructors highlights the role of teachers in promoting cultural pluralism and sensitivity. Oliveira et al.'s proposal recognizes the importance of teacher/student relations in creating an environment conducive to learning, as well as the perception of teachers as role models. The burden of proof for competence lies on foreign-born instructors. They work to alleviate students' apprehension by reaching out to the students, communicating effectively, and displaying professional preparedness and organization. However, an increasingly global world compels students to appreciate diversity without sacrificing critical awareness, i.e., preference for the familiar and agreeable.

CHAPTER 3

Academic Excellence

Disparities in conceptions of academic excellence between teachers and students illustrate the challenges African immigrant teachers face regarding classroom expectations. Differences in educational background create misunderstandings with colleagues and students alike regarding role expectations, classroom civility, and the process of enforcing academic standards. Watoya's experience as a foreign-trained teacher in the United States reflects this ambivalence: It is "frustrating at times but generally exciting, particularly when you have students who are committed to learning and to being guided." However, education transforms people's way of being, feeling, and knowing (Martin, 2007). Cross-cultural adaptations are inevitable and often unconscious although some differences persist. For instance, the emphasis on speech patterns crosses national boundaries. Simplistic conceptions of racial inequality in the United States, particularly within schools, emphasize the role of language in social status and economic mobility (Arnot, 2006; Carlson, 2006; Giroux, 1988, 2005, 2008; Martin, 2007; Ravitch, 1995; Ravitch and Viteritti, 2001). Most African immigrant teachers link education to particular speech patterns, dress code, and typically, Western mannerisms. In contrast, the United States myth of a classless society reflects much greater ambivalence on these issues. The flexibility in dress codes among faculty, staff, and students fosters collegiality. And yet, immigrants stand out for their conspicuous accents.

Students' academic success, or lack thereof, may stem from the roles of teachers, administrators, parents, and material disparities within and across states. Disparities in teacher/student expectations of one another, for example, as well as classroom decorum, complicate the teaching/learning process. Students are more receptive to teachers they view as "experts" as well as to those with whom they can readily identify. In addition, a teacher's expectations of classroom order and regulation may seem unnecessarily insensitive and inappropriate to American students. Such perceptions influence what students and teachers accomplish in classrooms. Classrooms are fraught with tension, when proving oneself takes precedence over proving a point. The expended energy and time involved could be directed to a more fulfilling purpose, particularly, acquiring requisite knowledge and skills.

Academic success becomes elusive when parties differ on how best to measure progress and the means for achieving set goals. In the United States, policymakers, educators, and communities advocate high standards but rarely define or apply these consistently (Ravitch, 1995; Ravitch and Viteritti, 2001). High school students receive a "U" grade that could be anything from a 0–65 percent. But do passing grades reflect a students' class attendance, failure to submit assignments, or inadequate performance on tests? Reflecting my hierarchically structured educational background, my academic expectations appear alien in a school structure that, seemingly, honors individuality and creativity over standard materials, teaching styles, or assessments. Accounts by various professors reiterate the differences in the training and expectations of most African-born teachers and their American students (Obiakor and Gordon, 2003; Traore and Lukens, 2006). As with Ravitch's calls for standards, many African professors experience frustrations in focusing on basics in writing skills or open-ended essay questions versus the use of multiple-choice examinations to assess understanding of course material. The choice may reflect familiarity with assessments that demonstrate comprehension of subject matter, for instance, the ubiquitous continual assessment tests (CATS) in Kenya. A student's grades reflect accomplishment as much as dispensed energy. Ravitch (1995) maintains that multiple type tests "subverted good instruction and critical thinking skills" (p. 102). The pedagogical focus on content over process causes endless acrimony. Abebe (2003) is known as the sharp professor who gives hard tests. Meanwhile, a department head accuses Uwah (2003) of giving "students too much information." Uwah's "tests and exams were mainly essay-type" (p. 65). He is further charged with being "either racist or insensitive to the feelings of minority students in a White environment." African-born faculties feel pressured by colleagues to "pass" students (p. 70). Yetunde's experience captures this dilemma:

> It seems to be hard for American students to consider Blacks as expert at anything upon initial contact. Students later respect my expertise but often tend to come to me as a last resort when seeking advice. Conversely, some Black and African students expect that our shared Blackness means

that I should give them an easier or free ride when it comes to academic rigor.

Students accustomed to incompletes, bonus points, or makeup work charge me with rigidity in enforcing standards and an insensitivity to personal requests and excuses. Ravitch (1995) admits that none of the college-entry tests taken by students in the United States are "considered comparable in rigor to the English A-Levels, the French baccalaureate examination, or the German *abitur*" (p. 17, italics in original). Like Uwah, Ravitch advocates what she terms the "best aspects of performance assessment: essays, projects, portfolios of student work, open-ended answers, as well as a limited core of well-crafted multiple-choice questions" (p. 21).

The following discussion explores differences in defined classroom outcomes in terms of teacher/student expectations of each other. Another area of contention is classroom etiquette and decorum. Are African immigrant teachers from militaristic school regimes that focus on order and obedience insensitive to the needs of American students who prefer greater flexibility and individual attention? My students at the college level as well as the high school classes I have designed and taught complain about my giving them, "too much work." Cecilia chided me for conducting boring classes that were too structured and therefore not fun. At one class, she alleged that my classes "are boring." Perturbed, I tried to keep a straight face as I referred to the class syllabus and my hopes for developing skills students would use in years to come—reading, writing, and an academic focus. This issue raises questions about students' acting out during lessons. Was Cecilia's accusation resistance to classroom requirements—read, write, and attend class—or did it reflect students' inability to follow through defined classroom objectives? Was I such a bore? Do students hand in shoddy work because they cannot write better, or is it that they do not care about school? These are questions all teachers wrestle with, often settling for a happy medium: cajole students into doing what fulfills class requirements.

Standards

The debate over national standards and assessments originates in a beleaguered past and with conflict of interests in the U.S. education systems (Apple, 1992, 1996; Ravitch, 1995; Salomone, 2001). Constituents run the gamut of parents, communities, educators, policymakers and religious groups drawing alliances that presume a "commonsense" faith in tradition and official knowledge relative to critiques of what constitutes patriotism. While proponents focus on the quality of education by highlighting the success and failures of individuals, some schools, states, and critics point to its simplistic approach to addressing social issues, as well as to the marketization of education (Apple, 1996; Giroux, 2005, 2008). National standards and assessments highlight the importance of establishing successes and lags in the system (Nord, 2000; Ravitch, 1995; Ravitch and Viteritti, 2000). Rigorous standards compel students to higher levels of academic excellence; states such as Massachusetts which establish high standards are more competitive and better prepare students for college entry knowledge and skills sets. In making the practice palatable, Ravitch (1995) ignores the impact of historical inequalities and conflicts of interest in the design and use of these assessments. Standards guide school curricula and pedagogy. In the United States, standards are voluntary and are continually redesigned for effectiveness, to identify areas of schools that require improvement. Colleges and universities rely on these high-stakes tests to assess students' performance (potential) much as do employers, an aspect advocated in President Obama's July 2009 "Race to the Top" program under Education Secretary Arne Duncan. The $4.35 billion stimulus bill contest had governors laying out impressive budgets to consultants and lobbyists, given the competitive, tedious process, and the intricacy/complexity of computations. The state of Ohio used the Parthenon Group, a consulting firm that was being paid with money from the Bill and Melinda Gates Foundation, to compile its report. With 18 finalists, Delaware and Tennessee won the first round in March 2010 (Starzyk, 2009). But these are aspects few dispute. Ravitch admits, "Many states have curriculum documents that list broad, diffuse objectives or behavioral outcomes or lofty goals, but these are rhetorical statements rather than content standards because no one is quite sure what they mean or how to measure them" (p. 14).

In schools and across states, students differ in access to qualified teachers, instructional materials, and even assessments. For instance, not all students take geometry and those who do are exposed to different grades of the subject. There is the fear by critics of the national standards movement that if the federal government designs assessments, it may settle for the least controversial and most minimal requirements to avoid compromise and eventually narrow the curriculum to what can be taught and assessed. Some argue that national standards undermine local and state control, forcing teachers into uniform instructional pedagogies regardless of differences in either teachers or students. How fair are uniform assessments in view of unequal access to education across groups?

Ravitch acknowledges the complexity of the debates, considering that not all students take either the Regents or SATs (Standardized Assessment Tests). Of greater concern, as Jeannie Oakes notes, is that "Black, Hispanic, and low-income students are disproportionately assigned to low-ability groups and nonacademic tracks, where they are denied access to educational opportunities afforded to students in the academic track" (Ravitch, 1995, p. 93). Ravitch also cites the complaint against teacher education programs in focusing on pedagogy at the expense of content knowledge. She maintains that "standards can be a lever for both excellence and equity." (p. 32). However, this is not so when high-achieving students are treated as "rate busters": "It is no secret that high-achieving students risk being called 'nerds,' 'geeks,' 'brainiacs,' and other epithets. Adolescents, perhaps imitating adults, respect good looks, money, and athletic talent" (Ravitch, 1995, p. 178). The focus on individuals and communities can obscure the impact of structural inequalities. Borjas (1999) maintains that the competitiveness of second-generation immigrants depends on the parents' social class as well as "the characteristics of the ethnic environment" (p. 146). Echoing Badillo (2006) and McWhorter (2001), Borjas (1999) highlights the importance of an ethnic group's "attitudes toward education and work." "Workers in two ethnic groups certainly differ in their occupational distributions, so that each child is getting different messages about the types of work that people 'usually' do, as well as making different types of job connections. And the two groups provide different types of role models as the children go about their everyday activities within the ethnic enclave" (p. 148). The cultural outsider status varies with location—group and settings. Typically, teachers educated in schools that emphasize content over process, may or may not favor the approach, depending on their receptivity. On the other hand, regardless of orientation, a teacher's pedagogical style can conflict with established approaches in individual schools, thereby relegating an individual teacher to an outsider status. Wesonga captures this complexity in explaining academic disparities in Kenya and the United States:

> Standards are relatively low. There was more demanded of us than we demand of our students today, even though expectations are higher. Interactions were with great[er] respect than [they are] now. During my time, we looked at teachers as keys to success unlike now when teachers are looked at as detractors. [His approach:] Taking a proactive approach to teaching that meets the needs of the students. Teach them according to their learning styles: for example, using technology, art, music.

Stevenson's (1990) comparative study of Asian and American students highlights the differences in self-concept with regard to academic success. American parents and students express confidence in academic performance, unlike Asian students, despite evidence to the contrary. I hear students speak of having "aced" (being confident of getting an A) a test only for results to turn out differently. Stevenson attributes the misperception to parental beliefs of what contributes to academic success: "American students, their parents, and—to some extent—their teachers believe that innate intelligence, not hard work, is the primary determinant of success in school" (Ravitch, 1995, p. 112). It may explain why American students devalue hard work unless it is tied to college admission or employment prospects.

The former schoolteacher, leader in teachers' unions, scholar, and professor Apple (1996, 2006, 2008), insists on the inextricable link between culture and politics. And while he dismisses labels as reductive, Apple positions his work as a critique of neoliberalism and neoconservatism. Apple (1996, 2008) maintains that critiques of national policies and practices—official knowledge, pedagogy, and assessments—is in itself a sign of patriotism. Schooling both reproduces and contests existing social structures, which may explain the conventional reliance on schools to solve social problems. The faith in schools as a panacea for social ills falls prey to blaming individuals and schools for social ills. Change is left to personal and market forces, a process that "legitimizes inequality" (Apple, p. 18). In addition, calls for a national curriculum and cautions against particularistic traditions infiltrating a national ideal ignores the selectivity of prevailing traditions, policymakers and textbook publishers (Apple, 1996, 2006, 2008; Ravitch, 1995; Ravitch and Viteritti, 2001). Establishing a national curriculum justifies "standardized instruments of evaluation" (Apple, 1996, p. 25). That race, class, and gender differences translate to differences in education access undermines any arguments for uniform assessments:

> Thus, when the fiscal crisis in most of our urban areas is so severe that classes are being held in gymnasiums and hallways, when many schools do not have enough funds to stay open for the full 180 days a year, when building are literally disintegrating before our very eyes, when in some cities classrooms must share one set of textbooks at the elementary level... it is simply a flight of fantasy to assume that more standardized testing and national curriculum guidelines are the answer. (Apple, 1996, p. 36)

These disparities in perception of social ills call for a national discourse on the "root causes of our dilemmas" (p. 87), what Apple identifies as "the relations of domination and subordination in the larger society" (p. 98). An incident with my students over an article on an exemplary student captures the dilemma of cultural/academic priorities, perceptual locations, and structural factors as these impact students' conception and receptivity to schooling. Janofsky's (2005) piece on the extremely gifted ten-year-old Misha

Raffiee created a contentious discussion in the class. Race may have been a factor in the students' reaction to the featured White girl with violin in hand, its case on her lap. The feature story had her in a spacious room with lined-up chairs, seemingly engaged in conversation with a male teacher. The journalist identified Misha's father as an associate dean at a university and her mother as a former bank economist. In contrast, our class of predominantly Black students met in a multi-usage computer room with a big center table surrounded by chairs that required rearrangement at each session. Classroom walls were bare and the class could benefit from more frequent emptying of trash cans.

Most of the students' responses to the article dismissed the gifted Misha for her younger age and grade at the time, an eighth-grader relative to their eleventh- and twelfth-grade status. The snide comments and snickers reflected the students' unease: "She is just an eighth-grader," Sarah called out. I focused on the student's achievements, oblivious to the historical racial undertones the discussion had taken. The lack of acknowledgment of Misha's youth and obvious intelligence or even achievements in the group surprised me. The article highlighted her impressive reading habits (six books in a month), violin and piano expertise, and insatiable intellectual curiosity. Misha planned to be a surgeon, given her IQ of 160 within a minority group of 72 million gifted children in the nation's public and private schools. Victor led the students in anger against being compared to a privileged White girl. There are more important things in life, the group insisted. "Which?" I asked. At some point during the heated debate Sarah reminded me that Black communities value talents other than school intelligence. "Isn't that true of other communities?" I interjected in the conversation swelling around me. My attempts to illustrate a diversity of interests and talents across race/ethnic groups even within the American racial hierarchy backfired. As an immigrant, my focus was on the factual details of the piece, and, typically, linked academic success to hard work rather than innate ability (Ravitch, 1995). The students seemed to read the piece from a background of racial segregation and privilege—in contrast to the predominantly Black students in my class, an extremely competitive high school across the street has mostly White and Asian students. In retrospect, it is an issue I should have raised in class to at least acknowledge the context for racial disparities in academics. Devoid of context, the students probably heard the usual question, "Why don't you be like them?" from another African-born black person. By implication, academic disengagement reflected individual/cultural pathology.

My high school students spoke of going to college, although in extremely vague terms—no mention of timing or specific colleges. While Mori (1997) worries about the lackadaisical attitude toward school, other scholars (Ogbu, 1992; Shor, 1996; Tatum, 1997; Willis, 1987) link students' resistance to "outwitting a dominant other" (Tatum, p. 25). But I wanted students to appreciate the importance of standards beyond neighborhood norms; they would compete against students of diverse abilities and nationalities. That day, the students walked out without the usual goodbye, avoiding my glance, although they engaged in a passionate discussion. Highlighting Misha's achievements among a Black student body reinforces the idea of White people's success and intellectual superiority, something critical theorists decry (Apple, 1996; Giroux, 2005; 2008; hooks, 1995). It builds on years of Black people being compared to a White majority and found wanting. The cultural rhetoric associating race to academic achievement overlooks individual Black achievement over the years. At the worst, the burden of cultural sensitivity runs the danger of a patronizing racism, whereby instructors avoid challenging minority students.

There is a danger of exceptionalism in highlighting minority achievements against a backdrop of a tradition of White people's success. Efforts by marginalized groups to reclaim historical achievements fall prey to conventional social hierarchies. Look at what he/she did. Just like the Whites or men. Touting women's achievements to demonstrate that one of two isolated individuals defy the myth of female ineptitude against a sea of prominent men isn't the point. Laudable is the fact that minorities (Blacks or disadvantaged groups) achieved what they did against all odds—a structural system's debilitation and denial of their humanity. As Achebe (2009) notes of Martin Luther King:

> I am not concerned here about marches and boycotts, great and important though they were, but rather about a man who struggled to conquer in himself both fear and hate, two of humanity's most destructive and limiting emotions.... The struggling is as important as the conquering, perhaps more, because it is *that*—the fact that our hero did not enter the stage fully formed and destined to win; that he began where most of us stand today, vulnerable to fear and prejudice and all the other frailties of our human condition.... That is what Martin Luther King should say to each of us, individually. (pp. 136–37)

Judson (1993) and Robinson (2004) note consistent patterns of school segregation despite the 1954 ban following the *Brown v. Board of Education* ruling. In northern states such as Connecticut, Illinois, Michigan, and New York, Black and Hispanic students attend segregated urban schools. The schools are also inferior to those dominated by Whites, Asians, and students from higher economic backgrounds. Robinson (2004) contrasts P.S. 6 on Manhattan's Upper East Side to students at P.S. 6 in the East Flatbush section of Brooklyn: "The Manhattan P.S. 6 is overwhelmingly white and includes only a smattering of poor students. Its East Flatbush counterpart is more than 92 percent black, with almost 90 percent of its students from families with low enough incomes to qualify for free school lunch" (n.p.). She attributes the persistent segregation to white flight and the segregation in the housing market, as well as the use of standardized tests to assign students to special programs. Citing Professor Claude Steel of Stanford University, Robinson acknowledges the cumulative impact of confining minority students to poorly funded schools, run-down buildings, and uncertified or inadequately trained teachers. In an essay contest marking the *Brown* anniversary, conducted by the Advocates for Children organization, students highlighted the value of diversity in schools, with some wishing for more "Caucasian students or kids outside of our neighborhood." Teaching in an urban school with predominantly minority students, Wesonga confronts this ambivalence daily:

> [In Kenya] [t]eachers were very highly regarded people. Even though not very well paid, but it was so rewarding to be a teacher. Every person I knew wanted to be a teacher. Today, teachers are not viewed by society as pillars that support future generations. None of the kids I teach wants to be a teacher. Not even my own children want to be teachers. Today, students are not seen as being as enthusiastic as in the old days. The impression they give is that if they had a choice, they would not come to school. They view education as trying to be "white" something that is not acceptable to most minority kids. That attitude makes a big difference between the old and the new school.... [He chooses to] [s]et high standards and expectations and try to push the kids as much as [he] can to reach [his] goals/expectations.

That most of my high school students planned to go to college demonstrated an awareness of higher aspirations; most were the first in the family to get that close to a high school diploma. Although students drew upon their Caribbean experiences in discussions, their college aspirations reflected similar concerns across the United States. Their certainty of attending college contrasted sharply with the apparent ignorance and disregard for specifics; this surprised me. Baruti finds it frustrating to work with "students who have low academic output and expect high grades." The eleventh-grade Sarah planned to study art but dismissed having to read or write any more than she already did. I called her attention to required core classes in colleges.

Even an art major would require familiarity with her subject's history and varied styles. I pointed out the need for her to hold her own among other high school students—in language, speech, manner, and knowledge base. I hoped she heard me.

Much like consumer choice in shopping malls, high school course electives in the United States education system are rare in Kenyan schools (Ravitch, 1995). In Kenya, secondary school students study thirteen subjects for the first two years. At the end of Form Two students take at least eight subjects including the five mandatory classes, mathematics, English, Kiswahili, and at least two science subjects. Mori (1997) contrasts access to higher education in the United States to that in Japan: "Most Americans take colleges for granted because they are always there" (p. 162). Contrasting academic standards in Sudan to the United States, Ahmad states:

> The U.S. teacher is very much prepared and equipped, whereas the teacher in Sudan is well prepared, but not equipped. The U.S. student is very much spoiled and very dependent on others for everything from having the pen to the books and never takes responsibility [for] his or her education until later on in his adult life, but in Sudan, students are more mature despite the difficulties.

According to the *International Handbook of Universities* (2010), the United States has about 1,600 public and private institutions which grant a bachelor's degree, with an additional 1,100 two-year colleges which often serve as a gateway to a four-year education. Conversely, Kenya has eight public and ten private institutions. Sierra Leone has two public and two private universities/colleges. Nigeria has the largest number of public (50) and private (10) universities/colleges on the continent, followed by Sudan with 29 public and 7 private universities/colleges. South Africa follows with 24 public and 13 private universities and colleges. Notwithstanding scholarship resources, the United States has a greater number of institutions of higher learning and greater access to scholarships for study. The disparities in higher educational access help explain most of the African immigrants' value of education, especially a university/college education. For many, education is the ladder to social mobility.

Despite the limited educational access in their home countries, African students find academic expectations less rigorous in the United States, coupled with a lack of "respect for the purpose of education." (Traore and Lukens, 2006, p. 24; DeVita and Armstrong, 1993; Obiakor and Gordon, 2003; Ravitch, 1995). Most of the pooled African immigrant teachers cited differences in academic rigor. "Academic standards are much higher and even though English is taught as a foreign language, the standards for teaching and the grammar taught is much more refined than the structures within the U.S. educational system" (Aarifa). Recalling her education in Nigeria, Amobi (2004) claims the school regimen made learning "an intense and even painful activity, a survival of the fittest, and those that were deemed incompetent were redirected to vocational occupations" (p. 169; Dodoo, 1997). Dingane links students' academic performance to discipline:

> Academic standards: The standard of education at the college level (at least in the subject that I teach [Economics], is higher in my country of birth than in the United States.
>
> Classroom interactions: Although classes are bigger in my country of birth, there is more discipline and interactions between teachers and students. Students also respect their teachers and hand in their work on time. In the United States, classes are smaller but it takes a while to enforce discipline in the classrooms. Students are also a bit sloppy when it comes to school work.

Ahmad has a different take on educational excellence in his country of birth and the United States:

> With respect to academic standards in both of my schooling the standards were very high, but due to ample material from pencils to technology the standards were much higher over here. [I]n Sudan the academic standards are not high because of learning material and technology, but the competition over limited opportunities in higher education is intense. Classroom interaction and student engagement in different activities are also affected by the availability of resources and comfortable classrooms. [S]ome argue that the role of the teacher is essential in classroom interaction, but what effort the teacher puts out can be hindered by the factors mentioned.

Besides the low incomes, large family sizes and prohibitive school tuitions along with the Kenyan government's claim of a free primary education (2003), which increased student enrollment by two million, and secondary education (2007), education in most African countries is extremely competitive. For many students, education affords them the opportunity for economic mobility, especially access to better-paying careers. At 41, Kayian Lengete, a mother of six from Kajiado Central District in Kenya, is enrolled in Form Two, a grade for fifteen-year-olds. Undeterred by jestings from contemporaries, shunned by several relatives, and mocked by politicians,

Lengete continues to invest in formal education convinced it is the key to a better life and social status. "Without education, life is difficult and no one can respect you" (Koross, 2009). Konneh's (2003) recollection of the parental rewards of "love, food and clothing" for the best performing child in the family is not unique.

Claims of free primary education (the Kenyan government has gotten a lot of mileage—funds and commendations—out of this from locals and foreigners alike) contrast sharply with the reality of most Kenyan students. Notwithstanding the lack of comprehensive statistics, a child's fortunes reflect the parent's socioeconomic status. Few parents can afford the inhibitive "extras" that need to be forked out over and above government-regulated fee structures. The extra expenses include mandated shopping lists, extra tuition fees, school trips, and lunches in day schools. In addition, schools are not evenly spread across regions. A student in Central Province and in major cities such as Nairobi has greater access to quality education compared to students in the nomadic regions of Wajir and Kajiado. In a report by the Kenya National Union of Teachers, 50 percent of students had not reported to school by February 2010. In Nakuru, children dropped out of school following a prolonged drought to work at casual jobs for food. The country is short of 70,000 teachers. In Nakuru one teacher serves between 70 and 135 pupils in a class despite the required limit of 30 to 40 pupils. The government has only released 30 to 40 percent of the Free Primary Education Fees (FPE) (Kibui, 2010). Meanwhile, Kshs 103 million disappeared from Free Primary Education (FPE) coffers. As Oriang' (2010) notes in her critique of government graft: "Some 8.6 million poor children are likely to lose out in the conspiracy to line the pockets of senior officials who can afford private education overseas for their own kids.... (Similarly) some 2.7 million bags of subsidized maize were sold to millers at great cost at a time when 10 million Kenyans were going hungry" (n.p.). Most Kenyan students have limited control over career prospects in the face of growing government graft and disparities in income and education access.

At a session on goal settings at the beginning of 2006, Alex spoke about his ambition: "I want to be the best I can so I will be determined, imaginative and consistent." It sounded like a pep-talk rally script. "How will you work toward these goals?" I asked him. "What is your deadline?" The rest of the group laughed at the shift in focus from the general to specifics: "What happens after June when you graduate? Will you stop being these things?" Sarah asked jokingly. Alex acted baffled by the interest his claim generated. "Do you understand our need for clarification?" I asked. "He doesn't," volunteered Paula sitting to my left. She appeared serious. I focused my attention on Alex. "How will you measure your progress toward these goals?" I probed him again. "When I pass my exams," he responded. "Good. So that is one measure of your success. Look at how well you are doing on tests. That is a start," I added. He appeared relieved at the affirmation. David planned "to work less to avoid stress, based on the doctor's orders," he added to the attentive audience. The comment elicited laughter from his classmates. He sat next to me slouched in the chair, head leaning back on the seat. "This less?" I asked pointed to his slouch. The class laughed. "How much less?" I persisted. "What grade did you get in the last quarter?" I asked. He mumbled something about an 80. "So how much less will be the next grade? 70? 60? A fail?" I asked. Hopefully, he understood the audacity of his response. His continued slouch was not encouraging. I redirected the discussion to the larger group, challenging students to think longer term, but, mostly, to make concrete and measurable goals. After class I drew David aside to remind him of my expectations: "I do not expect you to work that much less in my class." David failed the class despite one-on-one discussions in and outside the class, and despite my enlisting his twin who attended the same school and my appealing to his mother. I was shocked at his request to sign up for whatever class I taught the next semester.

In her discussion on the crisis of authority in schools, Hemmings (2003) claims teachers can be lax and inconsistent in enforcing rules, or can water down curricula to avoid intellectual rigor. Damon (2001) and Holmes (2001) blame it on the moral relativism prevailing in schools. The arbitrary conceptions and application of discipline within schools as well as between homes and schools creates moral confusion in impressionable youth. To avoid alienating students, the expediency of not fighting losing battles, or maintaining some semblance of order, "some teachers simplified curriculum and even eliminated certain portions of it, assigned easy-to-do seatwork, rarely handed out homework, and were quite tolerant of students as they socialized in class" (Hemmings, 2003, p. 423). The lack of consistency in enforcing discipline (too lax or too oppressive) across and within schools alienates the teacher who enforces the moral order. In this case, foreignness serves a purpose; students attribute an immigrant teacher's priorities to their foreignness. Students tolerate Aarifa's classroom demands—respect and academic rigor—ascribing them to her foreignness, despite her having been raised in the United States:

> Students found me too strict, old-fashioned, or harder on them. They associated my style of teaching with my background which they considered out of touch with American culture. Foreign-born parents, of all races, appreciated my style much more than American students and parents. Second-generation students also felt more comfortable with me.

Teachers trained in the United States also experience frustrations. Hemmings (2003) recounts the frustration of a teacher, Ms. Thomas, who adopted "normal upper track pedagogical practices"—literary text analysis and discourse, and intensive writing assignments. One morning some students "would alternate between talk and work. They would write a few words, talk with their friends, and then write a few more words. Others did not write at all. All they did was talk. Michael was the only student who worked quietly and independently on the essay" (p. 424).

Maria wrote little in class and sat quietly nibbling at candy most of the early semester. She was however distressed at her low grade for the class after the first marking period, confronting me in the school office one afternoon. Her concern for the grade appeared genuine, "I never miss class. How can I fail the class?" I reiterated the rubric explaining the class requirements—attendance, class participation, and written assignments. "I cannot fail the class," she said. "If that is what you want, you need to do more," I replied, calling attention to her limited class participation and dismal performance on writing assignments, and offered to work with her outside of class. "I am busy and have to leave right after class," she stated, which could have been true. Some students spoke of rushing off after school to part-time jobs. "If I can sacrifice the time to help you, the least you can do is set aside some time to review what is covered in class," I said to Maria. She smiled at the reminder but walked out without offering to meet with me. She never did. Except for occasions when I paired her off with a colleague, Maria sat next to me. As I went around monitoring students' writing activity during the class after our exchange, Maria asked if she could get a good grade the following quarter. "Of course," I responded. "Why?" I asked following up on her question. "Because I am trying," was her prompt response. "You will get what you work for," I reminded her. "It has nothing to do with whether you are my friend or not." I knew she was doing the best she could, compared to her performance at previous sessions. In retrospect, the reference to affectivity in my exchange with Maria reflected a cultural adaptation; rarely, if ever, would African teachers be as vocal in reference to affection for a student. The process of cultural adaptation for many immigrant teachers is often unconscious.

Raised in environments of material lack relative to those in the United States, most African immigrant professors find the apparent disregard for academics disheartening, a tremendously frustrating experience. The cultural dissonance also reflects upbringing. Appiah's (1992) Ghanaian proverb captures the complexity of cultural norms: "The matriclan is like a forest; if you are outside it is dense. If you are inside you see that each tree has its own position" (p. 192). Similar to African immigrant teachers, the

Japanese American Mori (1997) is frustrated by students' sense of entitlement and lack of perseverance as well as respect for authority, although she prefers students "who question too much rather than accept everything from teachers" (p. 178). Even oil-endowed countries such as Nigeria stress the value of education and classroom etiquette (Obiakor and Gordon, 2003; Owolabi, 1996). Students' resistance to classroom etiquette can frustrate well-meaning efforts by faculty to engage students or enforce intellectual rigor. Reflecting the ambivalence among African immigrants toward the United States, Ahmad admits: "What is attractive about the U.S. system of education is the organization, clear objectives, fairness of the education system and maintenance of quality standards. What is inhibitive is the limited social relation and lack of trust and confidence between the teacher and the students."

Classroom Etiquette

Since we reviewed a *New York Times* piece each week in the high school elective, each student took a turn reading a paragraph before the large group discussion and the text analysis for key themes and new terms. Initially, the read-alouds caused tremendous resistance among students. By the end of the semester, I was never short of read-aloud volunteers despite the pattern of shared responsibility with each student reading out a paragraph. At the second session when I first introduced the practice, David resisted my request for him to read aloud. I refused to give in to his resistance. Even students at college level express trepidation at reading aloud in the class, claiming to feel self-conscious. Some students claim to be shy. The resistance probably reflects a fear of being found wanting by classmates, particularly when one wishes to project an image of confidence. In extremely rare circumstances I have worked with students who could not read at least 80 percent of the words in any paragraph of a class textbook.

David stalled following my instructions that he read aloud. "You are holding the class up," I reminded him. There was an apprehensive silence in the group. He began reading after what appeared an eternity to me, during which time the class glanced back and forth at us, waiting. David's read-aloud broke the impasse. I was just as apprehensive, wondering what options I had, had he refused to read. All the students read aloud, round-robin style, and did so thereafter. By the end of the semester, students vied for the opportunity to read aloud. One day, Maria volunteered to read well before class began. She was ready to read the whole piece although we typically divided paragraphs to give more students a chance. "You can read, but each of you gets a chance," I informed her, pleasantly surprised at the initiative. Even

Karen, who had long avoided reading aloud, offered to read the conclusion that day. She eventually read the last three paragraphs of the piece. Karen resisted reading aloud, initially with giggles, then excuses of being shy, and finally accusations of my picking on her. "Oh, miss, go to someone else," she begged. I waited, insisting she read, "Get it over and done with," I urged her. She eventually conceded after an extended silence. The change in atmosphere in the group was noticeable. Jennifer, another resistant reader, offered to read three times that day.

My insistence on the practice, despite students' resistance, may have brought some along although the change in heart was probably due to the emerging bond, if one can call it that, within the group. By mid-semester, the random read-alouds were an established class ritual. Students can embrace academic rigor when required. In this case, the consistency in expectations (standards) illustrates the significance of classroom routines. But change is gradual and teachers are selective about what and how to enforce a routine. The selectivity in intervention could be due to expediency or availability of time and the urgency of an issue as the following incidents demonstrate.

It was Karen's first semester at the high school. She would arrive late but participated in class activities. Her response to the bickering in class was always a cynical look of exasperation coupled with a sense of resignation. She pointedly ignored the amorous Alex and Jennifer, both of whom sat at her side of the table. Her intolerance of Alex was evident on two occasions when I paired them for a project. My urgings only got them to move the chairs closer to each other. In one case, they both busied themselves with some scribbling and totally ignored each other. My success at instituting read-alouds contrasted with the failure to build a community of learners in this particular incident. Students' responses to each other and to course material reflected the sort of independence—openly defying a teacher's directive—that would be rare in my country of birth.

The day after Rosa Parks's death on October 24, 2005, we read a piece on her life. As did the rest of her colleagues, Maria mumbled complaints against the written pieces in class. For many of the students, having to write an essay at each class sitting was an unwelcome chore. Her resistance was more subtle than that of her classmates. She would say something to the student next to her or stare at me for a while as if hoping I would change my mind and cancel the writing activity. I experience a similar resistance to impromptu writing activities at the college level, typically couched in calls for clarifications such as "Are you collecting the papers?" Students would debate issues rather than write a reflective piece on the topic. In the teaching/learning process, a big task can appear overwhelming. Smaller tasks are more manageable. The paragraph or two my students write takes but a minute, definitely less than

15 minutes. Even a brief and succinct piece can be comprehensive and lovely to read. In a brief time there is a short piece from everyone in the class. The writing and subsequent read-alouds and peer reviews allow students to step into each other's lives, behold, perhaps question, and to better understand one another.

Eventually, Maria settled down to write her response, taking her time. Maria's reflection on the excerpt on Rosa Parks included the paragraph: "During an interview Rosa Parks said that there was not Civil Rights back then. Your focus was to try and survive day after day." After the exchange over Maria's failure to attain the required 60 percent to pass the first quarter, her grades improved significantly. She volunteered to read in class and spoke out more. One of the pieces she produced in class two months later was better thought out and better expressed. Responding to a piece by the *New York Times* columnist Bob Herbert (2005) on "A New Civil Rights Movement," one of Maria's reflective paragraphs read:

> Even today with the so called freedom for all in this American society doesn't really exist in the black community, and that's just what I think. Even after the Emancipation Proclamation and the ratification of the civil rights amendments during the reconstruction period which gave African-Americans rights and new liberties. We still live today with a shadow of racism, discrimination and racism. People think we don't see it but we do, and I think our new year's resolution should be to change that.

The experience with Maria demonstrates the danger of writing off students, ever. They can surprise you. The definitiveness in Kenya's grading policies with students' grades exclusively dependent on their performance on a one-time examination offers a limited assessment of intellectual ability. Similarly, in grading mathematics papers, teachers focus on the solution rather than the process (steps to it). This is unavoidable at the Kenya Comprehensive Primary Examination (KCPE) because the grading is computerized. However, even at this level, English and Kiswahili composition papers are graded manually. All other papers are computer-graded.

Whatever the reason, Sarah laughed during her part of the reading on Rosa Parks. "What is so funny?" I interrupted, shocked at the irreverence. Our ancestors made tremendous sacrifices for non-Anglo Saxon groups to enjoy the liberties of racial integration that we take for granted. Yet, was my sense of gratitude generational? My exasperation must have been evident, "Do you understand the seriousness of the issue?" There was silence in the room. Upon reflection, it may have been an expression of Sarah's unexpressed nervousness. I overlooked her feelings and chided her for the inappropriate response. In contrast, I offered emotional support to resistant readers who voiced their concerns as did Karen, Maria, and David. The former involved a cue that I did not pick up on. After the brief exchange Sarah offered to re-read the text. Victor responded with, "Oh, just go on." Sarah resumed the reading. She was the perfect student following the exchange: attentive, engaged, and focused for the rest of the class. It made me wonder what motivates students to learn. What impact did my expressed frustration have on Sarah's change in demeanor? In contrast to cajoling students to do the required, my exasperation probably indicated that she had overstepped her boundaries.

After the first month, I brought four dictionaries to class. These lay spread conspicuously on the center table around which we sat. Despite my urgings, by the end of the first class only one student had looked up a word in the dictionary during the writing exercise. The word "peonage" was in the essay on Rosa Parks. I used such moments to expound on the importance of building vocabulary. "Look it up in the dictionary," I urged students when they failed to explain the meaning of a word that arose in conversation or in the day's reading. There was no rush for the four dictionaries lying on the table. I waited. Maria picked up the last dictionary, but dropped it rather promptly. "Have you found the word?" I asked. She claimed the word was not in the dictionary. "Try again," I urged her. Sarah rose from her seat to look up the word, assisted by Victor four chairs to her left. Maria insisted the word was not in the dictionary. Sarah read out its meaning from the dictionary in her hand. Maria listened rather listlessly. "Maria, look it up in your dictionary," I insisted as she continued fumbling with the pages. "Give her the page number," I finally instructed the class, feeling frustrated but also to avoid losing extra time. They did. Maria took her time to open the dictionary. She put it back. I doubt she read the definition. The choice to intervene reflects a teacher's previous experiences in particular situations or with specific students. Class size and the availability of time also determine a teacher's flexibility in confronting an issue. In this case, I chose to continue with the lesson. Explaining a teacher's preferred style, Bashir highlights the focus of African immigrant teachers on product rather than the process of learning: "By and large, schooling in my country is taken much more seriously than schooling is taken here. There is a greater provision of teaching and learning resources here than in West Africa. A much more serious attitude is given to class, home assignments and exams in West Africa than it is here." Fast (2000) makes a similar claim about the value of education from his experience teaching mathematics in Zimbabwe. Ignoring the cultural rhetoric, Konneh (2003) insists that "Goodness and evil are not peculiar to one race or ethnic group" (p. 93). Owolabi (1996) concurs.

One day, I instructed the students to integrate a word from the dictionary that they hadn't used before and to underline it. I consistently urged students to raise the bar for themselves: do better rather than well enough. The class again responded to my instructions with silence; the pattern turned into a waiting game throughout the semester, although the gap between my instructions and the first scribbling grew shorter with time. "Can we use a curse word?" Victor interjected. He always had something to say, sometimes inappropriately. My "No!" was abrupt, "You know enough curse words already." He laughed and got back to the task. Victor was the best speller in the group. He once admitted to carrying around a dictionary; it helped build vocabulary. On that day he did have a dictionary in his book bag. He could be impudent, questioning my rationale for classroom activities with the usual, "Must we do it?" If not, "What do you want us to do?" For the most part, he did his work. He had a visible limp that made his walk labored. I watched his classmates slow their pace when he was in company. Victor would often break away from a group, although never in his classmates' company, to speak with me when we encountered each other outside of class. (He has since joined the university at which I teach and speaks with me whenever we meet). In the presence of his classmates, he was aloof with me. I honored his choice. About ten minutes into the writing assignment, I reminded Andrea about the requirement of integrating a new word from the dictionary into her essay. "I have them in my head," she said. She appeared ready for a fight. I let it go.

Responding to a growing concern about the academic performance of Generation 1.5—immigrant and international students—who may be fluent in conversational English but struggle with academic texts, Singhal (2004) advocates explicit instruction in academic writing. Literacy involves "the ability to read and write, but as well the ability to use critical thinking or higher-order thinking skills, communication skills, and research skills." (p. 4). To promote the discovery of the language components of academic English, Singhal underscores the need for explicit instruction of tools for "expanding and expressing the intellectual ability. Among the language comprehensive strategies she identifies are "notetaking, highlighting, paraphrasing, summarizing, outlining, and using a dictionary" (p. 6). Students should know how to locate and extract information from standard sources. They also need to distinguish between "relevant and irrelevant information; understand the writer's responsibility of attribution to avoid plagiarism; and accurately document primary and secondary sources" (p. 9). Teachers help students develop communication skills by promoting students' writing and oral skills in groups. For critical skills, students "learn to move back and forth between observation and inference, facts and assumptions" (p. 9).

Singhal views academic writing pedagogy as teaching students explicit skills in what to do before writing, what to do while writing, what to do after writing, writing aids and writing as communication, language, structure, and style, research and using sources, rhetoric modes and formats and evaluation. Most African immigrant teachers appreciate the significance of these strategies in acquiring facility in host country languages.

Aman's (2002) frustration with academic writing mirrors the experience of many African immigrant teachers: "As an Arab-speaking student, I was writing English in an Arabic style: long sentences with verbs at the end of the sentence and lots of flowery language and metaphor. [A professor] taught me to write scientific English—precise and succinct" (p. xiv). Tips for teaching Generation 1.5 students pertain primarily to diverse schools with significant numbers of immigrants in New York, Texas, Florida, Miami, and Illinois (Harklau, Losey and Siegel, 1999). The high school students I taught exhibited similar characteristics—fluency in speech but with tremendous resistance to writing as well as poor writing skills. Sarah's early comment about never having to read beyond twelfth grade illustrates the aversion to the art. It could also reflect the absence of a print-rich environment in the primary setting. Being surrounded by people who love reading can also foster a love of the art.

At every class session, I would review the requirements for each assignment, reiterating the need to identify facts related to the 5Ws and 1H (who, what, where, why, when, and how). By the end of the first month, the two-hour class met once a week. I reminded students of the latest strategy we had covered in previous weeks—argument and counter-argument. I suggested that they conclude the essay with a summary and counter-argument. They could then write seven sentences. "This is boring!" charged Sarah at one of the sessions, a smart but typically contentious student. "We want to have fun," she went on to say. Her eleventh-grade classmates joined in the resistance. The charges became a chorus: "Yeah, it is too much work." "Why do we always have to write?" "Why must we always write six paragraphs." "I signed up for this class to have fun but all we do is writing." "We are not learning anything," Cecilia added. I felt like a heel, dismissed and rejected. Besides my role in the teacher-education program, the frustration reflected my deflated hopes of helping prepare students for college. How could I have been that blind and wrong in my role as a teacher, I wondered. Giroux (1988) acknowledges students' frustration with "predetermined and hierarchical" classroom practices that ignore what interests and concerns them; not surprisingly, students are bored and become disruptive. Teachers such as myself focus on "maintaining order and control," rather than "teach[ing] positive knowledge," he charges (p. 122). The issue is: Who decides what constitutes positive knowledge?

The neoconservative focus on basic literacy masks the production and legitimatization of "oppressive and exploitative social relations" (Giroux, 1988, p. 147). There are more important things in teaching than the content of knowledge. In the United States the primary goal of schooling has been the creation of an industrial workforce and the development of character based on a chauvinistic Western tradition reflected in the Great Books canon. Not dissimilar is the focus of immigrant teachers on "basic skills, technical training, and classroom discipline" (p. 151). However, Giroux concedes that such efforts also empower students personally and socially. Students "consciously or unconsciously refuse to learn the specific cultural codes and competencies authorized by the dominant culture's view of literacy" (p. 157). The age-old debate between conservatives and liberals captures this dilemma. Critical pedagogy equips marginalized groups with the skills of "naming and transforming those ideological and social conditions that undermine the possibility for forms of community and public life organized around the imperatives of a critical democracy" (p. 151). On the other hand, students from privileged backgrounds understand the impact of a privatized, pessimistic, and capitalistic orientation. In critical theory terms, literacy becomes a cultural tool for naming and transforming debilitating social conditions (Apple, 1996, 2006, 2008; Florence, 2009; Freire, 2000; Giroux, 1988; hooks, 1994, 2003, 2008). The ensuing solidarity avoids privileging any one experience, literary tradition, history, form of knowing or being. Often overlooking perceptual locations(Black/White; male/female; rich/poor), immigrant teachers focus on defined class objectives—curriculum and appropriate class behavior.

The silence on political (controversial) issues may be a conscious choice to avoid charges of unpatriotism or, and probably more so, a lack of context for ongoing intercultural rhetoric. During my first year in the United States, conversations with a particular classmate always ended with a tirade about Puerto Ricans relative to "assimilable" immigrants (like me?). I neither knew nor could distinguish this group from the rest of the Americans. Baruti's ignorance of students' eating habits and relationships, whether intentional or not, is understandable. When in doubt reserve the comments.

One day, Cecilia made some snide remark that elicited laughter around the room. "You are malicious, Cecilia," I said. "What does that mean?" she asked with a puzzled look. "It means, 'mean,'" Andrea volunteered. The snide remarks continued. I ignored the commotion and waited. "You never teach anything," continued Cecilia. "I need to answer my phone," Victor interjected with a request. "Can I leave the class?" Notwithstanding the ban on cell phones in public schools, I never saw Victor with a phone in hand. I dismissed the request with an adamant, "NO!" "Can I go to the bathroom then?" he repeated, drawing the group's attention. Three students stopped writing to watch us battle it out. I insisted Victor complete the writing exercise before leaving class. He folded his hands and sat pouting. Some students sat unyielding. Sarah, Cecilia, and Andrea maintained a stream of personal note exchanges which I ignored. The conspiratorial glances, snickers, and side talk tempted me to confront the issue but I resisted the urge. It is a tough call. In Kenya, a teacher's punitive glance silences disruptive students who can be thrown out of class, suspended or expelled in extreme cases. Students thrown out of class stand outside looking mortified and fearful of subsequent consequences. In US public schools, students require passes to be in hallways and teachers are cautioned against leaving classrooms unsupervised. I waited patiently, focused on students who continued with the task. A third of the class appeared engrossed in the writing activity, shutting out the commotion around them. They were also the twelfth-graders who disassociated themselves from Andrea's eleventh-grade clique. Aminata's greatest challenge as an elementary school teacher is one of "retention and students' [inability to] focus." For immigrant teachers such improprieties by students pose a real challenge; a teacher has to consistently negotiate terms with a seemingly belligerent group of students (Mori, 1997):

> In my country, the teacher is respected to the point of being feared. I remember when I was a college lecturer, I used to arrive late, when the students would be preparing to go home. As soon as they saw me getting off the bus, they would run back to the classroom. We are talking about grown men, not high school students. The students were expected to respect each other too. The classroom was considered like a sanctuary for learning. No fights or hostilities were expected to go on in the classroom. Never. (Girikaze)

Yetunde reiterates Girikaze's view of the centrality of respect for adults, especially teachers, in African communities: "Teachers get more respect from students in my country. So do parents from students. Elders in general are believed to have more life experiences and insight, and thus are deferred to by youth." But this is changing with children talking back to adults.

That day, the most resistant students—Andrea, Victor, and Sarah—did not submit the last writing assignment which students typically dropped off at my side on their way out. Surprisingly Cecilia, who initiated the resistance to the assignment and who frequently complained about class activities, handed in her work. I wondered if the group knew that Cecilia did her work regardless. In his analysis on cultural diversity and school learning, Ogbu (1992) notes how some minority students "camouflage" their academic commitment by "becoming a class clown or jester." Braininess is acceptable for students who have other assets their peers value; without these other assets, the smart African-American student is "seen as a turncoat," influenced by teachers or White folks (Harris, 1998; Ogbu, 1992; Tatum, 2007). Harris maintains that children avoid being different; peer rather than adult approval is much more coveted. "Children see adults as serious and sedentary...for instance, when the teacher is being particularly bossy—they become sillier and more active. Students demonstrate their fealty to their own age group by making faces and running around" (p. 175). In Harris' estimation, the issue of race or in this case social status, is secondary to peer approval. Tatum's (1997) analysis of Black students' voluntary apartheid shows the inextricability of race and peer pressure on students' choices.

I always returned students' work at the end of the next scheduled class. Based on a paper's content and coherence, the student with the highest mark read their paper aloud to the class. Besides fostering transparency of the grading system, the practice publicly acknowledged a student's diligence: a different use of peer pressure. In my years of teaching the privilege has been shared among a number of students.

For African immigrant teachers, tensions that arise over classroom etiquette—disrespect for the forum and also individual students/teachers—constitute distractions from an academic focus. My cultural shock in the initial years appears, with distance and with some issues, extremely insignificant. Students ate during lessons and professors sipped beverages in class! On the other hand, a supervisor ranted and raved about a fellow African immigrant student who wore his hat in the library. We looked at each other in utter confusion, none the wiser for what the breach was. Later we would learn that U.S. protocol dictates that one remove his or her hat upon entering a house or gathering as a sign of respect. In retrospect, reflecting a post-colonial mentality of dress codes, Kenyan judges don white wigs and lunch-hour crowds feature men in black suits, white shirts and ties in sweltering tropical temperatures. Men remove hats in places of worship even as women keep their heads covered for modesty. At the time, none of us reflected that deeply on the tradition of taking off hats inside offices. These incidents demonstrate that something is not a discipline problem unless so defined by the teacher. Indeed, teachers have different levels of tolerance for social breaches. Aarifa acknowledges the differences in classroom etiquette in Ethiopia and the United States:

> There are no similarities, but rather only stark differences...with regard to other students, I believe that the students in my home country develop a similar level of camaraderie, but it is demonstrated differently. For instance, boys are very affectionate with each other and there is less focus or distraction due to heterosexual male/female dynamics. Also, parents do not have

to be called as often due to misbehavior or truancy; in fact, teachers and the community at large are considered extensions of the family and can deliver punishment, including corporal punishment, without parental consent.

Kofi's apprehension of the student/teacher relationship illustrates the frustration of teaching in the United States. In Ghana, there is a greater emphasis on discipline in terms of learning. Students respect teachers. He adds: "Children listen as teachers teach. [There] is absolutely no vulgar language in class." While reiterating Aarifa's concern about students' lack of respect, the male Kofi worries about cross-gender misinterpretations: "Teachers prefer not to get close to students for fear of [charges of] disrespect. Students could falsely accuse teachers of sexual harassment. Students could set up teachers."

African immigrant teachers want to be appreciated and also to have the satisfaction of helping students learn something. And yet, "pleasing students" appears undecipherable and impractical. Some students, however few, appreciate a teacher who holds them accountable and demonstrates the value of focusing on longer-term academic benefits even when the choice draws ire at the time. Traore and Lukens (2006) acknowledge the difficulty of enforcing discipline in American schools: "Teachers no longer automatically command the respect of their students (or sometimes even the parents of their students)...teachers must earn the respect of their students; and in some communities the testing of a teacher can be extremely difficult for a teacher who is not accustomed to being challenged or personally attacked" (p. xxvii-xxviii). Indeed, school authorities are increasingly limited in controlling student behavior; "the paddle and strap are illegal" (Milner, 2004, p. 18). James E. Rosenbaum calls teachers "lion-tamers without a whip" considering the ongoing negotiations for order and academic delivery many engage in (Ravitch, 1995, p. 119; Mori, 1997). In contrast, Harris (1998) acknowledges differences in the use of physical punishment within neighborhoods and across cultural groups. Bateson (2000) alludes to a "repressive discipline to assert control over children whose world was extremely hazardous" (pp. 187–88). Families in poorer neighborhoods and members of ethnic minority groups are more likely to use corporal punishment than would wealthy or European American parents, a claim the economically secure Japanese American Mori (1997) disputes. Her relatives appear more punitive than European American parents. In most African schools, the relationship between teachers and students is hierarchical and often coercive, particularly in the lower grades; teachers abuse their authority as a male respondent acknowledges:

> There was more respect for teachers in Africa. Teachers were always referred to as sir or madam. Interactions with teachers were limited to the

classroom except in cases of abuse where male teachers often took advantage of female students—some eventually became their wives. Teachers in Africa were a symbol of authority. Teachers could not be challenged on their knowledge—it was considered rude. To speak to a teacher, one needed permission. Students stood up to address the teacher. (Wafula)

Kanga (2004) exposes the pervasive and structural sanctions of sexual harassment in Kenyan society. Some parents trade daughters to wealthier adult propertied men. Despite the cultural silencing, media accounts reveal "chilling narratives" of rape, arson, and other forms of violence against females by classmates and teachers. To some degree, the United States legal system limits such abuses of power.

Most students in the United States expect teachers to consistently negotiate for compliance to classroom activities or codes of conduct, "questioning decisions at every turn" (Mori, 1997, p. 178). It is an ongoing battle, what Willis (1981) terms the "guerilla warfare" in schools, as teachers and students battle it out over school regulations. Sharon, whom I met first of the group, treated me like a prized pet, which could well have been the case. She helped recruit the group in the elective class I taught, selling my elective to her acquaintances. I was firmer with her to avoid her taking liberties. The class rule was that only one student could leave the class at any one time to use the bathroom. Sharon always asked to be excused after someone else left the room: "But I need to go NOW!" "You waited this long and can wait for two more minutes," I would tell her. She'd suck her teeth in annoyance, roll her eyes and engage whoever was next to her before settling down to the writing activity. The bathroom request was forgotten until something else distracted her. She worked better on her own but I frequently chose not to isolate her because of the energy the task took. At the second session, Sharon pulled out her makeup kit (it matched her pink–and–white pantsuit with matching sneakers), and proceeded to apply the makeup right at the working table. I was too shocked at the lack of etiquette to intervene. In later discussions, my colleagues assured me the incident was a breach. On one occasion, Sharon and her friend David maintained a running chatter that distracted the class. I demanded they separate and waited despite the tension as they first ignored my urging, then argued against the imposition, and finally pleaded for its withdrawal. Students glanced back and forth, waiting to see who would give in first. Finally, David scraped the chair behind him, causing enough ruckus to draw the attention of the whole class, before shuffling over to the chair next to me. It was a close call and the achievement not entirely due to a premeditated plan of action. For many immigrants, classroom choices reflect a resignation to the least evil or merely ingrained habits.

Handling students' requests or distractions reflected my priorities at the time. Requesting to use the bathroom each time the class settles down for a writing activity raised a red flag. And yet I would often allow interactions among students when the request did not detract the focus on academics, or I would use such requests as a teaching moment: "What if we all did what we want...?" In some cases, I allowed students a classroom break only after they completed the required work. To this they grumbled but did the work; often the urgency of their earlier request was forgotten by the end of the writing assignment. On the other hand, I would insist that students work independently on writing activities, aware that some required that level of concentration to absorb the new material. The pressure of accommodating students' requests that are not focused on academics is a challenge to most African immigrant teachers:

> The most attractive part about education in my country is the value attached to it. Education is perceived as the only way to move ahead, and everybody takes it seriously. When the nation is peaceful, every child understands that the classroom is a sacred place, after the church. The teacher is given high respect as the communicator of knowledge. Rarely is the teacher's authority questioned. The structure of education itself is another beautiful thing about the Burundi system of education. (Girikaze)

Such classroom contests for power unnerve teachers accustomed to a general consensus on tasks and procedures in their home country (Mori, 1997). A teacher's consistency in academic demands fosters competitive learning although the process takes much more effort. Bateson (2000) and Badillo (2006) link the watering down of curriculum and expectation of shoddy performance, tardiness, and incompletes to liberal racism. In this class, students gradually wrote pieces at each class setting, read aloud despite the initial resistances, and gradually took some responsibility for choices. Often, the issue involves fostering a culture of accommodation and accountability rather than the imposition of an immigrant teacher's values or denigration of students' primary experiences or preferences. Damon (2001) and Nord (2000) caution against succumbing to a quagmire of moral relativism to accommodate minority interests. Damon emphasizes the centrality of shared values: "[P]arents everywhere want their children to be honest, respectful, kind, responsible, law-abiding, fair-minded, and so on" (p. 138).

> Yet there is hesitancy today to assert the moral sense, or to use a moral language at all, in many homes and schools. There are several reasons for

this: some adults worry that shaming children wounds their self-esteem; some believe that moral teaching does not belong in schools; some believe that there are no moral truths anyway, or that it is hypocritical to preach them to the young when so many adults ignore them, or that in a diverse society one person's moral truth is another's moral falsehood. (p. 129)

American society has largely replaced religion with principles that Holmes (2001) and Nord (2001) claim fall short of "fundamental values of good citizenship" (Holmes, p. 199) as the example of parochial schools and spirituality in African-American communities illustrate. How can teachers design a moral ethnic acceptable to students? For immigrant teachers the choice is never easy. Many fall back on school rules for maintaining discipline, or in Baruti's case, rubrics in the syllabus to assess students' progress. It is a familiar route!

That urban minority students can and do perform to standards adds to the frustration of African immigrant teachers from more structured, discipline-oriented backgrounds. My high school students seemed unaware or unconcerned about the implications of a lack of diligence. The students talked about going to college with little mention of what it took to get there. Milner (2004) claims youth cultures resist visions of what schools should be. Willis (1981) attributes much of students' counterschool culture to immaturity and a focus on immediate gratification. The time spent socializing and at (sometimes needed) part-time jobs is time away from academics. Yet most students are able to socialize with friends and "most have a significant amount of money to spend on themselves" (Milner, 2004, p. 163). For some others, there is the danger and pressure of the streets, what Damon (2001) calls, "*anti*social engagements" (p. 124). Overall, peer acceptance or rejection "is often perceived to be much more important than academic success" (Milner, 2004, p. 23). Even smart students will eschew academics when such ambitions conflict with group norms. (Harris, 1998; Holmes, 2001; McWhorter, 2001)

Initiating discussions over what constitutes academic excellence with the high school group filled me with a sense of resignation. The students spoke of going to college, glossing over the required credits, particularly the embrace of excellence as opposed to just passing (anything but a failing "U"). Frustrated with the troubling academic standards, I wondered what else I could have done to foster the love of learning. The sense of failure as a teacher is hard to shake off when students begrudgingly tolerate school policies and the teacher's role as necessary evils. Since the battlefield classrooms never work for either party, the larger problem is how to establish an environment where students see meaning in what they are asked to do and one where mutually respectful standards of behavior are maintained. Ongoing discussions about the importance of hard work and appropriate school behavior are crucial. Peer pressure can function as a motivator or demotivator to academic success.

The critical educational theorist, Giroux (1988), derides this conservative focus on academic scores and character development at the expense of more immediate concerns—such as school dropout rates, sexism, and racism—that disempower students; an abstraction of knowledge that denies the concerns of "schools, workplaces, the state, and other major public spheres" (p. 34). He faults the mainstream system of education for abstracting knowledge and emphasis on traditional authority, both of which reinforce elitist conceptions of knowledge, privilege past traditions and future endeavors, but ignore prevailing "contradictions and tensions" (p. 125). A democratic ideal involves collective effort for a common good rather than reproducing the status quo. The process interrogates "what is" to envision inclusive ideals that question the rigid curriculum, "the way school time is organized, the political consequences of tracking students, the social division of labor among teachers, and the patriarchal basis of schooling" (Giroux, 1988, p. 79). Giroux advocates an emancipatory "pedagogy of critique and possibility." Respect is reciprocal; students from industrialized countries need to appreciate cultural elements that may not be evident to them in their primary groups, as immigrants do continually. Cultural accommodation is a responsibility for both teachers and students.

Teachers do a lot of waiting. They wait for the spark of interest in students' faces, something on which to build the learning experience. They wait for students to settle down and focus on the task at hand. They wait for students' responses to verbal and laid-out instructions. They wait for an end to disruptive behavior when this undermines learning. They wait and hope for an "aha" moment as an affirmation of the teaching effort. Teachers wait for students to excel academically and to outgrow the commonplace resistance to learning. Meanwhile, teachers seek out academic potential and motivational factors, at times staking boundaries of what is tolerable and at other times conceding to students' demands when these offer the required learning environment.

CHAPTER 4

Respect

Ongoing debates about respect demonstrate the complexity of social norms with regard to self-conception and social interactions. Most immigrants socialized in close-knit communities that emphasize external discipline are more tolerant of social regulations as an inevitable convention; order comes from formalized roles and status as demonstrated in Aminata's depiction of American students as "more vocal" compared to those in Sierra Leone. Foreign-trained immigrant teachers stress social etiquette and obligations while disputes over respect in class settings focus more on individual rights.

At the national level, calls for cultural pluralism have not tempered assimilation policies and practices. Within schools, an area of contention is authority, its conception and expression in social interactions. Most African communities stress respect in social interactions to be accompanied by language and postures sensitive to age, gender, class, and authority. The cliché of children being "seen but not heard" captures the underlying social hierarchy. In general, women defer to men, acknowledging themselves as subordinates. Authority figures offer patronage for deference and allegiance. Such hierarchical structures are supported by overcrowded schools and limited opportunities which create pyramid-like structures of privilege, with the masses at the mercy of the wealthy and powerful. The denial of concessions by an authority figure evokes in some students feelings of resentment and the need to prove their clout. Students perceive traditional displays of authority and their emphasis on external displays of respect as inhibitive and culturally insensitive. In general, they prefer teachers they can identify with , those with demonstrable expertise and also admirable qualities such as beauty, an athletic body, those who are well-dressed, or even teachers who are lenient in grading. Students' rationale for a contentious incident with, "Because I feel like …" contrasts sharply with a more deferential response acknowledging other people's interests to which most foreign-trained immigrant teachers are accustomed. Yet, Aarifa, a first generation African-American (Ethiopian descent), exhibits similar cultural tendencies common to foreign-trained immigrant teachers despite her American upbringing.

A teacher's perceptual location determines what constitutes a discipline breach. In reality, what comprises assertiveness in one culture represents disrespectful narcissism in other cultural contexts (Appiah, 1992; Bateson, 2000). The American emphasis on individuality and empowerment offers a different model of social interactions. What an African views as insubordination is lauded as assertiveness in most American cultures, and a teacher's demand for respect may appear an imposition and abuse of authority to students accustomed to speaking up against perceived injustices.

According to an online survey of 339 faculty members from nine geographically dispersed U.S. colleges and universities, student incivility is also directed "at women, the young, and the inexperienced." The study, presented at the American Educational Research Association, described student incivility like "passive behavior such as sleeping or texting in class; more actively disruptive behavior such as coming to class late or talking on cell phones in the classroom; and behaviors that appeared directed at the instructor, such as open expressions of anger, impatience, or derision." (Schmidt, 2010 n.p.). That the oldest and most experienced faculty members reported few incidents of incivility might indicate that some faculty members ignore incidents of incivility, or, as one survey subject admitted, "students seem to smell the vulnerability of the professor seeking tenure" (n.p.). Although scholars differ in conceptions of student incivility and the frequency of occurrence, such breaches complicate the teaching/learning process.

The passion with which people defend affiliates—blood relations or friends—as well as defensive attacks on perceived threats, raises concerns about perceptions as much as the tolerance of differences. Notwithstanding differences in the conceptions of respect, discussions typically focus on its lack, blaming other people's lack of respect. Milner (2004) notes how students call each other names, ostracize one another, yell across rooms and at teachers, waste resources, and mishandle school furniture, but yet complain about disrespectful administrators and teachers. I devoted time to class routines and expectations in the specially designed high school course. Resistance to class activities ranged from not having writing materials, frequent trips to the bathroom, audible complaints, incomprehensible comments, absences, poor quality work, or un-submitted assignments. "Respect," I once interjected, "is what schools value." The faces around the room stared back at me.

Were we talking about the same thing? Often, calls for respect or the lack thereof reflect upbringing. Deferring to adults denotes respect in African communities. On the other hand, most communities in the United States encourage assertive behavior, its lack implying insecurity or something questionable. The following discussion explores differences in the conception, application, and rationale of (dis)respect in class settings.

At the beginning of a class on rights and obligations, I called students' attention to the manner in which cultural differences within schools create tensions and misunderstandings. "We may or may not know what others expect of us. Sometimes people know what we want from them and yet do something to disappoint us. This makes us angry." Students' faces around the room stared back at me. "Look at us," I reminded them, pausing for effect. They waited. "Raised differently and from different countries, we are different, look different, have different interests and like things that some others hate. And yet," I concluded the speech, "we are compelled to work together for a significant amount of time each week." At that point more than half the class was looking to me, waiting.

"Teachers do not respect us," the students charged, breaking the lull. Their voices rose drowning out each other, oblivious of my call to order. Some laughed; they exchanged knowing looks. Alex called out the name of one of their teachers at the high school as an example of disrespectful teachers. The tirade stopped temporarily; his classmates' "Oh yeahs!" were in unison. In nearly drowned-out voices, accusers cited specific incidents to affirming yeahs, coupled with some dismissive comments and conspiratorial laughter. The students' consensus on the particular teacher was the person's dislike of Alex. Alex, one of the few male students in class, delivered concise responses to my questions, however rare. His assignments were in coherent English, reflecting his facility with the language. However, for most of the time Alex sat leaning back in his chair, basking in the devotion showered upon him by his girlfriend, Jennifer. They always sat next to each other in class. "Respect is important to the school too," I interjected. My comment struck a discordant note in the conversation. Our class discussions that day pitted one party against the other, another authoritative adult against victimized students.

Conceptions of Respect

Scholarly discourses on respect reflect a similar ambivalence over its definition with some focusing on what is observable in social interactions as opposed to the causes of, and individual motivations for, acting disrespectfully as well as the impact of its lack in school settings. Hemmings (2003) distinguishes respect from reputation among students with teachers focusing on the former. She associates respectability with propriety—speech, dress, and class. In contrast, reputation reflects an individual's self-determination regardless of the consequences. Youth with a "bad" reputation have greater status among classmates, while teachers honor and foster "good" reputations that reflect socially desirable behavior patterns. Reputation for males "is acquired by the limited use of English, standing up to authorities, showing up male rivals, and controlling women through multiple sexual conquests and harassments" (p. 427). Harris (1998) acknowleges the impact of peers on males to shun female company. She stresses that males are more cliquish than females. Black males cultivate reputations by adopting the image of being rich and tough, by wearing expensive designer clothing and jewelry, and by using hip-hop street talk. In contrast, female friendships "tend to be close and exclusive, though not necessarily lasting. Girls are less likely than boys to show hostility directly; they get back at their enemies by attempting to turn their friends against them" (p. 232). They are torn between the image of docility and an "in-control" tough girl: "The idea was to send clear signals that there were women who were in control when it came to eliciting attention and resources from men, handling female competitors, and otherwise taking care of themselves" (Hemmings, 2003, p. 431). These priorities contrast sharply with a teacher's focus on academics or harmony in class settings. The rhetoric of progressive education as developing creative and autonomous students overlooks the conventional preference for compliance, obedience, cooperation, attentiveness, respect, and orderly classrooms (Walkerdine, 1990). Which will it be? Teachers, she notes, are "guardians of an impossible dream" (p. 25).

While communities associate respect to civility, Lightfoot-Lawrence (1999) recommends reciprocity in relationships of unequal power such as teachers and students or doctors and patients. Giroux (1988) decries calls for deference to authority figures as a neoconservative cultural tool of oppression and exploitation. Given disparities in conceptions and tolerance, fostering respect and civility is an elusive goal, however legitimate the call for a healthy balance. Respect undergirds social interactions, determining the appropriateness of interactions and manner of speech as Hemmings (2003) maintains. Holmes (2001) links respect to responsibility and honesty, values that are prized in communal systems. Underlying these values is the "consideration for others" (p. 196). Sara Lightfoot-Lawrence's (1999) interviews of six professionals demonstrated the impact of family roots, temperament, and life stories on conceptions of respect. The traditional association of respect to civility focuses on externals—proper demeanor in relationships with authority, colleagues, and family; self-image; and proper use of space and property. African communities and schools emphasize the external nature of respect; children refrain from misbehavior because relatives, neighbors, and friends alike chide them for breaches in discipline (Appiah, 1992). Childrearing is a communal affair. It is an aspect African immigrant teachers can foster in class settings.

> Classroom interactions in my home country consist of the students standing up when the teacher enters the room, greeting the teacher politely, and a general attitude of deference and respect. Standards within the United States are diametrically opposed with my students talking to each other, talking on cell phones, cursing at the teachers, and treating teachers with much less respect than they would their own peers. In the end, with a great deal of effort and understanding, I was able to elicit a much higher level of respect from my students than my American peers. (Aarifa)

Students' level of preparedness for school-adaptive social skills such as respect or diligence varies either due to parental expectations, home setting, or teacher expectancy and inconsistency in enforcing discipline (Hemmings, 2003; Lane et al., 2006; Lawrence-Lightfoot, 1999). Citing Lightfoot-Lawrence, Harris (1998) focuses on peer pressure in respectful interactions. But there are limits to external coercion. Students choose to associate with those they view as similar, with whom they share experiences (Harris, 1997; Milner, 2004). Generally, the recognition of a common humanity or circumstance regulates social interactions (Harris, 1997; Jacobs, 1995; Lightfoot-Lawrence, 1999).

Respect, notes Jacobs (1995), is the unifying aspect of life: "When we have respect as a disposition, we enjoy the fact that justice is served, that others are not suffering, that we have done right by others" (p. 137). It involves attending to facts about people and their situations in order to achieve what is "ethically relevant." A lack of respect need not be malicious or cause physical harm. "It may be a matter of not bothering to acknowledge [students] as responsible, voluntary agents and regarding them instead just in terms of what difference to us or our concerns is made by what they do" (p. 142). While Dingane concedes the privilege of teachers in interactions in his country of origin, he recognizes the centrality of respect in interactions particularly among students and links cultural tolerance to respect:

> Respect for teachers is a MUST in my country of birth and in certain instances disrespecting teachers can lead to expulsion. Respect of other

students is similar in both my country of birth and the United States. For example, students respect and tolerate each other's cultures as well as political and religious views.

Charges of disrespectful adults by my high school students focused on behavior; adults failed to acknowledge the individuality of students over and above the students' compliance or the lack thereof to school rules. Paula charged me with disrespect for urging her to integrate more sources in her paper; she felt her work was good as it was. In contrast, the African culture appears repressive and hierarchically structured. "African students talked different, dressed different, and behaved different"; they are respectful to teachers, want to learn, and are diligent, which creates endless acrimony with classmates (Traore and Lukens, 2006, p. 52).

To most Africans, respect translates to listening to elders, not talking back, use of civil language, a conciliatory demeanor, or disciplined and mindful behavior. "Respecting oneself and others is such a key ingredient to identity development in adolescence" (Traore and Lukens, 2006, p. 161; Fast, 2000; Obiakor and Gordon, 2003). The embrace of such norms comes instinctively in smaller communities that foster intimate interactions. Accommodation to differences in traditional communities reflects social obligations and the primacy of cohesion. Appiah (1992) and his friend's perception of American culture captures the dissonance: "The most cultural difference" between Ghana and the United States, upon their arrival is the "aggressiveness...what he had noticed was not aggression but simply a different conversational style" (p. 130). The veneer of compliance can be deceptive though: "At first glance, many African students seem content in school, almost placid. Underneath their calm exterior, however, there stirs a potent mixture of hurt, anger, disappointment, and disillusionment, all rising from their schooling experiences" (Traore and Lukens, 2006, p. 96). Obiakor and Gordon (2003) link the passivity in African-born students in the United States to expediency. Caught between a dominant White group and a Black underclass, African-born residents face a dilemma: "they are expected to be *silent* and *invisible. When they are quiet, they are assumed to be 'inferior'; and when they are confident, they are assumed to be 'arrogant'.* Either way, their positive or negative responses carry devastating price tags and misinterpretations" (Obiakor and Gordon, 2003, p. xvii; italics in original). Neither invisibility nor passive aggression is conducive to learning (Appiah, 1992; Traore and Lukens, 2006).

Students' access to social networks impacts academic achievement, but so does their demeanor (Putnam, 2001). These networks include supportive structures within families, communities, and other social organizations, whether work or leisure related. Putnam's empirical study links the absence of such networks to crime, child welfare, access to higher education, civic responsibility, effectiveness of state government, and the tolerance of diversity:

> In short, teachers report high levels of parental support and low levels of student misconduct precisely in places blessed with high levels of community- and family-based social capital. This evidence suggests that the attitudes and behavior that parents and students bring to the educational process are even more deeply affected by the strength of community and family bonds than by the general socioeconomic or racial character of their communities. (p. 82)

Putnam cautions against "civic lethargy and social disengagement" in view of the distrust in urban areas because socially disengaged students tend to be dismissive of sacrifices devoid of immediate gratification or self-interest. Despite the erosion of communitarian values, the consistency in discipline from parents, relatives, and religious institutions reinforces teacher authority and therefore the pressure on students to behave appropriately. In Kenya, most parents support the authority of schools as necessary to the child's academic success; teachers collaborate with and are part of community events. Teachers are lauded for students' achievements even as school dropouts are vilified with the familiar, "they didn't finish (school)." School dropouts reflect poorly on communities, making collaboration between schools and communities inevitable. In the United States, Damon (2001) warns against a "debilitating climate of moral uncertainty" (p. 129) to youth "when moral instruction in the school is hesitant, haphazard, and wholly uncoordinated with the core values of the home and community" (p. 131).

While essentialist in portrayal, Traore and Lukens (2006) as well as Obiakor and Gordon (2003) distinguish community-oriented African systems from cosmopolitan, individualistic value structures in the United States. Overall, economic, political, and social contexts shape cultural norms. Kenya's regimented system of education reflects the community value for social cohesion and national harmony. Most schools stress order and obedience to authority. First generation African students in the United States find the lack of respect reflected in students' talking back to teachers and the frequent "use of profane language" objectionable. A similar unease is evident among African teachers. Baruti reduces students' misbehavior to "rudeness." Ahmad contrasts the demeanor of an "absolutely obedient student to a student who questions everything with no boundaries or borders" in the United States. Aminata's assessment is more cautious: American "students are more vocal compared to students where I come from." Most African immigrants grew up in cultures that emphasize respect to adults and elders (Traore and Lukens, 2006). The reverence for authority figures is not unique to African societies. Citing traditional practices in Ireland and Rome, Freud (1918) roots the reverence for authority to their representation of the divine authority. Communities believe that, as with the gods, cultural authorities including kings and queens possess power over matters of life. In terms of healing, their touch was curative but could also be punitive: "Charles I is said to have healed a hundred sufferers (of scrofula) at one time, in the year 1633." Bukusu culture extends the reverence to parental figures in regard to curses and blessings.

Siegel (1996) as well as Traore and Lukens (2006) note the frustration of Peace Corps teachers and the lack of respect upon their return to the U.S. system. Among most Africans, younger members of a community or within family settings refer to adults by title—Mr., Dr., Sir, Uncle, Aunt, Father, Mother, etc. The use of names implies a lack of respect for elders (Mufwene, 1993; Obiakor and Gordon, 2003; Owolabi, 1996). Most African communities forbid intimate interactions between "ascending and descending in-laws (fathers-in-law and mothers-in-law and sons- and daughters-in-law)" (Mufwene, 1993, p. 64).[1] American collegiality and aversion to monarchical authority stand in sharp contrast to the hierarchical relationships familiar to most African immigrant teachers. I once responded to a "yo!" from a graduate students, after some pause, unsure of who he was speaking to. While some students in the United States use the professional title with me, more of them fall back on "Ms. Florence" or "Miss," if at all. The absence of titles fosters collegiality but also blurs generational and authority lines, encouraging a familiarity that complicates a teacher's class discipline.

Immigrants are unnerved by the informality in the United States (DeVita and Armstrong, 1993; Owolabi, 1996). During a conversation with a student as we rode the subway, I asked about his family (a typical African inquiry to which the respondent talks about spouse, children, and livestock). He mentioned a "partner." Was the partner male, female, wife, or girlfriend? There followed a pregnant silence. I was not sure whether to pursue the issue for clarity. In the United States, people readily divulge personal information about relationships, even of spouses and partners but yet consider discussions related to money as too personal. Owolabi (1996) is shocked by the tendency to announce early pregnancy, something Africans consider an indelicacy. Kim (2003) claims Americans put on a "facade or mask" to avoid an "emotion draining" confrontation, a tactic that reflects "social pleasantry" with one party maintaining "social politeness" and the other, a desire to maintain "self-esteem." In contrast to Kim's (2003) claim, Mori (1997) links these evasive mannerisms to Asian communities. An individual's perceptual location explains the variability in cultural conceptions and expressions. Africans are reputed to "beat around the bush," to avoid blunt and confrontational talk in social interactions. Is this unique to Africans though? Qualities of assertiveness, blunt honesty, and individualism are in all cultures as much as the opposite, as the intimate exposures on Twitter and Facebook across the globe illustrate. The popularity of "letting it all hang out" in Internet Facebooks and, most recently, Twitter, contrasts with an obviously individualistic culture. Uwah (2003) notes a similar discrepancy in American receptivity to foreigners. The "perfunctory conversations" on superficial topics such as the weather, traffic, or ethnic affiliation" are no reflection of the state of relationships. Few of these associations translate to hometown, fireside dinners with American colleagues.

The friendliness and openness associated with American culture differs sharply from the prevailing "mind your own business" attitude foreigners find impersonal and disarming. Traore recalls the suspicious glances in response to her greetings on a Philadelphia subway. In African communities, "Ignoring people is a lack of respect" (Traore and Lukens, 2006, p. 112; Fast, 2000). Absence from the homeland creates a new awareness of unconscious beliefs and practices. I recently visited a girls' boarding school in Bungoma district. For the most part, outside of class students moved around or engaged in tasks in groups. Surprisingly, a group of students would lapse into silence at the appearance of an adult or teacher, including myself. "They do not greet people," I chided the Principal. She wasn't surprised, explaining that it was the students' way of expressing respect. Students respond to an adult's initiative, in this case, an acknowledgment of their presence, or continue their discussions with the implicit sanction by an authority. Once spoken to, most bubble over in conversation while others respond timidly to questions. For African children, the habit of maintaining a respectful silence in adult/authority presence begins early and is reinforced in schools and workplaces. The greetings are a mere formality in the United States, Mucha (1993) notes, typically followed with a "How are you?" but not expecting a detailed or honest response. That students rush past teachers, often with little acknowledgment, ignore directions, and speak out of turn can be extremely unnerving to immigrant teachers used to more deferential, "respectful" students. The breach is noticeable to immigrant teachers accustomed to students' offers to erase the board, deliver a professor's teaching aids as well as personal effects, and the habit of maintaining a respectful silence in the face of authority, the lack of which Kenyans would consider taking liberties.

Kim's (2003) claim of American superficiality in relationships ignores the price of dissension and individual efforts at maintaining the facade of social harmony in African communities. African communities are hierarchically organized based on wealth, status, authority, gender, and age. Each category has prescribed roles and obligations such as mother, father, elder, healer, seer, warrior, adult, child, and so forth. An individual's failure to meet their obligations undermines the existing order, inconveniencing those who depended on the person to fulfill the role. The penalty for breaches results in social ostracism in a culture centered on collectivity; it is a high price to pay for individuality. African communities shun children who talk back to adults, although similar behaviors are commended as assertiveness in the United States. For immigrants adaptation to the openness and assertiveness associated with U.S. systems involves a shift in cultural goalposts (Appiah, 1992). The shift is gradual and disorienting; a cultural outsider becomes an insider depending on the setting. Baruti contrasts her attitudes toward students with her colleagues' "casual and friendly" relations with students, a stance she embraces rather reluctantly. However immigrants like Girikaze, acknowledge their outsider cultural status upon returning to mother countries.

Rationale for (Dis)respect

Hemmings (2003) attributes classroom contention to a crisis that undermines teaching and learning. Similarly, McFarland (2004) illustrates how breaches or crises arise from students' passive or active resistance to an established structure, what Hemmings terms "a moral order." Authority undergirds educational policy and practice, shaping classroom activities. Teachers, students, the administration, as well as custodial staff and security guards shape the school culture. The crisis in authority arises from defiance or sabotage of this moral order by students and teachers. Without trust in a moral order, neither students nor teachers feel obliged to the other or committed to the process of learning. Students reject the moral order through a defiance of rules, disrespect for classmates, and decorum (Giroux, 1988; Shor, 1996). Harris (1998), on the other hand, roots students' choices to peer pressure.

The inconsistency and sometimes contradictory enforcement of a school's moral order is confusing to students who confront different adult expectations and flexibility as they progress in grade, and also within an instructional day because of the variability in teaching styles. The arbitrariness of discipline codes in schools contributes to the problem of students' lack of discipline (Glazer, 2001; Holmes, 2001). Citing Himmelfarb, Glazer (2001) links classroom indiscipline to tensions between traditional values, what he terms "assimilation," and the focus on individuality. Himmelfarb blames the inconsistency on "Professors of Education who are...more permissive than either parents or teachers" in enforcing discipline, stressing writing rubrics, and tolerating tardiness, practices that he commends in parochial schools (Glazer, 2001, p. 176: Viteritti, 2001). In high schools, some teachers foster assertive skills and flexibility while others prefer a more structured approach that emphasizes cooperation and self-control in order to minimize classroom disruptions (Lane et al., 2006). However, while some teachers persist in efforts to engage students, others "simply gave up. They conceded defeat and pretty much allowed students to do as they pleased" (Hemmings, 2003, p. 424). One of the teachers, Ms. Hathaway, commanded respect: "She made learning strategies explicit and practically manageable for students" (p. 432). Her teaching approach was structured with "'step-by-step' lessons and direct assistance," competence, and respect for her inner-city Black students, as well as faith in their ability to succeed. Another teacher, Mr. Cameroon, cares for students in ways evident in his engagement of students in learning and demands for civility during a heated civil rights lesson. On the other extreme students reined in a teacher's disrespect for the regime by complaining about the lack of professionalism and offensive language. The teacher engaged in "off-color discussions on sex, sexuality," overstepping codes of civility, claiming to "stimulate the real interest of kids" (p. 425). Linking class material to students' lived reality only goes so far. Reflecting their primary upbringing, African immigrants are reticent on handling issues of sexuality and intimacy but belabor those of diligence and respect. When I have intervened to stop sideline chatter during a student's class presentation, the scowls, head rolls, and grunts by culprits let me know in no uncertain terms that I was being heavy-handed. Similarly, Baruti and Ahmad are reluctant to intervene unless absolutely necessary.

Various factors explain the poor academic performance of minority students in at-risk schools, those Holmes (2001) calls "dysfunctional"; teachers condone or even reward "poor attendance, low levels of achievement, and parasitic work habits" (p. 198). Besides students' low academic scores and graduation rates, the school environment makes it difficult to recruit and retain well-qualified teachers and principals. These schools mostly serve minority and low-income students. Due to the high traffic within these school and limited potential for enrichment exercises, "Teachers at high-risk schools viewed self-control and assertive skills as more critical for school success compared with teachers at low-risk schools" (Lane et al., 2006, p. 164). Students in high risk-schools compete for limited opportunities, and worry about the danger of anti-social confrontations. Harris (1998) makes a similar claim in associating aggressive behaviors to racial categories, in this case, African Americans. Hemmings' (2003) focus on socially adaptive skills highlights students' behavior patterns that reflect choices of cooperation and assertiveness. Students acquire particular coping skills from primary environments that spill over to school settings. Raised in a competitive and threatening environment, students develop combative survival skills. Harris (1998) acknowledges the environmental impact on students' aggressive tendencies:

> The kids in the South Bronx are aggressive for the same reason that the kids in the Mexican town of San Andres are aggressive: because that's how the other people in their communities behave. It's not because of the way their parents treat them.... Because you can move one of these families to a different neighborhood...and the behavior of their kids changes. (p. 213)

The focus on immediate gains also reflects a lack of hope and longer-term prospects among Black youth. Sarah's dismissal of the extremely gifted ten-year-old Misha (Janosfky, 2005) reflects the disillusionment among minority students in a society of perceived double standards: White privilege over minority students' alienation. Aarifa advises African immigrant teachers to consider the importance of context and consequences in addressing classroom practices:

1. African immigrant teachers should not judge, but understand the history within the United States that has determined the conditions affecting their classroom interactions.
2. African immigrant teachers should familiarize themselves with the historical factors that have led to generational poverty in the United States so that they may empathize with students in urban academic settings; their students' behavior is a byproduct of the larger society and not indicative of a student's pathology.
3. Students should be educated about the differences in educational standards throughout the world so that they may understand that the African immigrant teacher's "difference" is both cultural and a method to educate the students in a manner conducive to the students' success.

Working with students groomed for their "evident or probable destinies" through a College Now program in a class on Small Business Management and Minority Entrepreneurship illustrated the ability of minority students to excel academically in affirming environments. Drawn from a range of neighborhood schools and predominantly of Caribbean background, the diligence of high-performing minority students contrasted with the group under discussion regarding class attendance and the quality of work. Academically successful minority students have a sense of place and destiny; they can afford to sacrifice a challenging present for a prosperous future. Harris (1998) attributes the differences to peer pressure; an academically challenging group maintains the label through peer pressure. Students compete against each other for excellence, a process that raises academic scores.

While Hemmings (2003), Lane et al. (2006), and Mori (1997) focus on external facts such as social structures or adults in fostering respect, Milner (2004) highlights the impact of peer relationships on teenage behavior. Harris (1998) reiterates the significance of peers in understanding student behaviors, disputing the conventional blaming of parents for recalcitrant children. Comparing childhood to imprisonment, Harris claims that both states develop a culture—language and other norms:

> [Prisoners] have a great scorn for those who suck up to the guard or who rat on their fellow prisoners. They have to obey guards' orders or suffer the consequences, but at the same time they do not want to knuckle under completely—they want to preserve some modicum of autonomy. So they delight in outwitting the guards, in beating the rules in little ways they can get away with. (p. 199)

Like prison inmates, children from the same neighborhood develop similar accents and word usage. They also embrace popular value structures besides defying authority as testing ground. These choices impact students' receptivity to learning and openness to a teacher's critique of them or their work. Calls for change to students evoke confrontations few immigrant teachers court.

Curriculum and pedagogical reform, however desirable, may alleviate but not eliminate "irrational" behavior patterns among adolescents. In confrontations with authority, youth gain self-respect from outright aggression or in assuming an air of indifference/invincibility—a destructive or disruptive exit from class, for instance (Milner, 2004, p. 58). Ambivalent about their identity, youth waver between respect for authority and the autonomous distancing that gains one status among peers. Initially, I worried about students' claim of boredom. It was an unexpressed sentiment in my youth. Claims of boredom are some students' excuse for blatant classroom deviance, a distancing of oneself from authority (Giroux, 1988; Shor, 1996; Willis, 1981). Students consistently subvert adult norms and authority by re-creating their own rituals and norms of acceptability (Harris, 1998; McFarland, 2004; Milner, 2004, p. 60). For some students, negative visibility is better than invisibility.

The quest for respect and dignity is evident among Black as well as White youth (Grant, 2001; Hemmings, 2003). Jefferson High students complained about security guards who are "overly friendly with kids." Similar complaints also identify the violation of "privacy in prisonlike surveillance," and fights on school premises. School overcrowding, poor supervision, insensitive teachers, prisonlike school facilities, and out-of-school police brutality contribute to the lack of civility in urban schools (Hemmings, 2003). Hemmings links disrespect among Black youth to an alienating and threatening environment. Students adopt aggressive roles to project a sense of power.

In contrast, White youth are frustrated and angered by their eroding socioeconomic status to society's accommodation of minority interests (Grant, 2001; Hemmings, 2003; Huntington, 2004). The dominance of White elites in all major American institutions has not filtered down to nonelites who "lack their assurance and security, and think of themselves as losing out in the racial competition to other groups favored by the elites and supported by government polity" (Huntington, 2004, p. 314). Not surprisingly, White youth feel threatened by the loss of traditionally masculine jobs that offered "their male forebears money and status"; it is an erosion attributed to affirmative-action policies. Adam's complaint about a lack of civility and the academic minimalism of Black boys reflects concerns regarding reverse discrimination: "Notice how most of them are Black. They are real loud and take their time to get to class. Administrators just ignore them. They don't do anything about it. They just stand around doing nothing while these kids wreck the school" (Hemmings, p. 429). For White youth violence becomes a means to gain the loss of status in a racially diverse setting. Peer pressure compels some youth to fight to avoid loss of status; fighting for respect functions as a rite of passage among youth. While acknowledging racial segregation, Harris (1998) attributes the social distancing to peer pressure; it "comes from within the group, not from outside, and it needn't be overt. Children seldom have to be urged to conform to the norms of the group" (p. 250). Overall, students "need respect to garner the social status, esteem, and protections necessary to give them some sense of control over their lives" (Hemmings, p. 426). A conciliatory demeanor threatens a student's survival in school, but also on the street where the weak or different are easy prey, another example of cultural disconnections.

Grant (2001) admits that the lure of the street overwhelms many teenagers' resistance in the absence of supportive social networks. Most skip school and spend inordinate amounts of time watching TV unsupervised; girls get pregnant while boys engage in petty crime and confrontations with authority as a way of asserting themselves, moving "without thinking from attitudes of deference to postures of defiance. But without other supports or voices to stay your slide, the attraction of the brothers increases." The college option is put off (p. 112). On the other hand, linear conceptions of academic success or the lack thereof deny the complexities of social problems (Carter and Goodwin, 1994; Gay, 2000; Giroux, 1988, 2008; Kozol, 1991, 1995; McCarthy and Crichlow, 1993; Morrison, 1993). To his credit Grant (2001) acknowledges the impact of historical factors on access and quality of education in African-American communities manifested in dead-end basic tracks, diluted curriculum, inadequate funding, overcrowding, and so forth.

Notwithstanding the ambiguity of the term "respect," the inconsistency in related discussions highlights the issue of self-interest in teachers as well as students. Both are more vocal in what they oppose than in what they advocate. Students at the high school at which I taught must be aware of existing disparities in education and probably buy into the conventional stereotype of minorities as academically challenged. They fall back on physique, clothing, and linguistic style for status among classmates. Opened in the mid-1980s, the high school is comprised of about 90 percent Caribbean students from working-class families; only a few students qualify for subsidized lunches. It offers only a college preparatory program for students. In 2006, the high school admitted 125 students from a pool of 2,646 applicants. It is a select group.

Across the street is a high school (9–12) opened in the 1920s that offers three Educational Option Programs (Collegiate, Humanities, Medical Science Institute, and the Bilingual Haitian Creole Medical Science Institute). Applicants to these specialized programs are screened for admission, a process begun about 30 years ago. These applicants are drawn from across the city, and the school bases admission on students' seventh-grade academic performance. The Medical Science Institute selected 300 students from a pool of 4,966 applicants in 2006. Students in this and two other programs that screen applicants are predominantly composed of White and Asian students. The fourth unscreened program draws students from neighborhood residents. Although entrance to this program is just as coveted as the other three specialized programs, the college preparatory program selects students by lottery, much like the smaller school at which I taught; most of them are Blacks and Hispanics. In 2006, about 475 students entered the college preparatory program from a pool of 772, since the school's capacity does not allow it to serve all neighborhood youth. Those not admitted must seek admission in other high schools.

How can academically underachieving minority students distinguish themselves? That students dealt harshly with each other—put downs, snickers, and ostracism or transient cliques—reflected their adolescent age but also the frustrations they faced in society. It was their way of claiming a sense of power (Hemmings, 2003). If academic excellence or an intellectually competitive environment were the overarching priority, my high school would have drawn more White and Asian students. On the other hand, my first experience teaching in an American high school meant second-guessing my instinctual responses and intervening when an incident crossed my emotional threshold. For instance, I insisted on writing and reading, yet entertained disagreements by offering a rationale for my choices. I considered reading and writing as crucial skills for academic success in an increasingly global economy. Most important was the reminder that students were socialized differently from me. Conversations with colleagues were a reassurance of territorial boundaries; for instance, they let me know that applying lipstick in class was inappropriate.

Cultural navigations are endemic to social interactions (Florence, 2009). It helps when schools reflect and reinforce home rules; however, for most students, even home rules require ongoing concessions. Students need to understand that fights are not the only means to gaining respect, and the rationale for appropriate behavior in different settings. Underlying concerns of disrespectful others is the wish for recognition in a relationship. Confrontations rip at the fragile sense of connection to other people when the real desire is for emotional bonding. While passing up the chance to put down an enemy threatens a student's sense of a violated self, it reflects the value for unity rather than division, collective rather than individual interests, and long-term rather than immediate gains in social interactions. It is not the "loss of a race" portrayed by an individualist approach of a real or imagined threatening other, "scoring points" (Hemmings, 2003). The African immigrant teacher used to sacrificing individual for collective concerns learns the importance of critique and students' empowerment; they develop a "comparative perspective" in cultural navigations. To fossilize respect as some historically structured power relations (the African way) absolves immigrants from the responsibility of the cultural adaptation involved in forging egalitarian ways of being and relating. Appiah (1992) advocates cultural accommodations that avoid defining the other culture as an objective standard and, therefore, superior, as African immigrants are wont to: "Unless all of us understand each other, and understand each other as reasonable, we shall not treat each other with the proper respect" (p. 134). It is a collective task, a challenge to immigrants and natives, cultural insiders and outsiders alike. This is the essence of the problem: the need to integrate appropriate/perceived values inherent in two different cultures, a change of beliefs and everyday practices that acknowledges the value in others. The alternative can be coercive hierarchies: teacher/students or elder/youth relations that undermine solidarity. Conversations on the inevitability of cultural adaptations and the rationale for tolerance creates awareness but also acknowledges the frustrations of living with difference.

CHAPTER 5

Resources and Relationships

Fifteen T-shirts, a room of one's own, or owning a car are luxuries which few Africans can boast of, which makes it difficult for new African immigrants to accept what they see as excess among American students. The material disparity is more obvious for Africans from war-torn countries or poorer regions. At the same time, differences in living standards across Africa mirror similar disparities with the United States. Perhaps reflective of socioeconomic class more than cultural differences, many African immigrants acknowledge the ambiguity toward possessions as much as they concede an uncertainty regarding cross-gender interactions. While some dwell on American's apparent need for instant gratification, others acknowledge similar longings within their home countries, despite lower living standards. Yet in African classrooms such excesses are not permitted to impinge on academics. But these perceptions of excess are changing as elite African parents indulge children with accommodations—pocket money, shopping sprees, boarding-school visits, and leisure time—denied them in childhood.

Despite resource disparities in schools as well as socioeconomic class differences among students, a general focus on immediate gratification pervades society in the United States similar to that in the African continent. Individual possessions define social status in schools and the society. In this light, different priorities between immigrant teachers and their students may reflect socialization patterns no less than living standards. Linking it to greed, hooks (2000) maintains that the obsession with possessions is evident among students of all social classes, in private as well as public schools. Students' choices in career or obsessions with celebrities and material possessions reflect a conventional preference for tangible and immediate results. In contrast, much of school involves sacrifice of the immediate, in time and effort, for later benefits—school success as well as economic mobility. Among immigrants, one's social status in the mother country shapes one's view of materialism in the United States.

Further disparities arise in the unease foreign-trained immigrant teachers experience toward cliques, but also in the public displays of intimacy within class settings. In contrast to increasingly informal or commercialized interactions, most foreign-trained immigrants are socialized in hierarchies based on age/seniority, gender, or family name that compel formality and distance in matters of the heart and body. Extended relationships based on kin or physical proximity reinforce communal over individual interests. Parental concerns about out-of-wedlock birth and, more recently, the HIV/AIDS scourge, adds to the angst. Foreign-trained immigrant teachers, much like the neoconservatives derided by Giroux (1988), worry about misplaced priorities among those still tender in age.

In his book, *Emile,* Jean Jacques Rousseau derided scientific progress for creating artificial wants that then obsess and consume individuals. His critique of a culture of consumption and purchased relationships applies to the United States and the African continent alike. The ubiquitous demand for greater wealth and status undermine integrity and solidarity. hooks (2000) highlights the "psychological torment" of "fantasies of a classless society, of a consumer-driven dream wherein you are what you possess. . . . Among young people, from grade school age kids to teenagers, to lack signs of material success is to be marked as worthless and to be the object of shame" (p. 82). In movies such as *Clueless, Anywhere But Here,* and *South Park,* the protagonists are rich and attractive. Among the poor and underclass, greed has:

> fostered and perpetuated the infiltration into . . . especially black communities, a predatory capitalist-based drug culture that would bring money for luxuries to a few, a symbolic ruling class. Suddenly-impoverished communities where life had been hard but safe were turned into war zones. Greed for material luxuries, whether a pair of expensive sneakers, a leather jacket, or a brand-new car, led individuals to prey upon the pain of their neighbors and sell drugs. (hooks, 2000, pp. 66–67)

On the other hand, raised in an African culture in which the personal—resources or relations—is consistently renegotiated, claims of "mine" and intimate/exclusive friendships appear excessive and juvenile. But there are disparities among Africans. I was recently shocked by an African immigrant friend's caution against drinking her teenage boy's orange juice during an overnight visit at the house. There were other types of juices and family members had preferences as I later discovered. It would be unheard of and considered "un-African" back home. Raised in a family of limited means, clothing and supplies are as readily shared as food. A fellow Kenyan, Wesonga, expresses similar sentiments: "Students have too much of everything material; as well as abundant moral support." In an apparent cultural accommodation, Wesonga makes "available everything students need and/or want even when inappropriately used." Aminata too acknowledges the material hardships of her childhood, "but we were content and we were able to succeed in school." The incidents exemplify differences among Africans as much as cultural assimilation in a more individualistic society.

While Jonathan Kozol (1991, 1995) highlights the racial disparities in American school financing, most African immigrant teachers are impressed at the resources poorer neighborhoods possess in the United States, as Dingane notes:

> There are huge differences with regard to material possessions between my country of birth and the United States. Very few teachers and students in my country of birth own cars, technological gadgets etc., whereas in the United States most students and teachers own and have access to material things.

Seemingly swamped with inordinate resources, some students discard reading materials, waste foodstuffs, and deface school property with little sense of accountability. On the other hand, how much oral, audio, and visual stimulation does one require? My college students hold onto cell phones much as asthmatics clutch inhalers. In hallways, I walk past students talking on phones with much urgency. Some continue nibbling away and sipping drinks amidst all this. On rare occasions, I see a book propped open on a student's lap as they lean against the wall with legs crossed or stretched out before them. But the issue of "excess" depends on one's vantage point. In American schools, round-the-clock custodians pick up discarded writing materials, half-empty bottles of drink and snack wrappers. The availability of custodians contributes to the students' lax attitude in maintaining cleanliness. Bateson (2000) acknowledges that " 'messiness' is a cultural construct rather than an eternal truth" (p. 240). A similar correction applies to material obsessions and narcissistic tendencies. For some students, it is a question of ingrained patterns of behavior. The following discussion focuses on materialism and a seemingly ubiquitous insatiable hunger for commodities across the globe, although the trend is checked in African communities by limited resources and traditional communal orientations.

Kenya's beleaguered and pluralistic post-independence history mirrors the history of many other African countries. Cultural changes in Kenya can be attributed to a range of factors including urbanization, relocations and settlements of individuals and families, the establishment and development of institutions of learning, and globalization. After Kenya's 1963 independence, the government urged *Wananchi* (citizens) to buy land wherever it was available. In addition, civil servants received and continue to get appointments anywhere in the country. Most of these migrations led to the acquisition of land and an eventual resettlement by parties. The resettlement and an increase in ethnic intermarriages create ongoing cross-cultural exchanges. A 2009 estimate locates 22 percent of the populace in urban centers with a growth rate of 4 percent. Further complicating the cultural mix has been the constant arrival of refugees from countries such as Somalia (173,702), Sudan (73,004), and Ethiopia (16,428). In addition, the 2008 post-election violence led to about 250,000 to 400,000 internally displaced people. The Kenya African National Union (KANU) was the single political party until 1991 when pressure from within and outside of Kenya compelled the then-president Arap Moi to allow opposition parties. In 2007, contention, with the loss of about 1,300 lives, arose from disputed election results for the presidency. Ethnic rhetoric continues to plague political campaigns. Kenya's population is 37.91 million with a growth rate of 2.7 percent. The unemployment rate is 40 percent of the population with about 50 percent of the population living under the poverty level (*CIA World Factbook,* 2010). Kenya's development of natural resources lags behind the demands of the populace.

Political independence failed to sever Africa's ties with the colonists. Globalization and trade liberalization policies limit any one country's sovereignty—economic, social, political, and cultural. Financial flows in and out of the country affect investments and job opportunities. According to the *CIA World Factbook* (2010), Kenya exported $4.479 billion and imported $9.031 billion worth of goods in 2009. Its debt is 54.1 percent of GDP. Improved communication and travel have opened up study options inside and outside Kenya as well as employment and cultural exchanges across the globe. Kenya has 3,360,000 Internet users, 16,304,000 mobile cellphone users and 243,700 landlines (2008 estimates). The economy is dependent on the export of primary products such as tea, coffee, wheat, and sugarcane, with fluctuating prices and demands. Financial fluctuations and the 2008 post-election violence reduced the GDP growth rate by 2 percent between 2008 and 2009. Major importers included the Netherlands (9.4 percent) and the US (6.4 percent) according to 2008 estimates. Kenya has 16 airports with paved runways.

The Iceland volcano Eyjafjallajökull's mid-April 2010 spew of ash and steam devastated Kenya's economy but also grounded about 100,000 planes worldwide, left thousands stranded, and jammed alternative transportation systems for the duration. The volcanic eruption, 5,000 miles away from Kenya, led to airport closures on various continents. Kenya's airport closure led to about 5,000 job losses and cost the flower industry $12 million due to cancellations of flights to European markets. Every night, about two billion pounds of fresh produce is shipped out of Kenya, an estimated 80 percent bound for mainland Europe and Britain. The cancellation left heaps of unused produce since few Kenyans eat the pricey supplies or even know what "flowers and courgettes" are (Gettlemen, 2010). According to the *CIA World Factbook* (2010), the service industry, which includes horticulture, contributes 62.3 percent of Kenya's GDP (30.57 billion and a growth of 2 percent), although 75 percent of the labor force is in the agricultural industry (2009 estimates). Global events have local impact on economic prospects.

After independence, residents in rural areas such as my neighborhood in Bungoma sold off family plots anticipating government takeover specifically around trading centers that developed into major urban centers such as Nairobi, Nakuru, Mombasa, Kisumu, Kakamega, Nyeri, Eldoret, Kitale, and Webuye. Others sold off land that had lain fallow to stay close to extended families. Economic prospects in emerging urban centers drew workers from across the country, most of whom settled in these areas. For instance, Central Province, with high-quality schools and industries, continues to draw more immigrants relative to the rest of the country. Over time, with the development of transport links, there have been increases in interactions nationwide. Globalization has influenced urban centers such as Bungoma in direct and indirect ways—remittances, telecommunications in and outside of Kenya, greater ease of travel, and the availability of a wider range of foreign goods from China and The United Emirates. "Kenyans living outside the country remitted $1.6 billion, which is an equivalent of $42 per capita or 5.4% of the GDP. . . . These Kenyans also point out that it is unfair for them to remit these huge amounts of money to pay salaries and perks for MPs who work less than 10 hours a week and get paid $500 an hour" (Okumu, 2010, p. 30).

Materialism/Consumerism

Natadecha-Sponsel (1993) is shocked that in the United States children from affluent homes with "a ranch house and BMW cars," work part-time at such early ages. She also attributes material obsession with "personal achievement and financial success" to individualism; parents encourage super achievements in life as exemplified by "Madonna, Tom Cruise, and Michael Jackson." hooks (2000) links the prevailing consumerism to economic progress and media propaganda. Not surprisingly, some youth value status and power rather than hard work. The question is how to establish a different environment in schools. For most African immigrant teachers, the habits of sacrifice and patience reflect primary experiences of growing up in environments of material lack relative to the United States, albeit, not always. Materialism in the United States reflects worldwide trends, argues Yetunde: "Worldwide, there is more materialistic behavior. [Nigeria] is no exception; however, comparatively, there is more embrace of access to material possessions defining the worth of a person here in America than in my home country." Pointing to the love for flashy cars, Owolabi (1996) views materialism as a shared plight between African Americans and African-born immigrants.

One day, David the twin came to class early. "I need to leave early today, Miss Florence," he called out as I walked in the door. Although he basked in his status of the "ladies' man" (they laughed at his jokes however irrelevant or irreverent), David hardly participated in class discussions. Students find niches for themselves among peers. Those typecast as brainy become more brainy. Meanwhile, the class clowns' tendencies become exaggerated with time (Harris, 1998). David's assignments were just as noncommittal: skimpy, with writing close to illegible. "My mother is taking me to IKEA to buy furniture for my repainted room," he volunteered. "During class hours?" I asked, suspicious of the excuse offered for missing class. I never knew whether the students told the truth or, with such outlandish claims, if they thought I was that gullible. I made no attempt to hide my shock at what I considered misplaced priorities. "We have to get the furniture," David added. He did leave early, having called my attention to it a number of times prior to his departure with a comment, such as, "Miss, I have to leave in ten minutes." He offered another reminder five minutes later. David's diligence in timing was impressive; he was the self-appointed timekeeper when he did show up for class. At the next class, he proudly announced the purchase of his choice furniture. It could have been some form of confirmation to satisfy my doubts. hooks (2000) recognizes that the pursuit of wealth or, in this case, possessions, can "breed ambition," and deflect the focus away from the students' emotional lack. "In their mind to be without money is to be without life" (p. 87). Shopping and material possessions offer a false, fleeting sense of self-worth. It is living the "good life."

Among African immigrants, the value for money and possessions reflects global trends, as Owolabi (1996) maintains. Third world nationals long for commodities that residents in developed countries can better afford.

However, Wafula and Girikaze point out the differences in living standards and disparities in wealth:

> There wasn't much by way of material possession so there was little to compete over. One was lucky to have the basics. Schools provided textbooks which were shared by students over the years as the tattered supplies in schools today demonstrate. Outside readers could have been considered material—such was protected from prying eyes. Popular literature like a James Hadley Chase novel could only be exchanged with another and returned upon completion; these were coveted possessions among youth in a country with limited library facilities. [He also notes how] in the U.S. materialistic competition is the order of the day. Students are constantly comparing their "threads" [New Jersey slang for designer labels] with others. Dress labels are the sign of social distinctions. (Wafula)

The abruptness of economic shifts from culturally isolated communities to global economies dominated by multinational corporations such as Nestlé, ExxonMobil, CNN, Nokia, Toyota, Coca-Cola, Philips, Citibank, and Microsoft, as well as TV programs, Total, international airlines, and so forth, bombard African countries with heavy-budget media networks and lure people with limited funds into prohibitive lifestyles. According to the *CIA World Factbook* (2009), Kenya's estimated Foreign Direct Investment (FDI) amounted to $2.053 billion, in addition to an external debt of $7.729 billion. Increasingly, the average Kenyan falls prey to illicit deals to support such choices. There are the religious fanatics who promise to double one's cash following prayer sessions, credit and land-grabbing scams, sexual exploitation, and, increasingly, incidents of criminal activity:

> There is a big gap between the haves and the have nots in my country. The majority of Burundians can be considered poor according to the American standards. Very few people can afford television (even in black and white); fewer still can afford driving a [used car or motorcycle]. However, middle income families can afford a cook and a maid. When I was in Burundi, people were not too materialistic. I do not know now. Globalization has had an influence on all the cultures of the world. (Girikaze)

Globalization has influenced indigenous cultures worldwide, as Yetunde noted earlier. The results are not always advantageous to the masses:

> There is more of a divide between rich and poor in terms of availability of food and access to it in my country than in the United States. Tastes

differ radically by class. The upper middle class and wealthy minority in my country have a high level of desire for Western goods, including food. Their tastes and eating habits mime those of the country's European colonizer even though the country has been independent for more than 40 years.

Generally, "goods and services become valued as much for the status they bring the owner as for the utilitarian needs they meet" (Milner, p. 156). hooks (2000) insists the desire for possessions reaches beyond basic needs. Children in public and fancy private schools are obsessed with wealth. "Already they identify with ruling class values, already they are obsessed with getting.... They simply believe they are longing for the 'good life' and that this life has to be bought" (hooks, 2000, p. 159). In addition, most likely out of guilt from extended absences, parents spend inordinate amounts of money on children. Harris (1998) attributes adult habits to keeping up with the Joneses. Milner (2004) focuses on the desire of adults for youth and agility; parents live vicariously through their children; "children are their status symbol" (p. 165). Some try copying teenagers' lifestyles and clothing. This, Milner acknowledges, complicates parental control over teenagers. Further, some parents help their children take on adult characteristics—dress, cosmetics, language, and body movements. Kweyu (2008) raises similar concerns, within Kenya, of pampered children becoming "insufferable brats." In this case, addressing students' issues requires an acknowledgment of adult influence on behavior (the cultural factor?) (Badillo, 2006; Borjas, 1999; McWhorter, 2001). To regulate status symbols within schools, Milner proposes mandating uniforms, limiting and regulating the use of cell phones in schools, fostering civility, a de-emphasis of traditional status symbols such as sports and cheerleading, reducing the power of money and commercialism, and reducing the significance of peer status by widening their circle of relationships. These are all good intentions, but intervention requires a political will that few parents or schools exhibit. Harris (1998) advises using peers to correct student behaviors. As Milner does, she advocates the use of uniforms to discourage cliques. Harris however recognizes the tendency among youth to rebel against authority and established norms as a way of distinguishing themselves.

Milner (2004) attributes teenage behavior to the organization of schools and youth status systems rather than on hormones, psychological development, parenting styles, or demographics. To explain the obsession with cars, clothing, and hair, Milner links teenage status to the broader society, especially the pervasive consumerism. The value for newness is evident in the American habit of tearing down the old for the new in building, relocations, car trade-ins, and even serial marriages (Mucha, 1993). Mucha wonders about the waste of seemingly presentable "empty, run-down apartments in American cities" (p. 22). Today's youth, whether rich or poor, "do not think about a range of class positionalities. To them one is either rich or poor and there is no in-between, nothing matters" (hooks, 2000, p. 84). The adult world is no different. Penthouses, gated communities, and exclusive neighborhoods are associated with upper classes as are ghettos, projects, across the tracks with lower classes (Milner, 2004). While certain behavior patterns among my students surprised me, I could readily understand their class consciousness. Urban minority students imitate wealthier classmates and value possessions over the required sacrifices of time and energy in academic endeavors. Students at the high school rushed over to the nearby avenue for lunch, rejecting the dropped-off subsidized lunches in the main office. "Isn't it expensive to eat out?" I asked. Students insisted they had money to spend. "Whose?" I asked. The responses varied, with students' claiming to have money from sources ranging from part-time jobs to parental remittances.

Phones

The issue of immediate gratification in schools, oral or audio, reflects social patterns in the wider society. I once sat next to an angry passenger on the number five train, as she talked into her cell phone. She wanted to know if her party would be home when she arrived. It was close to 11:00 p.m. Not long into the conversation, she began yelling at the person, expletives included, to get out of her house. She hung up, only to call back again. It was a repeat conversation. She gave the person an ultimatum. I thought, why did she call back? Before I got off the subway, she called and took calls from the party about five times. Crammed into a subway car, we all, or at least I, listened in to what I considered a really private conversation. The discomfort with personal space, whether in terms of asserting rights or defending private interests, reflects cultural upbringing. African culture derides the mention of sexual or bodily functions in public spheres except within ritualized settings such as circumcision rites. But what constitutes cultural tolerance? Claims of personal boundaries in many African communities are tempered by the value of harmony as a sign of respect for the group. It could also be a fear of displeasure. Despite displays of shouting matches and fist fights in school playgrounds, frequently the maligned walks off to avoid further antagonism instead of prolonging an exchange, although this may be common among female rather than male students. In marital unions, wives more than husbands remain passive-aggressive during confrontations despite their feelings to the contrary. In the United States, such attitudes appear escapist and dishonest; individuals avoid confronting an abusive other for intruding on personal space. To some, it reinforces abusive power and lack of self-esteem. The public determines boundaries of acceptability and appropriateness to behavior in various venues.

Wesonga claims phones, "Distract students from their educational focus." He therefore prohibits "students from bringing and using cell phones during class." Aminata does not have to deal with phones in classrooms because of prohibitions in elementary schools. By contrast, amidst public school bans against cell phones and DVD players "because they pose a distraction," with students illicitly "loading answers, mathematical formulas and notes onto their iPods," the Union City school district distributed iPods "as part of a $130,000 experiment in one of New Jersey's poorest urban school systems" (Hu, 2007, p. B1). Similarly, the "Brearly School, a private school on Manhattan's Upper East Side, has used iPods to supplement foreign language textbooks and its music, drama and English classes" (p. B6). In the United States, debates over students having cell phones in school range from issues of security to frivolous distractions. On the other hand, the African craze for cell phones seems unchecked although few can afford such luxuries, particularly in K–12 settings. National outrage over examination cheats in Kenya raised the issue of cell phones as easy tools for transmitting coveted details. Although African immigrant teachers own cell phones, they all complain about the distraction of cell phones in school settings. Wafula and Aarifa bemoan the invention: "The worst scientific innovation for students has been a cell phone. There is nothing singly as disruptive to classroom decorum as the cell phone. There have been attempts to ban them in schools to the chagrin of parents" (Wafula). While Yetunda claims cell phones create "minimal distractions and disturbances but I also warn students to turn off their phones," Aarifa stresses the distraction posed by cell phones:

> Cell phones have created nothing but mayhem and havoc. The time spent taking cell phones away from students, the distraction caused by phones ringing, students texting each other, and repeating the rules regarding cell phone use greatly detract from time meant to educate. Simply stated: cell phones have created an exponential increase in time spent dealing with behavior rather than education.

Girikaze also demonstrates the frustration of accommodating the use of phones in classrooms: "I hate cell phones so much. I even have a cell phone policy in my syllabus. I allow students to put their cell phones on vibrators. Still, I get disturbed whenever one or the other student goes out to respond to a phone call. I tell students that they have to be considerate of each other; however, it never seems to work."

Dingane has a policy on cell phone use during class: "Although I enforce the SOYC 'switch off your cell phone' rule in my classes, cell phones still ring during lectures, and thus have been very disruptive. Such behavior is punishable in my country of birth." For teachers the challenge is in creating schools for which academic content is more important than cell phone conversations, text messaging, or sexting.

Students' liberties appear excessive when one is on the receiving end. I recall the yearning for storybooks in times long blurred by failing memory. I have no recollection of ever owning a storybook. At a high school away from home, I longed for books my wealthier friends owned. We would read borrowed novels under lifted desk lids during a lesson. I recall the day a teacher discovered my indiscretion. My world collapsed. The hopelessness was overwhelming. I rushed to the teacher after class begging for a reprieve. "Could I please complete the chapter at least?" I pleaded. Oh, the audacity of youth. It was the longing for a book; an immersion in a world unimagined, then, the loss of it. I have no recollection of the book or its contents, merely the sense of exhilaration and then profound loss. Reflective of zero tolerance policies for breaches in many schools in Africa, Baruti prohibits "cell phones to be used in class!" Ahmad has found his middle ground: "Cell phones always have been the source of distraction in the classroom and all laws failed to limit the use of cell phones because always students find a way to sneak phones into the classroom.... [He admits] I make clear no cell phones period in the classroom and any phone I found I kept until one of the parents came and got it and let the student promise that he/she never use it again."

Pinxten (1993) is not surprised the telephone was invented in the United States where phones or, most recently, computers offer round-the-clock "emotional and intellectual contact" in formal and informal settings. The technologies provide an illusory sense of having the world at one's fingertips. They also foster prepackaged sound-bite-style interactions, what Pinxten terms "a value for the facts." In the United States, one packages oneself in catchy eloquent phrases for self-promotion. "There is no cultural room for anguish, fear, angst, or ambiguity here. These are topics one deals with in the privacy of therapy" (Wasserfall, 1993, p. 109). The range of choices for pastime activities and the rapid pace of life in developing countries contrasts with the more Rousseauian "natural" existence of men picking their teeth or spending hours talking to kin under shade trees. Women pick vegetables for cooking, shell beans or maize, and thresh millet for grinding, often tedious, arduous, and monotonous tasks. Increasingly, people's access to phones in villages replaces tiring travel and long journeys to visit far-removed kin.

But then limited resources confine pastime activities to energy-saving and small-scale engagements. One learns patience in cultures in which a tea-making process using charcoal stoves or firewood takes 45 minutes at the least. Sleepless nights mean endless thoughts in the dark as one waits for the dawn. For many Africans the slow pace of life reflects a lack of alternatives rather than a preferred lifestyle. The yearning for easy and more exotic lifestyles is evident in urban as well as in rural areas.

Food

Most of the high school students chewed gum or nibbled at something during the class. Students typically sipped at soft drinks and munched on potato chips or snack bars while others ceaselessly chewed gum. One day, Alex brought a three- or four-course packed lunch to the class. I ignored Alex's infraction because he still paid attention, randomly engaged in discussions, and wrote up the required essay. Each day, a medium-size blue lunch bag is delivered for students on subsidized lunch, and each evening there are leftovers in the main office. I never saw members of my class with the familiar lunch packages. At the nearby avenue about four blocks away, I see students crowded at the bodega for fast food at all hours of the day. The high school allows twelfth-graders to walk over to the avenue for lunch. While youth are often hungry, where one eats, what one eats, and with whom one eats define one's status among peers. They lean over and share each other's food or request to do so although not hungry. And yet some students starve themselves in order to look attractive (Milner, 2004). hooks (2000) links the insatiable hunger for food in children to greed: the "endless longing for sweets, longings that lead to hoarding, stealing, or some combination of these" (p. 63). As a teacher of science and health, Wesonga maintains that U.S. "[s]tudents today have too much food and in a variety of tastes. As a result, they eat too much and uncontrollably." He advises "students on the effects of eating too much or rather abusing food."

Introduced during the 1930s Great Depression to "assist desperate farmers, the [subsidized meal] program was extended to schools in response to the malnourished among army recruits." Today, the U.S. Department of Agriculture spends $8.3 billion a year to provide free and reduced-priced lunches for 30.6 million children whose families are at or below 30 percent of the national poverty level, about $26,845 for a family of four" (Pogash, 2008, p. A14). The participation percentage rates of 40 percent for New York and 37 percent for San Francisco reflect national trends. New York serves about 860,000 free or subsidized meals each day. Pogash links students' eating habits to economic status. Even deserving African-American and Hispanic students would rather go hungry than compromise their nicely dressed clothing and matching shoes, and their well-to-do image among classmates. In contrast, recent immigrants from the Dominican Republic, Mexico, Central America, Russia, and China as well foreign-born students from Thailand, India, Myanmar, and Hong Kong in San Francisco appreciate the free lunch. A student from India dismisses the idea of the institutional deliveries as a stigma: "The food is good" (p. A14). Students raised in environments of relative material lack appreciate the services offered in their adopted country. Aarifa's and Bashir's summations mirror the experience of many from the African continent. Material shortages are a reality which most Africans learn to tolerate:

> There are food shortages in my home country and food is not given to students on campus. Also, there isn't the level of availability of fast food close to school campuses. Lastly, the students in my home country have a much better idea of what comprises a healthy diet especially since malnutrition is a dire problem for the country. (Aarifa)

> [On the other hand,] in West Africa people are not as affluent as they are in the United States. Also in the United States, students here, at the college level, seem to pay greater attention to their part-time jobs than to their classroom activities. It is difficult to compare materialism in the United States and among West African students who can't place emphasis on something they lack, in this case material possessions. (Bashir)

The complaints about hunger pains among children and adults in a continent devastated by warfare, economic inequalities, corruption in public office, as well as natural hazards are understandable. In my home district, Bungoma, the percentage of people living below the poverty level is about 56 percent, with an average doctor-to-patient ratio of 1:60,000 (www.ace-africa.org/index.php?=bungoma). At our neighborhood primary school, a few women sit on their heels along the fence or at the gate, next to small bundles of sugarcane, black-sooted pots of boiled maize, or pots of porridge to lure the few students who can afford the required Kshs 5–10 (less than $.1) for a lunch treat. Most students hang around and appeal to charitable classmates in the hope of receiving coveted leftovers. The rest wait until they get home for their meal of the day unless one counts wild fruit that some students pick on the way home. Focusing on the boarding experience Wafula notes:

> Food in African schools was horrible to say the least—but at least healthful—fresh vegetables albeit cooked poorly. Students ate at an

appointed time. Bread and butter was considered a rarity and a luxury. In the United States, students are constantly eating even in class. Vending machines line not just the common hallways but dining room walls. Students are constantly eating.

Owolabi (1996) contrasts the round-the-clock availability of food in the United States relative to his country of birth, Nigeria. Ahmad offers a rationale for these eating habits:

> Since food is available round-the-clock in the United States, it leads to eating habits that border on addiction. Students complain about hunger more than five times a day. Food is available in Sudan but it is not the responsibility of the government to feed students. Most of the students bring food from home and in a few cases students can buy from the school cafeteria or adjacent food market close by school since safety is not issue in Sudan.... [He admits] "I do not allow any student to eat in the classroom in here. In Sudan the whole school has a certain time to go out and eat.

Girikaze claims to have adjusted to the United States system with regard to eating habits.

> Regarding food, I think we should condemn the U.S. system. However, in a system that is legal frenzy [sic], I can see why students who are not able to arrive in time for breakfast should be allowed to eat in class—not to chew gum though. I learned not to be offended by that. Their teachers do the same in our classrooms, anyway. I did it in grad school, too. Ha, ha, I guess I have quickly adjusted to that one.

Indeed, African immigrants who travel back to the home country are viewed as foreigners exhibiting cultural practices or beliefs from the resident country, particularly demands for immediate gratification. It also frustrates these "been-tos" that villagers fail to appreciate the urgency of life.

One day I raised the issue of chewing gum in class. "Do you chew gum all the time?" I asked frequent and obvious offenders. There was no immediate response. I went round the room identifying gum chewers by name, albeit jokingly. The majority of the students were chewing gum that day. The ones who spoke up attributed it to hunger pangs. I hoped so. Later I included Paula. "You too are chewing but it is hard to tell." During the discussion, Andrea and Sarah expressed their disapproval openly enough with teeth sucking, sighs, and mouthed comments. "Are you always exasperated?" I asked Andrea. "What does 'exasperated' mean?" she asked. I suggested she look it up in the dictionary. Her friend Sarah readily supplied the meaning. "It is what you do often, sigh, grunt...." leaving the sentence incomplete. More teeth sucking from Andrea, but I was getting used to it two months into the relationship. With a long grunt, she got up, turned her chair around and went on with her work (I hoped), her back to me.

Most African immigrants are ambivalent about the consumerism in U.S. society but feel drawn to the freedom of speech. The economic prospects are also an attractive lure for social mobility. Although over 50 percent of Kenyans live on less than a dollar a day, the wealthy enjoy lifestyles that would be enviable to most Americans. Earnings in the United States appear impressive compared to the standard of living in the old country (Traore and Lukens, 2006). Despite limited job prospects—taxi driver, garage or home attendant, hair-braider, and service industry worker—most African immigrants view the United States as a land of opportunity, often unaware of the "inherent prejudice of American society, which is based on racial inequality, racial exploitation, and racial humiliation" (p. 41). For many African immigrants the priority is economic survival and the ability to support family members here and back home. The World Bank estimates the figure is double the quoted $10 billion ub-Saharan immigrants sent home. According to Okumu (2010), Kenyans alone account for 1.6 billion of the remittances. Most African immigrants rely on informal transfer payments—Western Union and MoneyGram—rather than cheaper bank-to-bank transfers, because family members back home do not have accounts (Hash, 2008). The distance and cost of migration limit the number of African immigrants in the United States but also eliminate options of going back, unlike European or Latin American immigrants (Daniels, 2004; Obiakor and Afolayan, 2007). Rich is relative; immigrants who appear marginalized in U.S. settings are the bulwark of communities in home countries.

I was in the classroom before 2:00 p.m. at what was my regular practice for the high school class. A group of students streamed in, calling out greetings. "Good afternoon, Dr. Florence," they called out. It was the first time any of them had referred to me by the title—politely and by name. That day, I had changed my sitting position from one end of the table to the middle. Sharon leaned over to offer me a share of her potato chips. "Dr. Florence, have some." However short, there was an uncomfortable silence following Sharon's offer. The rest of the group turned to watch me. I am not one for eating in class although I never prohibited students from the practice. It was a moment I could not pass up. I leaned over the table to take out a couple of potato chips from the packet Sharon extended to me. Acceptance at last? It was the sixth class. In retrospect, students' resistance to class routines—read, write, discuss—toned down considerably. Students are more perceptive of teachers' value systems than they let on.

Relationships

Ethnic links shape cultural identities in African communities much as cliques of race, gender, or class characterize high school settings in the United States. Ahmad attributes limits to cross-gender interaction in his country to "conservative Islamic traditions." The following discussion explores the impact of student/student and student/adult dynamics in class settings. However, transient classroom cliques affect the atmosphere by either fostering collegiality or creating tensions that hinder intellectual exchanges. Often students pointedly ignore or curse each other out. They ostracize classmates with a lower status and reinforce the popularity of some students in social interactions. Following explosive exchanges among students, teachers have difficulty focusing students or engaging them in collaborative projects.

Milner (2004) distinguishes instrumental relationships based on an identifiable purpose from expressive relationships that "involve emotional intimacy and attachments" (p. 63). Not surprisingly, the former relationships are transient and can overlap, particularly associations based on interests and activities. Academic tracks and cross-racial as well as class groupings fall under this category. Some youth may work across cliques but readily resort to distancing from acquaintances outside of class. A student's involvement in romantic relationships enhances their status within a group (He/she has a friend!), and yet cliques limit one's range of relationships. There is a double standard here. Indeed, there are more derogatory labels for sexually active females (slut, whore, prostitute, even madam can be misunderstood) than for males. While multiple relations reflect a boy's popularity, classmates chide girls who are intimate with a number of boys; some view it as a sign of disloyalty. Milner agrees that puberty, biological maturation, and psychosocial development heighten the desire for intimacy but attributes the concern for relationships to the status system, a desire to be with and gain from rather than an enduring love for the other. Supporting Milner's position, Harris (1998) views the rejection by "a jury of peers" as paramount but also something few children easily rationalize.

Jeffrey and Sharon seemed inseparable in the high school class I taught. Andrea commanded her own group. Her followers reflected her mood. Cecilia appeared in need of an anchor, initially following Andrea around and later transferring allegiance to Sarah when the previous alliance soured for some reason. She would edge close to her "hero" Andrea or position herself to allow visual connection in response to some occurrence. Sarah walked in with Andrea one day. It was a familiar picture; they came in together or, if apart, Sarah pleaded with Andrea to sit close by. One day, Andrea rebuffed Sarah with "No, I want to sit here [elsewhere]." Sarah focused her attention on Andrea throughout the class, looking to Andrea before responding to a question or mumbling a comment during class discussions. Likewise when Andrea rebuffed Cecilia, the humbled Cecilia spoke little that day and avoided Andrea's glance for much of the class. In one of the conversations on weekend activities, Cecilia chided Andrea with: "You used to call me all the time." There was nostalgia in the accusation. Andrea's mumbled dismissal was not encouraging.

The side comments were irritating when Andrea and Sarah followed up the distraction with laughter or extended giggling. I got around it by separating them for paired work. The sharing of knowledge, secrets, and rumors among cliques demonstrates intimacy and trust. Insiders are separate from outsiders by what they know or have access to about each other. Secrets typically involve some form of deviance notes Milner (2004). Most recently, this includes sexual involvements or substance abuse. The subtle and obvious appeals to Andrea's acknowledgment illustrated her leadership status in the majority eleventh-grade group. The rest of the eleventh-graders marched alongside, followed, or if ahead walked sideways to participate in her conversations. In class, they rushed to sit next to Andrea, or, if she arrived later, pulled out a chair for her. Initially, it was disconcerting to observe their obvious appeals for her recognition. It was almost as though she gave the order for them to speak and sanctioned their response.

Andrea appeared the smartest, although testy, in social interactions with all of us in the class. Her bestowal of favor on one of her clique uplifted their spirits and freed them to greater class participation. For those Andrea ignored the class could not be over soon enough. My relationship with Andrea was a rocky one. Initially, she came to class and did the work but called out responses or expressed audible complaints about assigned work, engaged in side- and cross-talk, essentially learning at her own pace. One day, Andrea announced she'd be away for the next class. "It is personal," was her response to my inquiry about her unusual absence. It was the one class Andrea missed the whole semester. When she did return, I asked her about the weekend event. Casually, I thought at the time, Andrea spoke of her parents having an [open-air] exhibition. She had to be there. "Good," I said, commending her for helping out her parents. Her curt response made it sound like an unwelcome burden and my concern inappropriate. Where to draw the line?

Cohen (1994) commends group work as an effective strategy for teaching heterogeneous student groups. Aware of the diversity in ability, linguistic, and interest levels among students, she maintains that the interaction helps develop students' cognitive, interpersonal, as well as linguistic skills. Cohen, however, cautions against the danger of status-ordering in groups whereby some dominate the process because classmates view them as experts at a task based on teachers' responses or the student's grades in class. The aura of a student's competence in one subject, say math or science, extends to other fields however unrelated the required skills. In some cases, a student's "high social standing outside the school" based on "athletic competence or attractiveness and popularity" extends to classroom interactions (p. 32.). In other cases, students acquire status for their physique, agility, or popularity. Harris (1998) adds to the list students with "force of personality, imaginativeness...sense of humor, and a pleasing appearance." (p. 177). Schools reinforce social hierarchies with classmates paying more attention to White, male, or purportedly "sophisticated" students. Wafula acknowledges the sexism in Kenyan schools and society:

> Now that I look back at male student behavior toward their female counterparts in Africa, most could be now considered abuse. Males dominated in everything. Relationships were one-sided and hierarchical. Female victimization was rampant. In the United States, there are mutual offenders. The sense of equality is more pronounced among relationships.

In pre-industrial societies, women were socialized to be submissive to men. Young girls had some leverage in discontinuing a relationship. Most educated females are more independent than their ancestors. While Wafula focuses on gender, Aarifa highlights the issue of sexual orientation among Ethiopian students:

> Compulsory heterosexuality is the norm in my home country but does not produce the same level of distraction as it does in the United States for students. Also, since homosexuality is considered both a sin and perversion, men are much more affectionate with each other without the fear of being considered perverse. For boys and girls, they do not suffer from the same pressures by their peers to engage in premarital sex, they are not exposed to the levels of sexual innuendo and license as within the United States media, and boys and girls treat each other with much more respect since they are expected to view each other as human beings rather than a means to sexual ends or fulfillment.

Bashir emphasizes the conventional apprehension toward cross-gender relations in African communities: "West African authorities are trying to keep a distance between male and female students which is not a practice here. Parents too do all they can to prevent the 'accident' [pregnancy], that usually results from free and informal interactions between male and female students. At the secondary [high school] level, many schools are still single sex." There are more coed elementary schools than high schools although tertiary institutions are mostly coed. Wesonga seems to view gender separation as a solution to the prevailing identity confusion and sexist abuses:

> In the old times, there were distinct boundaries between males and females but not in a negative sense, but in a respectful manner. Females were left to be by themselves to feel comfortable in what they talked and did. Today there is too much of what I consider to be invasion of privacy. Females are treated with hardly any respect at all. [His solution]: Conduct class discussions about the need for respect for females as well as males.

Insecure students (wannabes or those who appear somewhat weak) bolster their roles by denigrating those excluded by the group as a form of social distancing. They disparage other groups for their own self-esteem; their own group is posited as more desirable and superior (Harris, 1998). Kim (1993) attributes the superficiality of adult relationships to a similar rationale; to avoid emotionally draining confrontations, individuals act pleasant despite personal misgivings. Overall, "the most [academically or socially] vulnerable receive the most verbal and physical harassment" (Milner, 2004, p. 88). Frequently, the "ugly" are ostracized as much as the physically handicapped. Milner also acknowledges that "weaker" students offer a nonthreatening scapegoat. They cannot retaliate.

The second class session focused on identifying countries on a world map I hang up on the wall. Students located countries on the map and discussed conventional perceptions of peoples from countries such as Afghanistan, Nigeria, Canada, Germany, Yugoslavia, and so forth. Andrea was the most knowledgeable in locating countries. Most of the students knew little of where different countries were located but appeared nonchalant about it. What became evident were the brutal stereotypes of different cultural groups represented in the United States. Ironically, African Americans fared worst in the assessment. None was represented in the class. The group claimed that Hispanic girls "came out" (with regard to sexual orientation) earlier than other groups. I wondered how the students knew for sure. I realized the need to address the issue of stereotypes at the next class.

Susan M. LoTiempo's (2005) *New York Times* piece on physical disability offered a fitting foundation. Lotiempo recalled the pleasure of being seated under the amplifier at Paul McCartney's Beatles' concert at fifteen. For her birthday, forty years later, her 20-year-old daughter bought a $278 ticket for another concert with Sir Paul, at the same venue. From where the ushers seated her, all she could see were "gyrating backsides." No amount of cajoling got Ms. LoTiempo moved to a better view. She left before the end of the concert weighed down by years of backstage maneuvers to get her into public schools, restaurants, airplanes despite the American with Disabilities Act.

In our discussion on disability, students identified Victor in hushed tones, perhaps as a reflection of their acceptance of him. Initially, all the students denied knowing someone with a disability. In contrast, he identified his grandmother when I asked the class to name a relative or neighbor with a disability. Victor's diligence, especially the association with the popular Andrea, guaranteed him status within the group. Milner (2004) acknowledges that a student's reception of the others depends on the perceived use to them: as supporter or threat. Put-downs of those within one's status or above it are more useful but also dangerous because of the possibility of retaliation. It is easier to undermine another in their absence than to their face. Thus, youth belittle each other for some real or imagined infraction to align themselves with the popular group and so improve their own status (Milner, 2004). It may explain the eleventh-grade clique's avoidance of any member who fell out with Andrea, the group hero as the following interaction demonstrated.

I planned to continue with the lesson on cultural heroes to link it to existing heroes and unacknowledged heroes in individual communities before addressing individual responsibility and personal accountability. To recapitulate I asked students to name some cultural heroes. The names of the Haitian revolutionary leader Toussaint, Martin Luther King, Rosa Parks, Cesar Chavez, and Gandhi came up. It was always the same students who spoke up—Sarah, Victor, Sharon, and Jeffrey (absent from the last class that day). I instructed students to write down the names of five cultural heroes. Two (Victor and Andrea) came up with five names within a space of three minutes. The rest of the students struggled with the task, with Maria only naming one hero, Mahatma Gandhi, by the end of the activity. After about two minutes into the activity, in response to my question about the number of cultural heroes students had identified, Victor claimed to have five names down. The claim raised discomfort among the rest. He had been coming in on his own of late and may have fallen out with the group. "Well, write more!" Andrea snapped back to Victor's chagrin.

The passionate relationship between Victor and Andrea affected the whole class. There was a lightness in the room when the two were on speaking terms; it allowed me to cover more material. Andrea, the smarter and most popular one in class could be extremely protective of Victor whose pronounced limp hampered his movements particularly when going up the stairs. That day Andrea cursed him out when he claimed to have completed a task under five minutes. It began with a "You think you know everything!" from Victor and progressed to death wishes and uncalled-for curses between the warring parties. His annoyance was evident. After the "You think you know everything!" claim, Victor piled up charges of Andrea's imposing role in class, "She must tell everyone what to do. She thinks she knows everything." The class was quiet during the heated exchange but then so was I, shocked by the vehemence of the verbal assault in my presence as the teacher. In most African cultures, the presence of an adult compels a truce between battling youth. Tensions cease out of respect for the adult rather than a closure to the contention. The tacit acceptance around the room showed the class's complicity in the slandering of personalities. Andrea hoped Victor, "slipped on the ice and died." "Enough of that and back to work," I interjected, shocked at the vicious exchange and realizing my presence was no deterrent. In retrospect, despite my discomfort at the verbal assault, the exchange hadn't deteriorated to expletives. "They are like that," Cecilia responded, smiling.

In schools, students coordinated class, as well as arrival/departure schedules. I recall Sharon's admission to having "recruited" her friends for my class. Her classmates laughed at the admission. I was aghast. "What did you expect?" the assistant principal responded rather dismissively when I later raised the issue with her. Isn't that assigning too much responsibility to a student? What is a teacher's role? How could a student know the learning needs of her classmates well enough to determine their eligibility for a class, even an elective course? Similar trends are evident in colleges; students advise each other on the selection of classes and professors for a range of reasons. Many college students rely on the rateyourprofessor.com website and the advice of acquaintances for course selections. In Kenya, students warn classmates about the idiosyncrasies of particular instructors ahead of time. The difference is that Kenyan students have limited options: fewer course sections to choose from and no change or transferring to another college. It boils down to "Be warned and beware."

Much as adult affiliations to professional associations symbolize one's status, youth fixate on whom they walk, talk, or associate with. The accessibility to fashion trends crosses class lines does not completely diffuse status lines. On the other hand, less obvious norms and rituals such as accents, demeanor, body language, and notions of taste and style are more difficult to copy (Milner, 2004, p. 31). The "insiders" frequently "change and complicate norms" to exclude outsiders through disassociation or denigration. Presumably students from lower socio-economic classes switch more easily from designer to "hip-hop" styles than do upper-class students. Poorer youth are "even more preoccupied with current status symbols in the national media than are their better-off peers" (Milner, p. 139). My urban high school students denigrated recent Black immigrant groups from the Caribbean for dressing shabbily; their clothing did not match! And they had an accent! In a rather subdued voice at the time, Sharon once spoke of the harassment she endured when her family first moved to the United States from the Caribbean Island. "But now, they can't tell!" she proclaimed with pride. I could, but that was not the point. Among her peers, Sharon was assimilated to American culture. At times students turned on each other for some undecipherable reason, although these cliques never lasted long. Adults are no different. Social gatherings tend to be ethnically or professionally homogenous (Dussart, 1993).

Public Displays of Intimacy

Jennifer was the model of a disciplined student in some respects. She was quiet, too quiet sometimes. Most of her time was devoted to coddling Alex in class. Alex's speech and written work reflected either a richer literary background or commitment to learning. He listened, participated when called upon, but otherwise sat quietly or leaned over the table or toward Jennifer. She would caress him sometimes, speak to him soothingly on occasion, and offer him writing materials when the class had a writing assignment. At one session, I intervened directly, "When you sit for your SAT (Standardized Assessment Tests) she will not be there to do your work." Jennifer and Alex ignored my urgings. Later, I walked over to where they sat and cautioned Alex against reviewing Jennifer's work instead of getting his work done: "Focus on your work. I will work with Jennifer." It was typical of the two; Alex waited for Jennifer to begin the assignment and reviewed her work before working on his own piece. He produced impressive but extremely short pieces given the limited time he devoted to the assignment. On occasion, I sat close by to ensure compliance. Alex had difficulty in starting assignments. It may have been a way to cover up Jennifer's difficulty in comprehending written assignments. She waited for his approval of whatever she wrote before moving on. He always began his assignment after she made progress with her own work. Some cultures frown upon public expressions of intimacy among immature youth and especially within school settings. Isn't it distracting? Maybe not for students from cultures which make allowances for premarital relations. Yetunde makes a similar distinction in the tolerance for cross-gender interactions in African societies:

> There are both co-educational and single sex education schools. Some schools rigorously separate males from females, and no universities have coed dorms. Open relationships between males and females is discouraged in the pre-college years but in college, not discouraged, except in very few conservative religious colleges where there are formal rules forbidding such affairs, and even walking together in some cases, and there are very strict dress codes which are believed to be important to defending chastity and morality.

Girikaze is surprised that "at the university level, there is a lot of dating and commitment among college males and females. In the United States, it does not seem to be the case." As early as the 1970s, in Burundi's bordering country, the University of Rwanda had a coed dormitory. In contrast, the Kenyan University of Nairobi maintained the ten-to-ten visiting code in female dormitories until the 1990s. Guards in women's dormitories prohibit male company before 10 a.m. and after 10:00 p.m. It is at colleges and universities that most African youth experience freedom from parental control over time and spending habits.

Notwithstanding maturity, Girikaze ignores parental restrictions in African communities to cross-gender relationships outside of family kin. There is the fear of girls getting pregnant and losing the chance for higher education (Smith, 2000). Colleges offer most students an independence few enjoy within family and neighborhood settings. Rarely do communities sanction public displays of intimacy, particularly in rural areas. For the African immigrant teacher, public romances create discomfort as intrusions of the private into public forums (Appiah, 2006). In schools, Americans instinctively clump down on excesses in liberties while immigrant teachers quibble over when or how to intervene. I intervened when the behavior distracted students from a classroom activity. Within one's cultural group, a teacher's response is more spontaneous and immediate primarily due to shared cultural norms.

Questioning the right of public romance in Meerut, India, Sengupta's (2006) *New York Times* article reported on physical and emotional harassment in response to interactions between cross-gender unmarried couples or single women in public parks. Police officers "yanked the couples by their necks, as though they were so many pesky cats, and slapped them around with their bare hands" (p. A4). Ironically, crime and violent rapes of females receive little publicity or prosecution in such cultures. Younger generations as well as organizations such as the National Human Rights Commission publicly express outrage at these traditional Hindu mores that violate individual rights. In discussions of Sengupta's article, my students were shocked at the seemingly archaic prohibitions of premarital intimacy in the current era. Class discussions that day highlighted cultural contradictions over intimacy issues across the globe. The silence following the reading was insightful; the students understood how arbitrary social mores can be. Perhaps the greater shock to the students, was the denigration of familiar practices including the taken-for-granted cross-gender interactions and displays of intimacy among youth.

In the last decade, Mungiki, a banned religious sect comprised of dissatisfied youth in Kenya's Gikuyu-dominated Central Province spearheaded female harassment (Murunga and Nasongo, 2007). The sect has terrorized "underdressed" women, stripping them naked in streets and publicly encouraging female circumcision. There too public outrage tones down such cultural impositions. In the past, matchmakers initiated contact between eligible couples. On wedding days, relatives, neighbors, and friends lavish presents to honor the family for "protecting" the bride if the girl was a virgin. Indeed, virginity set the price for a bride, while society tolerates infidelity in men. In contrast to the traditional "miniscule pieces of animal skin or tree bark or beads" worn in the past, the cultural aversion in African communities to revealing clothing (miniskirts and tight jeans) appears disingenuous. Haphazard appeals to the African way begs the question of authenticity and relevance.

Parents

In a session on social obligations and rights we explored the expectations students have of schools, and what, in their view, schools expect of students in general. In an ensuing debate over uniforms, to illustrate the impact of policy on classroom practices, David the twin called out, "Nobody can force me to do something!" I was shocked that none of his classmates challenged him on the claim. "No?" I asked in obvious disbelief. "No!" he responded no less certain than the first time. "What about the police?" I reminded him, still trying to recover from his evident lack of realism, as well as audacity. "Don't they limit your choices?" I pressed on, my shock evident. Silence. "No one can force me," he repeated, though with voice much mellowed. A third-year college student made a similar claim in 2010 during a discussion on Paulo Freire's work, *Pedagogy of the Oppressed*. The cockiness surprised me. Even her classmates gasped in shock. "Why do you stop at red traffic lights?" I asked, "To view the scenery? Talk to passersby? Adjust your driving mirror?" She didn't respond. I heard similar audacious assertions about tasks, with students claiming they are "A" students. That a student makes such claims despite consistently poor performance in particular subjects is cause for worry unless they excel in other subjects (Holmes, 2001; Ravitch, 1995). Seemingly perceptions defy reality. Even if true, flamboyant claims about one's ability and skills are considered poor taste in most African communities. Indeed, recipients of commendations tend to play down the attention, with a "God is good!" There are those who believe the visibility draws bad luck. We later focused on family obligations that most students dismissed with exasperation, accusing adults of being unyielding and inconsistent. It was an engaging discussion, however polemic; students pitted against me, the teacher.

On the day we talked about parents, the students' high-pitched dismissals and exasperation at our discussion on rights and obligations were instructive. Later discussions bashed "mothers" for their inconsistency, myopia, and lack of understanding, among other things. References to family in the adolescent group I worked with were rare unless solicited, in which case the responses were dismissive and laden with exasperation. Students complained about the unreasonableness and inconsistency of parents: "They tell you to speak out and berate you when you do speak out against them!" "Why do parents put so much pressure on children?" Lisa, the usually reticent student, complained aloud. The nods in the room echoed her classmates' sentiments to her voiced concerns. I felt condemned as an adult along with other authority figures—parents, teachers, and administrators. Like the parental figures, my intentions and injunctions were ambivalent. I wanted to empower them, but within limits. I often expected much from them, disregarding their (im)maturity and different socialization patterns. Students had a writing assignment each day; it related to the readings of the day rather than being a free-form composition. After all, how important was my class in their lives or aspirations? And yet assigning easy tasks may please students at the time but does little to prepare them for more challenging academic tasks at higher grades (Abebe, 2006; Amobi, 2004; Badillo, 2006; Damon, 2001; Glazer, 2001; Holmes, 2001; Mori, 1997; Ravitch, 1995, 2001; Viteritti, 2001). At the college level, I face similar resistance to graded in-class assignments and the demand for extensive literature reviews for classroom research projects.

To explore rights and obligations in society, I split the group between those who came on time that day (mostly twelfth-graders) and late-comers who tended to be eleventh-graders. Armed with construction paper and markers, each group was to list what they expected of parents and what parents expected of them. Follow-up discussions centered on demanding and unreasonable mothers. A number of students wanted to know if I had children. The question kept recurring. I used the phrase, "speaking on behalf of mothers," in previous discussions. "Do you have children?" demanded Victor, interrupting my instructions for the assignment as usual. "Shut up," Andrea called out, "she has told us she is a mother." Andrea's claim wasn't true but I let it go. I tried to explain the position of mothers as wishing the best for their children. "We (mothers? Adults?) have lived through most of these challenges that you claim are unique to your age. We want to save you the pain and waste of opportunity." At the end of the class Maria wanted to know if I discussed what transpired in class with my children. "I live alone," was my response. The room settled into a conspiratorial silence. Maria had a snide smile on her face. I felt condemned. They complained about single mothers. I did not even live with my children!

At the next class, I revisited the issue of demanding and unreasonable mothers. "What about fathers? Do you have more stable relationships with your fathers then?" I asked the class. After a moment of silence Karen and then Maria volunteered the fact that fathers were absent from homes. "How can you get angry with someone who is never there?" Maria called out. The somber question was laden with longing for missed opportunities. Andrea and Karen admitted to having an even more tumultuous relationship with their live-in fathers. Fathers are more demanding, both agreed. The rest of the class followed the discussion keenly, as though the revelation shattered the myth of a stable two-parent family. Class discussions can evoke problems that go beyond defined outcomes, specifically subject matter for individual courses. Teachers are hard-pressed to address these issues in the confines of time and school demands for factual transmission as well as character-building.

Karen always sat apart from the rest of the class. Later I discovered it was her first semester at the high school. The other students studied as a cohort from middle school. Karen's face knotted in a grimace at some things her classmates did or said. The students complained about parental pressure on students to attend college. These reminders never ceased. It was clear these parents wanted something better for their children with regard to schooling: "First [parents] tell us to be ourselves but then keep telling us to go to college." "Why don't they let us choose for ourselves?" "We are grown-ups." "We know what is good for us." "They are old and do not realize that things have changed." Although reflecting conventional views of minority academic underachievement, I found the students' resistance to school disturbing. I wondered how the value for upward mobility in minority communities since the 1960s civil rights movement had changed, but refrained from pressing the issue. Distinguishing expressed care from intrusion into students' privacy is no easy matter for teachers, not just immigrants. Occasionally, students volunteer extremely intimate details, but as quickly rebuff a teacher's attempt to explore the issue in depth. Where to draw the line? I finally spoke up, reiterating my earlier claim of parental concern: "We were once young like you and thought we had much ahead of us. Now we know better and wish to save you that frustration." Their silence was hard to read.

What constitutes appropriate parental or social intervention? Kim (1993) questions the arbitrary application of individualism in American society. The man or woman who succeeds against social and economic circumstances becomes a hero, yet the same individual "takes a 180-degree" turn in attributing failure to external factors:

> Americans too readily blame others for all sorts of things—from inadequate educational achievements (for example, "The school failed to teach me how to read" or "SAT questions are gender/race-biased") to murder (for example, "I plead not guilty by reason of insanity") to alcoholism (for example, "I inherited alcoholic genes"). The expression "I am sorry" comes out naturally from the mouths of Americans. (p. 17)

It helps to identify causes and establish priorities to best address an issue. The practice of passing the buck by students, parents, administrators, and politicians, although politically expedient, merely compounds the problem.

African cultures value kinship ties and social harmony or "restrictive religious and political ideologies," in contrast to what Ojeda (1993) terms "American notions of egalitarianism and informality," evident in the use of first names or nicknames for adults. Within communities, the appropriateness of social relations depends on age, gender, and social ties. These social hierarchies dictate an indisputable chain of command (Appiah, 1992). Kinship ties mean shared resources and collective work. Even in post-independent Kenya, an African's identity is primarily relational (sister, brother, uncle, daughter, son, father, mother, uncle, aunt, grandparent, father, and so forth). Communities also specify privileges and obligations for each stage of life and social roles. The obverse is a self-effacing attitude toward individual achievement. Individuals attribute success to luck, divine intervention, and external support. However legitimate, the dismissal of personal accountability undermines motivation and sacrifice to some degree.

Since cultures are dynamic, cross-cultural interactions or educational access lead to a gradual realignment in group relations and values (Appiah, 1992; Bateson, 2000). Although Kenyan communities hold elders responsible for the welfare and survival of the family, economic changes in the twentieth century altered family structures (often) making elders dependent on younger working members for survival. However, children are expected to revere adult figures. In many African communities children are "to be seen not heard." Youth talking back to adults raises eyebrows and elicits headshakes of disbelief in an audience; frequently, many express a nostalgia for the good old days. My socialization and educational background made some students' behavior in U.S. class settings difficult to comprehend. On the other hand, I would be labeled too assertive in African communities. Students in the United States probably found my expectations just as alien. This is the essence of an immigrant teacher's dilemma. However, disparities among students' attitudes toward school or demeanor (recall the shocked response at Paula's denigration of her mother) illustrates a similar ambivalence toward each other.

CHAPTER 6

A Window of Time

Classroom tensions compel teachers to reflect and act as *Immigrant Teachers, American Students: Cultural Differences, Cultural Disconnections* illustrates. Teachers, as often as students, articulate frustrations over each other's choices or expectations. Since classroom decisions tend to be immediate, choices reflect learned attitudes and behaviors as much they reflect logical decision-making. Despite the emotional upsets, these incidents offer forums for reassessment of views, acknowledgment of differences, and decisions about future interactions.

Immigrant Teachers, American Students: Cultural Differences, Cultural Disconnections acknowledges the impact of primary experiences on beliefs and behavior patterns while advocating awareness and individual responsibility for choices. Teachers no less than students require a give-and-take approach in daily interactions (Giroux, 1988; Shor, 1996). Too often, parties adopt an adversarial us-versus-them attitude, which leaves little room for understanding, growth, or learning. Schooling compels cross-cultural exchanges and accommodations; individual tastes, priorities, and expectations change with age, relocations within national borders, and everyday social interactions (Bateson, 2000; Minnich, 2005; Martin, 2007). The teaching role involves not only transmission but also a reflective transformation of personal beliefs and practices. While the discussion raises issues experienced by immigrants in general, the focus is on the African immigrant teacher. Overall, pitted against one another, individual versus community interests appear extreme to advocates despite evidence to the contrary.

Despite years of socialization—informal and formal—particular incidents compel individuals into decisions that reflect immediate concerns as well as ingrained beliefs and habits. In particular, students often view correction as an imposition of unfair discipline, while teachers cite established rules and standards in order to maintain order. Decisions and actions are immediate and involve risk with a potentially enduring impact. Overall, habitual patterns of behavior offer personal anchors for day-to-day choices. Teachers, no less than students, fall back on familiar conceptions and behaviors, whether for expediency or as a matter of principle, as the following anecdotes portray. During an incident, few teachers or even students engage in a reasoned analysis of what is happening or the best way to handle the situation. It would help if teachers could handle situations with reason. Typically, individuals interpret situations from a particular lens and respond from habitual patterns of behavior. For instance, some people avoid talking back when confronted, while others lash out at the first indication of real or imagined disrespect. Mori (1997) acknowledges the dilemma of "living between two cultures" and the decisions on degree of tolerance for what is "well-intentioned or otherwise" (p. 47).

On the day of the confrontation cited in chapter one, Paula arrived about 20 minutes late to the two-hour class. She did not have the shoulder-strap bag she usually brought along. Minutes later, Paula requested to pick up her book, having left it in the guidance counselor's office. "How long will it take?" I asked. "Five minutes," she replied. I conceded. She did return within the five minutes but with neither the book bag nor the notebook. Her classmates had already settled at the computers researching select cultural heroes during an independent activity. I pulled up a chair at Paula's side to explain the assignment before stepping away. Less than 15 minutes into the Internet search, Paula called out, saying she was through with the work. After reviewing the work she had done, I urged her to integrate more sources and details into the essay. Paula initially kept her eyes glued to the computer monitor ignoring my presence in the chair next to her. The look on her face when she later turned to me showed her distaste and checked anger. "I have done my work!" was her response. I stepped away from her. What evoked the anger? It could have been the implication that her work was not good enough or some incident prior to that. Teachers respond to exhibited behavior not always sure of the rationale behind students' choices or discontent.

The use of personal space reflects status in distinguishing insiders from outsiders among youth no less than adults (Bateson, 2000; Milner, 2004). There is a cultural element to the issue of territorial boundaries. Perhaps reflective of communal orientations, Africans are more at ease with physical proximity than Westerners. In churches, parishioners typically huddle together on pews even when there may be open spaces elsewhere. Kenyans stand closer to each other in interactions and engage in physical contact more frequently, which can be misconstrued in the American culture. Kofi's concern about students' false accusations of inappropriate conduct by male teachers ("He/she touches people" or "They stand too close to you") captures this cultural incongruence.

Space is segregated or monopolized by cliques—race, class, gender, talent—within and outside of schools. Cliques of students monopolize particular areas of the class, cafeteria, hallways, locker rooms, football games, and concerts or neighborhood cafes. Of school buses, Miller notes: "High-status students sat at the back because it was harder for the driver and others to see them, and because they paraded by everyone else as they made their entries and exits" (p. 54; Willis, 1981). In the class, Andrea was always surrounded by her eleventh-grade clique. The twelfth-graders sat apart and acted more maturely than her classmates. Teenage use of space to define intimacy and status reflects similar trends in the larger society's association of physical to social distance. In neighborhoods, floor spaces, streets, parking spaces, or even territorial boundaries serve a similar function in defining status or group allegiance. Whether it is the expansive office space, residence, or car, adults also stake their claims through physical space or sizable and extravagant possessions: "The rich tend to live on top of the hill or in penthouses; the offices of top executives are never in the basement; the powerful have larger offices, desks, and cars" (Milner, 2004, p. 55). The expression of social status through access and the extent of social spacing on the basis of gender or age—physical and emotional—reflect dynamics noted by Milner (2004); for instance, at public ceremonies in African communities, dignitaries, adults—particularly males—sit in conspicuous places (Appiah, 1992). It is no different in the United States.

Paula's hunched posture and dismissal of my presence during class and threat to drop out reflected claims to emotional and physical territorial space. Stepping away from Paula gave us the emotional space for reflection, but it could also have been an avoidance of growing tension on my part. The problem of establishing relationships is complicated. Empathy requires mutuality and connection but also restraint and distance, notes Lawrence-Lightfoot (1999). She maintains that in interactions every word, gesture, and silence is significant. Although difficult, sometimes the wise thing to do is nothing.

Natadecha-Sponsel's (1993) analysis of individualism in American culture highlights the relationship among issues of space, possessions, and intimacy relative to Thai culture. She links America's use of space to its "cultural value of individualism." Children accustomed to private spaces and possessions early in life develop emotional and economic independence. African cultures exhibit similar values for collectivity and the priority for social harmony described by Natadecha-Sponsel. In contrast, American children typically eat from separate plates and parents rarely chide children for leftover food in restaurants. Communities that value independence and assertiveness tend to be more tolerant of difference. In class settings, American students tend to assert their rights, often at the expense of classmates or the required decorum in class settings; for instance, Andrea's call to Victor to "Shut up!" disregarding classroom etiquette. Although classroom monitors and school prefects wield tremendous power in the Kenyan educational system, it is a delegated authority assumed in the absence of teachers and administrators, the real authority figures. Classroom monitors organize and censure students' behavior within an established pecking order system of relations.

That day Paula did the six-paragraph (two or three sentences each rather than the recommended four plus) essay and resisted having to do more work. "I am not like them (the rest of the eleventh- and twelfth-grade students in the class). I read and write more and faster." How dare I insist she revisit her work? My reminder that revision is always good appeared to anger her further. I stepped away to give her space. Less than five minutes after the exchange, Paula walked over to where I sat typing at one of the computers chained to tables along the wall. She handed the typed essay to me with a damning, "Here is your work and I am dropping your class," audible enough for the whole class to hear. I took the paper from her and turned back to the task at hand. She stormed out to return less than 15 minutes later, confronting me as I wandered around the room to guide and monitor students' work. At least she let me finish with the student I was assisting. Standing less than a foot from me, Paula announced, "I am leaving your class because you are rude. No one shouts at me, Paula. (She thumped at her chest with the fingers of her right hand.) No one." Still glaring at me, she continued with a list of allegations concerning my disrespect. I stepped away from her. She came behind me, apparently not finished with what she had to tell me. "I thought you left the class," I reminded her. "I need a note from you and my mother to drop your class," she informed me rather curtly. "Get a note from your mother and one from the school. I did not register you in the class. Go back to whoever registered you and have them withdraw your name," I replied, getting exasperated with her comments. In retrospect, I could have insisted on a private discussion after class earlier in the exchange. Paula's interruption and audacity stretched my patience. She stomped out a second time. Meanwhile, around the room the rest of the class worked away in apparent rapt attention, although more likely drawn by the exchange rather than engrossment in their writing assignments. Teacher/student squabbles leave the class delighted but disoriented. Students take sides either as expected protocol (show some respect for the teacher) or as sabotage (Go get her!).

They rarely accept challenges however legitimate from lame-duck teachers they have little respect for.

At the end of class, following the litany of accusations and bafflement on my part, Paula's voice appeared to mellow enough for me to explain my priorities. She accused me of imposing unrealistic standards on students. Which ones? Was writing a six-paragraph essay too high a standard for a smart girl like her? I asked. She did claim to be the smart one prior to the confrontation, I reminded her. My requirement of four-paragraph essays at the beginning of the semester encountered tremendous resistance. This is not a college class, a few students reminded me on occasion. "No," I agreed, "that is why I asked for just four paragraphs." We progressed to six based on the four Ws and H (why, who, what, where, when, and how) format. Later, we included a summary paragraph of the main points and counterargument. "Whether or not you stay in my class, remember one thing. Eighteen is too early an age to close off oneself from learning," I concluded in the exchange with Paula.

McFarland (2004) views students' resistance as a social drama replete with players, progressive plot structures, and audience with discernible conclusions. Each classroom conflict reflects three overlapping levels at which parties operate: the academic, social, and person frame. Typically, teachers focus on the academics. Lane, Wehby and Cooley (2006) as well as Giroux (1988, 2008) admit this conflict in priorities—academic performance, behavior decorum, and social interactions—within class settings. The students' cooperation and self-control skills facilitate instruction. McFarland acknowledges the subjectivity in perceptions and choice of action in warring parties. Students appeal to classmates for support by talking to willing ears or linking the incident to a former breach by the teacher. The ploy works if the class views the culprit as representing their views, that was the case with Cecilia's resistance to in-class writing activity. A few students failed to turn in their work although she herself did so, unbeknownst to her clique. In contrast, Paula got neither support nor acknowledgment for her confrontations with me. I rarely saw her hang out with other members of the class. Overall, the contention halts a teacher's effort and rewards non-conformity in students. On the other hand, teachers appeal to the class by linking desirable behavior to "prohibitions and rule violations...harder tasks, failing grades, and detentions" (McFarland, 2004. p. 1279). Teaching involves the transmission of facts but also the establishment of relationships between teachers and students.

The danger with public conflicts, which should be avoided, is that both teachers and students become defensive, and, consciously or not, appeal to the audience for support. It is harder to hear the other party if one is avoiding the loss of face. Each feels justified in their perception of the situation and stance in the matter. Individuals acquire value structures from prevailing norms and practices, specifically what American students expect in social interactions. Teachers rely on official guidelines to design syllabi as well as in establishing class norms. Students learn state- and city-defined material within a set duration. Determining what is appropriate raises the issue of whether teaching is an art or a science. Notwithstanding defined school policies, each teacher applies rules and regulations with some amount of flexibility. These structures allow teachers and students to negotiate for territory in social interactions.

Professional standards prescribe means and ends to classroom interactions. Students' complaints about assigned tasks or a teacher's role derail this focus on academics. "Challenges usually characterize teachers as corrupt or inept and the classroom activities as ineffective" (McFarland, 2004, p. 1267). Specifically, teachers establish and set boundaries to curb inappropriate behavior and reestablish their authority over the process and product of learning (Giroux, 2005, 2008; hooks, 1994). They may use tough talk, cajole, ridicule, or make sarcastic comments, threaten punishment, or appeal to the personal frame.

By giving priority to social or personal issues, students undermine a teacher's focus on tasks, lesson contents, assessments, or teacher authority (McFarland, 2004; Shor, 1996). While attending to students' personal issues and content matter are not mutually exclusive, finding the right balance is a major challenge for teachers. Students can engage in an elaborate and extended discussion of clothing and television programs. The gripes about a topic or lesson's lack of relevance are one such example. McFarland includes students' jokes about their "teacher's appearance, mannerisms, dress, weight, and speech patterns" in the category of personal issues.

Classroom Misunderstanding

Drawing on McFarland's tripartite model for understanding and addressing classroom dissonance, both Paula and I were aware of and drew upon the academic, social, and personal frame in our interaction. Although both immigrants (I later discovered), Paula's longer-term residency in the United States may explain her assertion of rights in contrast to my accustomed hierarchical student/teacher interactions (Borjas, 1999). Herein lies the conflict. In my role as teacher, I challenged but also assessed Paula's performance based on established guidelines—grasp of lesson, class participation, and written assignments. She too appealed to the academic frame in justifying her absence and substandard work, later pointing to the confusion over registration. Regarding the social frame, both of us looked to the validation of

Paula's classmates although our expectations differed. I hoped they would stay out of the exchange, which they did. I presumed Paula expected her classmates to support her charges against me, something they failed to do. Without the audience at the last exchange, our engagement reflected a more personal appeal to reason and understanding. Despite the lack of obvious concession or apologies by either party, we both conceded to an unqualified closure. Neither of us referred to the incident in later meetings.

Based on McFarland (2004) and Milner's (2004) assessment of adolescent behavior patterns, especially the importance of peer approval, my challenge of Paula's work may have implied an inadequacy that threatened her sense of comfort. Publicly urging the twelfth-grade Paula to improve the essay challenged her status among her classmates, the majority of whom (11 to 15) were eleventh-graders. Although Paula's "insubordination" was ignored by her classmates at the time, her public confrontation and accusations probably helped recover her compromised status. Paula could afford to be more conciliatory away from her classmates.

Students may act out to feel powerful among friends, or as a matter of habit. Teaching, as one of Lawrence-Lightfoot's (1999) respondents notes, is loaded with risk: "Adolescences often define themselves by testing, by flirting with danger, by pushing up against the rules and defying laws of gravity. To be in sync with that, as a teacher, you sometimes have to take a leap of faith...and you must often make the decision to leap in a millisecond. Timing is everything. There is always the possibility that it will not work out" (p. 116). Consider a teacher's decision as to when and how to intervene in a classroom incident. Because respect needs nurturing, an adolescent's confusion calls for time spent exchanging stories of their dilemmas with teachers as some sort of sounding board. Discussions centered on models of respect or the lack thereof allow for a critical engagement of what is or isn't appropriate over and above taken-for-granted patterns of behavior. Such exchanges highlight differences in perspectives but also the need for cross-cultural understanding. For instance, the use of profanity may be tolerated in a family or neighborhood but inappropriate in class settings. One of Lawrence-Lightfoot's research participants warns that "storytelling can be both inspiring and dangerous, both empathic and narcissistic" particularly when "you project your own needs and expectations on those who are listening" (p. 223). Immigrant teachers can provide contextual stories for classroom expectations contrasting familiar practices in teacher-student relations to evident behaviors. The trick is how best to foster a habit without belaboring the point. The caution avoids students' familiar exclamations of, "Oh, not again!" Hemmings (2003) warns that talk of respect is ineffective without an established "moral code that fosters mutual respect among teachers, students, parents, and administrators" (p. 434). She calls for dialogue around the concept and implications of civility codes. In her research students showed a greater willingness than teachers and administrators in debating the crisis in authority. Hemmings (2003) recommends teachers' "sensitivity to students' individual characteristics and their social class, racial, ethnic and gender backgrounds" (p. 434). In contrast, Appiah (1992) cautions against one-sided demands for cultural accommodation.

Conventional debates on inclusion focusing on students as minors to titled teachers ignores liberties taken by students as gendered, classed, and raced individuals (Walkerdine, 1990). Specifically, social privilege or the lack thereof shape interactions among students and teachers. Walkerdine's study illustrates how boys as young as four explicitly and subtly dismiss female teachers and students. There is also the issue of perceptual locations. In the cited incident with Paula, she viewed me as the imposing and culturally superior English teacher relative to her American identity. My blackness offered no solidarity between us in her estimation.

Advocates of culturally relevant pedagogy such as Delpit (1995) underscore the importance of "teacher-centered practices that make explicit the learning and language skills" for minority students with "less power and familiarity with White languages of power" (p. 434). Delpit focuses on differences in rearing patterns between White and Black families. While Africans are explicit in cautioning children or employing punitive measures against behavior breaches, "experts" advocate "appealing" techniques over a commanding tone (Owolabi, 1996, p. 63). Regardless of the source of conflict, the more teachers know their students on a personal level the easier it is to challenge them to a desirable cause of action. Based on McFarland's framework, my appeals to Paula's age, intellect, and future during our private exchange fell into this category. At that time, I avoided imposing my authority in order to focus on what benefited Paula on an individual level. My "sharing" of what had worked for me fit into this framework. It was a talk between equals: a heart-to-heart interaction.

There is a reciprocity in the acculturation process (Appiah, 1992; Bateson, 2000; Drechsel, 1993; Giroux, 2005, 2008; Martin, 2007). Civility, much like the students' ability to dress appropriately for different occasions, involves choice and attention to social settings (Bateson, 2000; Mori, 1997). As a student, Amobi's (2004) response to her alienation in graduate school settings was to immerse herself in the prevailing education discourse, poring over books and articles for familiarity with the intellectual terrain. "Knowledge gave me voice, and my ability to view the commonplaces of teaching and learning from two cultural vantage points gained the attention and respect of empathic and even antipathetic" colleagues and professors (p. 172). In her case, enlightened teachers "widened the community border to make it inclusive and complementary" for her otherness (p. 173). She advocates a "bridge-building" approach to acculturation. "Otherness" becomes a learning resource in confronting students with the unfamiliar, a different story: a cultural cross-border experience that broadens their sense of reality and being (Bateson, 2000; Mori, 1997). African immigrant teachers can affirm the uniqueness of students within classrooms aware of their own cultural outsider status in a new and challenging environment; they embody the richness of cultural synthesis. Literature abounds on the alienation of minority students' experience in U.S. schools. Educated in colonial-style systems and aware of the danger of cultural parochialism, many African immigrants embrace mainstream Western values for upward mobility (Achebe, 2009). For instance, students accept the need to learn English as the official language. School uniforms are a requirement in all K–12 grades. Teachers are respected as surrogate parents. Rare are sentiments of dissent against an authority mandate such as, "Well, that is what I feel like…" expressed by youth or tolerated in institutions and by adults.

Standards versus Relationships

I accidentally encountered Paula a month later. As usual, she had her iPod earphones on. She immediately pulled out the plugs before calling out a cheery greeting. That was a surprise. We stood facing each other at the entrance staircase the high school and college share. "You gave me a U [unsuccessful—below 65 grade point]," she said. It could have been a question or statement. I waited. She repeated the phrase, raising her voice at the end. "You got a U," I responded, "You did not do much work in our class. You attended only five [out of fifteen] classes the whole semester and submitted only one assignment." Paula attributed her absence and lack of commitment to the confusion regarding her registration. "I was never sure about belonging to your class." I reminded her of our previous discussions and her insistence that she had never "dropped" the class despite her threat to do so. It took me aback that despite the threats and subsequent class absences, Paul did not drop the class. As with the excuses that students give for class absences, tardiness, or missed assignments, immigrant teachers like myself are torn between accepting a student's claim and the frustration of enduring skepticism. Paula's actions contradicted her claim. I am reminded of a graduate student's confession about a common practice of gaining concessions by giving excuses of deceased relatives, preferably, grandparents. Not long after the confession, one of the classmates missed a key presentation to attend a grandparent's funeral. I explained to the class the reason for the concession, prior to the make-up, having explicitly prohibited make-up for class presentations. The student's angry looks throughout the class in response to the announcement were disheartening. In Kenya, grief is shared. Indeed, colleagues, neighbors, and friends contribute to ease the burden on a bereaved member. Often, students deny having heard me discussing course requirements, particularly with regard to deadlines and penalties as stated in the syllabus and rubric. When I have pointed out an item in the syllabus, the response is a nonchalant, "Ohh!, but I didn't think it was serious." On occasion, a supervisor sides with students claiming that I might not have "explained the assignment properly." It must be the accent!

The blatant lies to excuse tardiness or missing assignments shocked me as did questions of integrity. I considered such an excuse extreme. In a Kenyan context, discovery, which is quite likely (talk of death always involves relatives who can expose the culprit during unrelated discussions), would result in dire consequences. The fear of reprisals checks many students' choices. Or maybe it is just me! "Is there make-up work (she used the term makeover)?" Paula was exceptionally polite that day. She pointed to the office with a last pitch, "[Teachers] are changing grades now." "Paula, you should have worked during the semester for the grade you now desire. I cannot change your grade," I responded. She turned and walked away from me. Four of her classmates made similar requests for a grade change in subsequent days. At later meetings with Paula, all I got was a scowl. Paula dismissed me.

Like Paula, Lisa was a loner despite having been with the group since junior high. I recall our first meeting. She joined the group at the third session. We walked up the stairs to the third-floor class after I stopped by the office to pick up the key. Her response to my question about her previous class absences was a shrug and a smile. She had pending work (for an incomplete) from the previous semester. "Is it complete?" I inquired, close to a month into the fall semester. "Oh no," she responded promptly, with a furtive smile on her face. Lisa attended 4 out of 15 classes, showing up halfway through the class on one occasion.

The week after our last class, Lisa walked in on me as I sat working at a computer. I turned when I felt a presence behind me. (My workspace faced the wall.) It was her first visit to my office. I asked her to pull up a chair. She did, pulling it close enough for us to see into each other's eyes. "You are not in class," she began, looking rather serious as she slumped into the easy chair across from me. It was shortly after 2:00 p.m.; the class met at 2:00 p.m. every Thursday. "No. The class ended last week," I informed her. "Ohh. What did you give me?" she asked, changing the topic. I informed her about the procedure of submitting grades to the office rather than individual students. Later I would learn she had been to the main office at the high school prior to her visit to my office. "You did not make the passing grade, having missed so many classes and assignments," I reminded her. She did not appear surprised or perturbed by the news. "Give me makeup work," she requested. Just like that. "You had a whole semester to work toward the grade," I told her, letting her know that in all fairness I would then have to extend the same concessions to her classmates. "They do not know," was her prompt response. "I do and so do you," I said. For about 30 minutes we talked back and forth about the importance of class attendance and involvement in class activities. It turned out she had missed out on other classes. "But they gave me makeup work," she reminded me. "I cannot change your grade but I urge you to avoid a similar mistake in other classes," was my summing-up comment, attempting to salvage a lesson out of the predicament. "Oh, but they do not teach anything," she said, referring to the classes she was in the habit of missing. The high school offers preparation classes for the Regents and other qualifying examinations, but few go to the Saturday sessions. "I went once. It was boring," Lisa explained. My urgings appeared irrelevant. At this point Lisa sat back slumped into the chair, chewing gum and sipping at her drink. She wanted me to know she needed the credit from my class to graduate. "Have you applied to any colleges?" I asked. "No," was her response, yet she planned to go to college. I sat there trying hard to hide my shock at the revelation. It was the twenty-first of December. "What are some of the colleges you plan to apply to?" I asked. She had no response to that either. We sat facing each other with little more to say. After five more minutes of silence, I informed her I would have to get back to my work and did. I turned back to the computer with Lisa sitting behind me chewing gum and sipping at her drink. She got up and left some time later. When she finally walked out, she ignored the farewell despite my calling out her name.

 The apprehension of acclimating to a new language and adapting to American social norms adds pressure to the immigrant teacher's ability to understand and respond to students' needs. Further, professional demands augment the teacher's angst in establishing credibility. Finding the right balance between transmitting crucial facts and enforcing discipline, as well as pleasing students by accommodating their needs and interests, is difficult for any teacher. Are African immigrant teachers insensitive to students' cultural differences? Perhaps not, considering the competitive environment most minority students confront daily from their better-off peers or immigrant students competing for education and employment prospects. Few of these minority students can afford to be lax about academic requirements. There are minority students who embrace intellectual rigor and excel in both challenging and affirming environments (Duster, 2009; hooks, 1994, 2003; hooks and mesa-bains, 2006; Holmes, 2001). Touching upon the age-old debate over standard English (Ravitch, 1995), Delpit (1988, 1995) recommends explicit instruction procedures—academic and social skills—for underprivileged (Black) students to prepare them for White-dominant economic and political systems. Schools help such students acquire the knowledge, linguistic skills, and behavior patterns—what Delpit (1995) terms the "White language of power"—that offer minority students alternatives as well as a competitive advantage in otherwise marginalizing environments. "In this country, students will be judged on their product regardless of the process they utilized to achieve it. And that product, based as it is on the specific codes of a particular culture, is more readily produced when the directives of how to produce it are made explicit" (p. 31). She chides progressive White liberals for playing down their power over students by avoiding teacher-directed approaches under the guise of "pleasing" students. They use "veiled commands" for which students are labeled disobedient in case of breaches. Meanwhile, children raised in structured environments view the denial of teachers to express "overt power" by using "a more egalitarian and nonauthoritative classroom atmosphere" as a lack of authority. For instance, a teacher makes the following suggestion to a student who has submitted shoddy work: "You might consider redoing this assignment," or "I will change the grade, if you can give me a revision of the paper by next week." What the teacher really means is: "This assignment needs to be redone." Delpit (1988, 1995) insists that the issue is not a choice of process over product teaching approaches, but rather, helping students "understand the need for both approaches, the need to help students establish their own voices, and to coach those voices to produce notes that will be heard clearly in the larger society" (p. 47). In disciplines other than language arts, the objective is to expose students to basic concepts and related skills rather than focus on Socratic-style discussions to elicit participation from students whose opinions are unformed.

Educational critics such as Giroux (1988) decry the cultural imposition of middle-class lifestyles, speech patterns, and language at the expense of minority cultures. Giroux finds the neoconservative focus on basics devoid of social critique "patronizing and theoretically misleading." Regardless of when and how individual teachers strike a balance, Delpit's caution against obliging minority students at the expense of teachers holding them accountable to mainstream standards and classroom etiquette reflects the priorities of African immigrant teachers. In society, graduates compete against colleagues trained in other cultures and concede to demands from a wider, perhaps more rigorous, constituent of supervisors. Schools need to prepare students for a competitive corporate world and a culturally pluralistic society:

> There is no social promotion [in Burundi]. Struggling students are even expelled (not too good) or given an opportunity to repeat the grade. The assessment system is also balanced. Students take exams seriously. Exams are administered at the end of every semester, and the promotion to the next level is based on the average of the exam grades throughout the year.... Finally, I treasure the fact that Conduct is considered like a core course. If a student gets a failed grade in Conduct at the end of the year, they get automatically expelled from the school, and it is very difficult to get accepted at any other school. I wish the same practice could be implemented in the United States. (Girikaze)

In *Black Teachers on Teaching*, Michele Foster (1997) makes a case for Black teachers in predominantly Black schools despite legitimate calls for integration by the civil rights movement. The denigration of the Black race—teachers and students—persists in the United States (hooks, 2003; hooks and mesa-bains, 2006; Nieto, 2004). For the most part, Black teachers share this legacy and address racial bias as role models who overcame overwhelming odds to achieve more empowering self-definitions. These teachers recognize, but avoid excusing, the counter-school cultural behaviors of Black students—indolence, resistance, and racial inferiority:

> Teachers have to realize that black students—or all students, but I'm talking about black students right now—are very clever, especially with white teachers. Too many black students have learned to play the game, to play on a teacher's sympathy in order to get away with doing nothing.... All students will con teachers if they let themselves be conned. But it's often easier for black students to con white teachers because the students know that the teachers will pity them, feel sorry for them, and make excuses that these can't do that, or that there's a problem at home.... It particularly disturbs me when I see black teachers letting black students get away with doing nothing. (Foster, 1997, pp. 47–48)

Gay (2000) cites culturally responsive programs such as Kamehameha Early Education Program (KEEP), the Multicultural Literacy Program (MLP), and the Webster Groves Writing Project (WGWP) to underscore the success of culturally relevant pedagogy in engaging disenfranchised students. The programs use multiethnic literature in reading and writing; they help students acquire skills of focus and clarity in arguments. Her proposal for building on students' primary cultures to enrich subject matter or class activities and interactive learning is not unique to cultural groups. Most teachers agree on the importance of promoting educative experiences, correct habits, and students' cognitive development. However, given the increasingly global nature of communities, due to world travel and migrations coupled with communication networks, American students need the "international" exposure to a range of cultural habits and practices. In addition, although Foster's call for Black teachers appears to include most African immigrants, this research shows the cultural disparities within the racial group. There are White American teachers who are more familiar with minority students despite the racial differences. They pick up on cues of students' resistance faster and intervene in more culturally appropriate ways. On the other hand, teachers trained in the United States are also stumped by some students' choices and deeds in classrooms—frustration at the lack of propriety and diligence as much as by the tardiness among students.

Lake (2009) warns colleges against relying on "legalistic codes of conduct," despite pervasive infractions ranging from substance abuse, mental health issues, cheating, and a lack of respect for academic integrity. In his view, discipline issues reflect cultural changes, specifically, differences in value systems between instructors and students. Like Bateson (2000), Lake attributes academic integrity to generational characteristics of what he terms, "millennial students," born after 1982. Benton (2009) refers to the group as "snowflakes." Both Lake and Benton note a disdain for penalties, with a sense of entitlement to rewards and accommodations: "Highly complex rule systems with harsh consequences are foreign to people who have been praised for even the smallest success and whose mistakes have often been glossed over as part of a process of becoming 'a better me'" (Lake, 2009, A31). Reared in homes and schools that reinforce their specialness and uniqueness, snowflakes expect accommodations believing it is normal (Benton, 2009). Lake advocates developing MAPs (Master Academic Programs) that allow mentors in "institutions to individualize their expectations" (A 32). It is another of the teacher accommodations Mori (1997) attributes to lack of trust in authorities. Reflecting immigrant teacher sensibilities, Benton (2009) calls for a teaching style "that demands excellence and that our students, beneath the surface, actually want more than inflated praise, permissiveness, and mediocrity" (p. A41).

As Benton (2009) notes, a teacher is pressured into focusing on consequences (or political correctness), at the expense of "maintaining high standards as a categorical imperative (p. A 39). The "snowflake" analogy depicts students unaccustomed to critique in homes much as in schools. Each is "special," "unique and beautiful," as are individual snowflakes. There is some truth to it, but its extreme can foster narcissistic tendencies. The sense of irreproachability in Paula when I challenged her about promising to and then not showing up with her book bag when she stepped out of class, reflects similar sentiments. Even the mother appeared to have little control over her daughter's behavior, or so Paula claimed. Paula's exasperation at my attempts to raise her academic ambitions mirrored similar rebuffs from her classmates. My students voiced anger, mumbled among themselves, pouted or in Paula's case, stomped out of class in opposition to requirements for more details or better written assignments. Surprisingly, students express outrage at a "butchered" paper with red checks all over it. In most African schools such critiques are commonplace; indeed, many would welcome the chance to redo a piece of work at the urgings of a teacher. Consider again the fall back on, "I have issues." However legitimate, such excuses for infractions, missing class, or not participating in class because, "I had a bad day," or "I am tired," are commonly heard in U.S. classrooms. Watoya advocates three crucial elements in preparing foreign-trained teachers in the United States: "1) knowledge of American culture and attitudes toward foreigners; 2) use of technology in the classroom; 3) mentoring period under an American teacher."

Both Badillo (2006) and McWhorter (2001) decry the academic minimalism associated with minority cultures. According to Herman Badillo's *One Nation, One Standard: An Ex-liberal on How Hispanics Can Succeed Just Like Other Immigrant Groups,* calls for cultural sensitivity (link class material to students' lived realities) within education are a hindrance rather than a help to underachieving minority students. Badillo's critique equates culture to racial/ethnic differences. While primarily concerned about the Hispanic community's lack of agency and accountability, Badillo (2006) extends his critique to the Black community. Born in Puerto Rico and educated in the Bronx, Badillo has been a congressman, borough president, deputy mayor of New York, chairman of the City University of New York, and is currently a senior fellow at the Manhattan Institute. He denounces the sacrifice of high standards as the insidious racism of White liberals. A student's inability to read, write, and speak Standard English has little if anything to do with culture. There is a point to Badillo's critique. Lowering standards by avoiding tasks that expose a student's inadequacy, making excessive concessions, and skipping difficult parts of a lesson to avoid putting pressure on or frustrating minority students is patronizing.

Frequent accusations of insensitivity, "You are not nice," and negative course evaluations in response to enforcing requirements put pressure on teachers to justify grades less than an "A" for students who slack off during the semester and wonder at the insensitivity of being denied makeup work and other forms of accommodation. In addition, reminding students that they repeated a question previously raised with "Do you recall X's question?" elicits negative reactions and sometimes charges of "You hurt my feelings." Picking on students at random to keep the whole class, rather than the diligent few, engaged in the discussion, has drawn charges of inconsiderateness at all levels—high school, undergraduate, and even at the graduate level. Graduate students take me on with the "You humiliate me" charge for exposing their gaps in knowledge. Fortunately, with or without the probing, some students come up with enlightening contributions to the discussion despite their not having volunteered a response. Other students claim the approach keeps them focused, aware they could be called upon at any time.

McWhorter (2001) attributes Black students' academic underachievement to a cultural crisis—victimology, anti-intellectualism, and isolationism (see also McCarthy, 1990). Playing the race card condones "weakness and failure" in Blacks. Academic excellence is portrayed as a White thing. Raising similar concerns a decade earlier, Ogbu (1992) notes how Blacks create an oppositional culture, what he terms cultural inversion, regarding "certain forms of behavior, events, symbols, and meaning as inappropriate for them because these are characteristics of white Americans" (p. 8). Admitting he initially gave Black students "as much slack as possible," tolerating academic underperformance, skimpy work, poor attendance, and even offering makeup work, McWhorter concludes that:

> The reason [Black students] do not try is not because they are inherently lazy, nor is it because they are stupid. Furthermore, while many of these students are quite obviously disinclined to dedicate themselves meaningfully to school, just as many give their best effort, but are unaware that white and Asian students' efforts come from a level and depth of commitment beyond theirs. The reason black students so rarely hit that particular bar, while such a disproportionate number are disinclined to even try, is that all of these students belong to a culture infected with an anti-intellectual strain, which subtly but decisively teaches them from birth not to embrace schoolwork wholeheartedly. (p. 100)

It is not a matter of social class; these Black students at Berkeley know what wine to order with white chicken as McWhorter insists. Although eschewing academics is not exclusive to Blacks, the implications for minorities, who are already marginalized in society, are dire. The loss of $800 to one who has $10,000 is no comparison to one with $1,000 to spare. In the United States, there is greater concern for the academic underachievement among minorities than White and Asian students.

As an African immigrant teacher, my instinctual focus is on the academics, preparing students for the intellectual rigor in store, given their aspirations for college. That education improves students' competitive advantage in social and work settings reflects my own faith in the power of education to broaden one's perspective and improve career prospects. It explains my Herculean efforts to foster a love for learning in students, despite ongoing resistance in class settings. On the other hand, the awareness of differences in social expectations with U.S. students checks my (over)enthusiasm or impatience with expressed choices when these differ from what is familiar. Wesonga's imperatives contrast sharply with Milner (2004), who attributes teenage behavior to youth status rather than biological processes:

> [First] Give serious attention to multicultural issues in education. Young teachers need to be schooled well in this. [Second] The psychology of adolescence from the educational point of view. Understand well developmental changes and how to handle people going through various stages of growth. [Third, study] The socio-economic effects on human development and learning/education. In my view, these three points are key and crucial in the preparation of future teachers. They should be emphasized in schools of education.

Besides differences in social expectations among teachers and students, confusion comes from inconsistent cues in interactions. The competitive individualism in the United States explains the conventional ambivalence toward welfare programs. To what degree are individuals accountable for their status in life? Similarly, some students readily blame institutions for poor academic performance—boring or terrible teachers as well as racist policies and practices. Inconsistent cues in interactions pose further challenges for immigrant teachers. Not all students are slackers. Each class has students who either value or dismiss the learning experience. Some appreciate the academic challenge while others view it as an imposition on personal space (Holmes, 2001). Drawing upon Milner's (2004) analysis of social space, infringing on other people's territorial space reflects an assertion of power over the person or an invitation to intimacy. When Paula and Lisa approached me to request a change of grade, both stood/sat physically closer and spoke in conciliatory tones despite a semester-long emotional and physical distancing. A teacher's role and accompanying power is more obvious at the end of the semester when they evaluate students' performance. Students are more generous in their use of the professor title then.

The interaction above demonstrates students' awareness of demands beyond personal wishes. Students know what constitutes appropriate behavior with adults or in school settings. Because choices have consequences, diligence pays off in good grades. In a world of competing interests, students need to make responsible choices. In addition, not all teachers capitulate to students' expedient requests. The difference in teaching and conversational styles causes endless acrimony for less flexible teachers. Ultimately, there is an appropriateness to social behavior involving ongoing negotiations for what works best in different settings.

Epilogue

Immigrant Teachers, American Students: Cultural Differences, Cultural Disconnections illustrates the impact of acquired norms in classrooms. Specifically, stereotypes of cultural groups, perhaps more than firsthand knowledge, shape mutual expectations, and a discussion on of cultural dynamics demonstrates the complexity of cultural identities and cross-cultural discourse. Prevailing cultural identities are neither definitive nor homogenous. But these "invented traditions" often masquerade as "national mythologies," in considerations of race, gender, and religion. (Appiah, 1992). Cultures shape identity but are not as determinist as the advocates of culturally relevant pedagogy imply. Though culture provides the rationale for group cohesion, members tend, in reality, to be selective in their allegiances. Badillo (2006) dismisses a link between acquiring standard (spoken and written) English and cultural traits, but links the success of Asian students to an assumed cultural valuing of education, contradicting himself in the process. McWhorter's (2001) focus on Black underachievement reflects a similar bias. Yet these authorities' personal successes, no less than their criticisms of fellow minorities, presume human agency. Individuals, as well as entire cultural communities, make choices that have consequences (Appiah, 1992; Borjas, 1999).

On the other hand, nostalgic appeals to a bucolic past often mask disenchantment with existing structures. Because of inherent dynamism, cultures often lack clear demarcations of previous, present, and foreign norms. Africans have much to contend with: an overwhelming economic, cultural, and political developed world, growing populations and pressures on diminishing natural resources, charges of corruption and lack of transparency among nationals and the developed world, and so forth. Vestiges of colonial conceptions and practices linger on in postcolonial African countries. In reclaiming indigenous traditions and practices, scholars draw upon existing literary traditions most of which were (are) written by Europeans who still have greater command over publishing facilities. African immigrants acknowledge similar cultural trends in their home countries often with reservation. To the chagrin of older and more conservative relatives, youth are less restrained in promoting their interests at the expense of the group's influence over their lives and choice of careers. As with all youth across the globe, African children want good lives, fun, electronic gadgets, and personal space, elements long considered Western and foreign, and often overlooked by African immigrants to America, who see these traits only in American youth. Appeals to communitarian systems and extended families often reflect ideals rather than reality. Ethnic rhetoric presumes a cultural homogeneity that increasing intermarriages, relocations, and global communication networks defy. The African? The American? These are fleeting identities in a changing world.

Disparities in cultural priorities among teachers and students reflect primary experiences in homes and schools. Raised in communitarian arrangements—extended families and an emphasis on social obligations—many immigrant teachers value harmony often at the expense of assertiveness in social interactions. Respondents represented in *Immigrant Teachers, American Students: Cultural Differences, Cultural Disconnections* acknowledge the challenges they confront in their host country. Advocating conciliatory strategies to counter misunderstandings, respondents placed the onus of cultural accommodation on African teachers without making demands on students and institutions of learning. Classroom expectations of students may differ between domestic and immigrant teachers. The immigrant as cultural outsider is expected to assimilate into their host country (Oliveira et al., 2009). However, domestic teachers and students need to adapt to "foreign" norms to retain a competitive advantage in an increasingly globalized world.

Environmental factors shape students' level of preparedness as well as beliefs and behavior patterns in school settings but also in residential areas (Bateson, 2000; Borjas, 1999; Mori, 1997). Both Harris (1998) and Hemmings (2003) note how students growing up in physically and emotionally threatening environments, where the weak and deferential are easy game, adopt combative survival skills. But not all do. Ogbu (1992) also acknowledges the impact of cultural inversion: the view of education as a White thing has a negative impact on the choices of minority students. In the case of White youth, perceived threats from eroding privilege and overcompensation to minority interests create resentments and competition that strain classroom interactions. These influences shape interactions among students and teachers who represent or are perceived as representing different cultural groups. The success of minority students, however few, demonstrates that cultural factors are not deterministic in an individual's prospects. Students do not automatically succeed or fail academically because of belonging to either group. On the other hand, what constitutes adequate parental or social intervention? What about individual liberty and responsibility?

Minority students dominate in urban schools with dilapidated buildings, limited resources, and a greater percentage of teachers with provisional teaching licenses. Poor academic achievement in such settings reflects disparities in educational resources as much as race/ethnic academic capacities and students' political will. Some critics attribute the academic underachievement of minority students to structural biases in contrast to economically privileged Whites and some Asian students although Giroux (1988) views it as resistance to the disempowering school structure. The philosophical analysis ignores practical consequences of such choices. Students who can least afford to do so, graduate unequipped for an extremely competitive world, particularly in the labor market. Further, critics of alienating school environments point to the bias in curriculum and pedagogical strategies which reflect middle-class "traditions, linguistic patterns and lifestyles." In contrast, the call for culturally relevant pedagogy focuses on students' conceptual and operational skills; teachers integrate background knowledge from students' lived experience. Tatum (1997) advocates solidarity among students with similar (debilitating) experiences, particularly academic hurdles. But this raises the issue of cultural parochialism.

Globalization and increased migration introduce cosmopolitan practices into local cultures. That urban minority students mingle with classmates and teachers from different cultural orientations, and will compete against an even more culturally pluralistic labor force, raises the issue of what is culturally relevant. Global communication networks, most especially emerging social networks such as Facebook, LinkedIn, Twitter, and the blogsphere, create a youth culture that exhibits greater similarity across national borders. What is different today hardly remains so for long. That governors Arnold Schwarzenegger of California and Bobby Jindal of Louisiana, as well as the former U.N. Secretary General Kofi Annan, are household names or that President Barack Obama occupies the highest office in the United States shows a change in historical racial hierarchies. African immigrants, whether as teachers, corporate employees, or missionaries in the United States are a radical break from previous trends when Europeans streamed southward as the cultural experts. Further, U.S. citizens working in foreign countries consistently confront cross-cultural practices. Schools should offer forums for cultural exchanges and adaptations by highlighting the cross-cultural challenges of disparities in social definitions and expectations. Silence on the impact of cultural imperialism reinforces prevailing social hierarchies. The challenge is for American students to engage other groups as "autonomous" Others rather than exclusive cultural idiosyncrasies (Appiah, 1992). Appiah urges African-American students to explore "the space of cultural politics... (and) resist facile reductions of modern African cultural groups" (p. 70). As various scholars acknowledge, cultural dissonance emerges from an individual's entry into unfamiliar environments whether those of class, physical relocations in and beyond national borders, gender domains, age, language, and so on. (Bateson, 2000; Giroux, 2005, 2008; hooks, 2008; hooks and mesa-bains, 2006; Mori, 1997; Shor, 1996). Each compels a renegotiation of familiar habits and practices with primary norms serving as reference points; in essence, both teachers and students accommodate each other's idiosyncrasies voluntarily or begrudgingly. Critical pedagogy exposes students to the "spirit of debate and analysis... for students to learn how to theorize, while affirming and interrogating the voices through which students speak, learn and struggle" (Giroux, 1988, p. 67).

Over and above conventional cultural nights offering an array of traditional garb, food, and activities, schools can create forums to address prevailing stereotypes of represented groups such as Italians, Mexicans, Japanese, Africans, Jews, Muslims, Caribbeans, and so forth. (Florence, 2009). Acknowledging the impact of negative stereotypes on students' performance and classroom interactions enhances self-understanding and empathy. At the least, the dialogue creates awareness if not outright change in attitudes and behavior. The class discussion on the aversion to public displays of intimacy in India shocked my students. Students could appreciate the difference but also arbitrariness of cultural norms and individual responsibility in reinforcing debilitating practices exemplified in xenophobic racial, gender, or religious rhetoric. Teacher-led discussions on what constitutes appropriate classroom behavior allows students and teachers insight into differing perceptions of events and role expectations. Giroux (2005, 2008) and Nord (2000) caution against the uncritical acceptance of the authority of experience. Introducing students to oppositional texts broadens personal experiences even as it challenges accepted truths or familiar habits as normative (Giroux, 2005, 2008). Nord (2000) expects teachers to expose students to opposing views, fairly. The looming question is, Who decides what is fair? Nord entangles himself in the debate of equal representation even as he acknowledges the dominance of influential voices and ultimately, a teacher's choice. Relying on traditional texts as critical theorists contend overlooks historically excluded voices (Apple, 1992, 1996; Giroux, 2005, 2008; Glazer, 2001).

Society

In their research on Islamophobia in the United States and the West, Gottschalk and Greenberg (2008) as well as Jackson (2010) root the historical and conventional vilification of Islam to ongoing political and economic contests. That Islam and Arabs are portrayed as the Other to Christianity, modernity, and democracy is no accident. In early 622 C.E. Mohammad, the founder of Islam, moved to Medina and established a state, assuming the functions of leader, including military operations. Medina Muslims also grew economically as they took on nations and travelers for material booty. Mohammad's religious and economic legacy, specifically Arabic solidarity, extended beyond his life. The group displaced the formidable Byzantines who "dominated the Mediterranean Sea for centuries." Paradoxically, both groups attributed success to the prominence of their gods. If one's god granted victory then a counterforce explained failure. The Christian Crusades drew upon a similar logic. Gottschalk and Greenberg attribute subsequent conflicts to disparities in political power and economic wealth rather than religious identities as the driving force. In a characteristic pendulum swing that would continue in years to come, the Crusaders captured Constantinople in 1204 only for it to be retaken by the Turks in 1453. Consider the imperial changes in Afghanistan politics—British, Russians, and now the United States. The rise of European imperialism in the nineteenth century arose from dominance in science, economics, and the military. In addition, conquered nations drawn to the Western ideology of supremacy reinforced their own subjugation although not always explicitly or willingly. Opponents to Western ideology emerged as "backward, traditional and regressive" relative to the emerging European norms (Gottschalk and Greenberg, 2008).

Today, more than 1.2 billion identify themselves as Muslims with a majority residing in South and Southeast Asia—Indonesia, Pakistan, India, and Bangladesh—rather than the Middle East, although the media focuses on anti-Americanism in the latter. In addition, the silence on religious interactions and interrelationships among Judaic, Christian, and Islamic theologies build on perceptions of religious dualism. Islamic achievements in economics and literacy have been superseded in the twentieth and twenty-first centuries by negative Islamic portrayals due to Western policies of Soviet containment, oil, Zionism, and fears of terrorism (Gottschalk and Greenberg, 2008).

Calls for cross cultural/religious pluralism are undermined by dualistic portrayals of complicated global relations:

> A large proportion of Americans rely on the mass media for news of the world, but this collection of news and entertainment agencies operates under most of the same ingrained perspectives as their audiences. Their

reporting reinforces these views, challenging them only at the risk of losing popularity, ratings, and commercial success. Political cartoons also reflect many of these perspectives as they too are edited and selected by the same system. (Gottschalk and Greenberg, 2008, p. 8)

Raising a similar concern, Jackson (2010) maintains that media focuses on the "exceptional over the ordinary" in associating Muslims with terrorism (p. 7). Despite the range in experiences of Muslims across the world, media consistently portray the group as a national threat. Mainstream vilification of the Other legitimizes biases against the group and reinforces representations of the defining groups as the norm. Gottschalk and Greenberg contrast cartoons of masculinity in Islamic men as "malevolent and uncontrollable—as opposed to positive directions such as heroism and protectiveness" (p. 101). "Exotic" and "Oriental" Muslim women are "either teasingly clad or tantalizingly covered" (p. 106). In terms of morality, Muslims are portrayed as either "moral militants" or "sensually insatiable" (p. 108):

> Whether one views representations in contemporary U.S. media as directly educational to youth, or as more reflective of common beliefs and attitudes deemed acceptable or normal in mainstream society, it remains clear that controversial minorities are vulnerable to stereotyping in this domain that has at least an indirect influence on young people and that must, therefore, be taken into account by multicultural educators as partly constitutive of students' background knowledge and experience. (Jackson, 2010, p. 3)

Jackson argues that stereotypical imagery of Muslims makes them "vulnerable to prejudice and discrimination in the public sphere" (p. 6). It is understandable that teachers such as Ahmad avoid speaking about religion or their Islamic identity in U.S. classrooms. Reinforcing existing cultural misapprehension, the destruction of the World Trade towers heightened religious tensions between the West and Islamic countries. In general September 11, 2001 justified, for many, the negative portrayal of Muslim Americans. Sledge (2010) attributes the xenophobic selectivity in the opposition to the Islamic Center in New York to disingenuousness and factual inaccuracy. Jackson (2010) stresses the impact of stories on impressionable youth for whom distinctions between fantasy and reality are blurred.

Mainstream discourse on culture focuses on marginalized groups and values within society. Whether it is a construction of whiteness, gender, or class, a dominant group creates a hierarchy that normalizes its experience and meanings, albeit, at the expense of the other. In contrast, Achebe (2009) and Morrison (1993) highlight the impact of social hierarchies on those who hold, resist, explore, or alter these notions. Morrison illustrates the reliance of social constructions on "the mind, imagination, and behavior of masters" (p. 12). While the choice offers reprieve from a seemingly divided self, it suppresses what a defining master considers undesirable, limiting, vulnerable, or blinding. Besides stumping growth, the denial leads to further neurosis. Social hierarchies dog relationships in public no less than in private spheres. A capitalistic patriarchy still limits the political and economic advances of women and Blacks in the United States (Bateson, 2000; Morrison, 1993; hooks and mesa-bains, 2006).

Differences in perceptions of what is right or appropriate occur even within families. Intermarriages compel cultural exchanges as much as the blurring of traditionally distinct categories of race/ethnicity, nationality, or cultural practices. United States citizens participate in cultural rituals including St. Patrick's Day or Caribbean parades no less than Christmas celebrations with its gift-giving trend. Mother's Day, an event initially unique to the United States, is celebrated in countries beyond its borders. Chinese takeouts or Mexican burritos are as commonplace as apple pie in the United States. That "White men like Buddy Holly learned from Black jazz musicians" dispels the belief of "rhythm [as] a racial characteristic" (Bateson, 2000, p. 90). The "unthinkable" becomes conventional with time. Cultural pluralism in United States public schools demonstrates the convergence of cultures and a need for cultural adaptation at the individual and social level. Huntington (2004) captures the essence of immigration: "The more people who bring to America different languages, religions, and customs, the more American America becomes" (p. 363). The same applies to cultural changes on the African continent.

While African immigrant teachers view certain forms of "assertiveness" as narcissistic individualism in other cultures, these habits appear across the globe; Africa is no exception (Bateson, 2000). Besides sanctioning cultural rhetoric, nostalgic appeals to the "African way" undermines relations with U.S. students whose choices reflect their lived reality (Uwah, 2003). The increase in global communication networks, migrations, education prospects, and growth of a middle class in African communities contributes to the erosion of parochial value systems. There, too, youth are more independent, materialistic, and hedonistic than elders approve of (Kweyu, 2008). The experiences of cosmopolitan Kenyans differ significantly from people who lived in the early 1950s, or current rural residents in relatively isolated communities. Bucolic appeals to the "good ole days" reflect a growing ambivalence toward changing cultural norms across the globe. Youth no less than adults confront different languages, wrestle to decipher unfamiliar gestures, question alternative conceptions of reality, national identity, and, recently, worry about climate changes from exposure to ideas across the globe, no thanks to mass media. Frequently, nature provides reminders of how the local impacts global events. In mid-April, the Eyjafjallajökull's eruption in Iceland sent up fumes as high as six kilometers. The volcanic eruption disrupted the world's aviation system with many European countries such as the U.K., the Netherlands, Germany, Ireland, and France closing down their airspaces. As noted earlier, the IATA estimates a loss of S1.7 billion. Passengers got stuck across the globe. About 2,000 Belgians were stuck in Egypt and Tunisia. About 3,000 French tourists were left in various destinations. Kenya's fresh fruit, vegetables, and flowers took a financial hit too. The volcanic eruption led to airport closures, waste of fresh produce, and flowers amounting to an estimated $12 million financial loss to the industry. In general, reality trumps perceptions. If shared experiences and symbols shape cultural identities, claims of "American" or "African" presume a fleeting norm. In an overwhelmingly connected world—physically and in cyberspace—youth exhibit greater similarity in tastes and information than they do with other members of their country of birth.

Individuals choose to either cling to fading cultural elements and the myth of cultural stability or embrace the inevitable in confronting a precarious future becoming "prisoners of the past." As bodies age so does knowledge (Bateson, 2000). To borrow the late Howard Zinn's apt summation; it is hard to stand still on a moving train. The Igbo saying, "He who doesn't like it in Owerri, should relocate" cautions African immigrants against cultural parochialism (Uwah, 2002, p. 18).

Notwithstanding increasing percentages of children from cross-cultural intermarriages, defensive cultural parochialism is impractical in the twenty-first century. Harassment and honor killings of females primarily due to public displays of intimacy in countries such as Jordan or India are undermined by mass media, migrations, and global cyber-links. Responses to premarital romances range from raised eyebrows to harassment across African communities. How viable will such restrictions to "indecent displays" or cross-gender interactions be when youth communicate in a language which most elders are ignorant of or unfamiliar with? Cultural exchanges in schools, workplaces, and communities expose students to cosmopolitan norms and rituals. Appiah's (2006) dismissal of campaigns by cultural purists is a poignant reminder of the inevitability of cultural adaptations. Tatum (1997) cautions against waiting for the perfect moment to intervene: fostering critical awareness breaks the silence on cultural biases.

Schools

Despite historical antecedents of limited access to education for minority racial groups in the United States, simplistic portrayals of cultural groups denies each group the moral responsibility for shaping history, and, at the classroom level, an awareness of the transformative power of educational experiences (hooks, 1994, 2003). Students interact with classmates who differ from them in language, religious affiliation, and social class as well as tastes in food and clothing. Socialized in particular value structures, teachers no less than students interact with colleagues and students alike despite differing expectations. Human interactions compel individuals into cultural adaptations on a daily basis; students and teachers alike adapt to or disengage from unfamiliar beliefs and behavior patterns. Changing one's tone of voice or speech patterns during verbal exchanges is not always a conscious process. But we do it. I recall moments of searching for an "American" phrase to express a sentiment in order to break through a frustrating exchange. While schools privilege middle-class traditions, linguistic patterns, and lifestyles, schools also expose students to norms and practices beyond the particulars of family or community frameworks that challenge Whites no less than minority students (Appiah, 1992; Bateson, 2000; hooks, 2008; Martin, 2007). For their part, African immigrant teachers live with an enduring apprehension of missing a dance step in a choreographed piece, unlike former colonials who operated with the confidence of a winner among the spoils (Bateson, 2000; Fast, 2000). Ahmad identifies three issues as crucial to African immigrant teachers: "Command of the subject area; Patience; and Accept the student within a teacher-student relationship. Their rights are protected by the legal system." As an immigrant from a developing country to a developed nation, Ahmad is aware of playing a secondary role in social interactions, compelled to assimilate the host country's norms and practices—the language is different, food, people's mannerisms, job demands, and so forth. The angst arises from an immigrant nature of second-guessing themselves. What impact do students' negative course evaluations have on one's job security? What if I am overstepping boundaries? What if I am saying something that could be misconstrued as unpatriotic, a political (terrorist) threat, or anti-American? Consider the issue of political correctness. There never is a clear-cut list of what it constitutes until one stumbles into it. Given the global paranoia of terrorist threats, there is always the fear that whom one supports at home could implicate them in suspect activities. What if an association or individual or family one sends money to or even through, ends up on a terrorist watch list? It makes an individual immigrant the ally to disputable ends. Travels to the mother country and back add to the anxiety among immigrants. What if immigration and customs officials deny entry to an individual returning to the United States? In addition, African leaders have a habit of fingering opponents as terrorists, consistently portraying political opponents as a disgruntled minority. Overall, African immigrants worry about food, shelter, and clothing similar to any other resident in the United States. Juggling balls? What adds to the burden is that during any one period, the balls change in size and number.

Fast contrasts the admiration of his students for the West to the negative stereotypes among expatriates associating "horror stories about travel in the 'dark continent,'" to the conventional "Welcome to Africa," sentiments (p. 101). As far back as the colonial era, Africans embraced an imperial curriculum reflecting whiteness as superior and desirable (Achebe, 2009). Dingane cautions African immigrant teachers in the United States to brace themselves against stereotypes, the inevitable cultural shock, and having to face a challenging work environment:

a. Stereotype: Most Americans view Africa as backward and with an illiterate population, so it takes a while for an African immigrant teacher to break that stereotype.
b. Cultural Shock: They should be prepared for a cultural shock in the classrooms, different teaching methods, short semesters, arrogant students, etc.
c. Work environment: Colleagues are sometimes very aloof and unhelpful. Some may not even want to socialize with you or publish joint papers.

Effective or affective? In daily interactions, teachers and students negotiate academic milestones; immigrant teachers try to capture and retain students' attention as well as elicit participation in which students comply or resist. Overriding daily negotiations are state and federal standards as well as standardized tests; academic years have start and end dates and specific subject matter at each grade level limits teachers to specific tasks and classroom objectives (Giroux, 1988). This adds to the complexity of the situations. Each country has its priorities despite similarities in calls for an educated citizenry. Each designs assessment procedures that shape learning practices: distinct cultural goalposts. Students fail or pass a class based on a prescribed measure of academic success. Playing by the rules, African immigrant teachers attend to such demands with less flexibility than some American-born students desire or are accustomed to. Working away in the faculty computer center recently, I listened with some apprehension to a colleague's recount of serving pizza at a make-up class the previous week, and offering Dukin' Donuts that morning during an in-class test. She was disturbed that the students did not eat the donuts she brought in. They may have been more concerned about the test or the calories count in the food, I suggested. Reflecting W.E.B. Du Bois' faith in Black people's competence to counter racism in the 1960s, Yetunde focuses on professional competence to alleviate personal apprehensions:

Be on the cutting edge of your discipline
Be ready to work at least three times as hard as everyone else
Be confident and self-assured, and be comfortable with selling yourself as an expert in your field.

Meanwhile, Aminata advocates training teachers in classroom management. Teachers need to "be professional and have a good grasp of subject matter."

Amobi's (2004) cultural "bridge building" approach advocates clarification of classroom expectations as most syllabi attempt to do; stating policies, assignments, and repercussions for students' failure to deliver. Similarly, Baruti uses the rubrics in her syllabus both as guide and shield against students' complaints. Yet, with all good intentions, teachers can't provide for all eventualities in teacher/student interactions. Factual exchanges may amount to little where there is an emotional gap to be bridged, as the incident with Paula demonstrated. Arguments over who or what is right are generally futile in contentious relationships. Often confronting the misperceptions is a priority to further amicable exchanges: "[R]ace and history and metaphysics do not enforce an identity: that we can choose" (Appiah, 1992, p. 176).

The frustrations of African immigrant teachers reflect a need to understand U.S. students just as much as the desire to be a good teacher. Bashir focuses on common areas in the American and African educational systems:

1. Teaching and learning is serious business, not fun. African teachers have to make U.S. students understand this.
2. The social distance between teachers and students is not as great here as it is in West Africa.
3. Many "special ed." students are likely to be considered normal students by African teachers if the system can empower teachers to enforce discipline and parents can support teachers in the steps they take to enforce discipline.

While the process of cultural bridging takes time and commitment, it is not solely a teacher's responsibility (Appiah, 1992; Florence, 2009). Students can make or break a good teacher. As with most relationships, there is a give-and-take approach to problem-solving. Schools comprise diverse cultural groups, each of whose needs matter although none are met in their entirety. The cultural hierarchy (superior/inferior; immigrant/native; White/Black) hinders social interactions as the teaching/learning process. Both Wafula and Girikaze offer philosophical approaches to African immigrant teachers in the United States:

> First they need to know that this society is vastly different from African society. That there is no free lunch in the United States, that they will be viewed exotically by white Americans and with disdain by African-Americans. It is swim or sink. (Wafula)

Girikaze offers a three-point slogan:

> Discipline: Expect to be disrespected
> Language: Expect to be misunderstood
> Prejudice: Expect your knowledge to be questioned.

Differences in perceptions of reality and social expectations show the need for negotiations about what is most appropriate. Besides the inevitability of diversity, misinterpretations in social interactions reflect differences in cultural cues because teachers and students often perceive and respond to incidents based on primary experiences and beliefs. The challenge is to acknowledge the diversity in perspectives and social expectations in order to develop cross-cultural competencies. Making explicit the rationale for learning strategies such as the importance of tolerating difference in classrooms comprising students and teachers from different countries, religious beliefs, and ability levels is one such example. Delegating the choice of social definitions and cultural practices to authority figures (or official mandates) as traditional communities are wont to do absolves teachers and students of the responsibilities for creating settings in inclusive classes as well as societies. If someone else dictates what is right, individuals are reduced to the role of puppets in a system. No less demeaning is the portrayal of students as maligned victims. Students can be manipulative (Benton, 2009; Foster, 1997; Lake, 2009). They make choices that lead to bad consequences. They are responsible beings.

While Black scholars (hooks and mesa-bains, 2006; Tatum, 1997) underscore the role of racism, Harris (1998), Hemmings (2003), and Milner (2004) attribute students' choices and behavior patterns to the influence of peers. In their estimation, peer approval overrides parental injunctions. Peer groups within schools or neighborhoods exhibit particular values; they constitute a cultural group with defining structures of meaning. These groups often embrace values reflective of environments in which they operate. Students from wealthy or economically disadvantaged families will downplay their class affiliation if they are in the minority. Children adopt the language of their peers rather than that of the parents. The peer group's lure lies in its relevance as opposed to what students perceive as typically conservative parents. Teachers often highlight desirable achievements of individual students to challenge the rest; the attempts, although imperfect, interrupt a cycle of social exclusion (Tatum, 1997). Harris (1998) recognizes this as an effective strategy to foster desirable attributes through peer pressure. Grant (2001) and Putman (2001) extend the obligation to families and communities for greater social networks: "Projects that cross generational lines, that put new relationships with adults, are critical to refreshing the supply of social capital" (Grant, 2001, p. 116).

The focus on peers and cultural influences on students' behavior patterns reflects different locations, in this case, the priority of community versus individualistic interests, value for, rather than the dismissal of, educational pursuits, materialism, or views of cross-gender relationships. Individuals operate from a range of positions—race, class, gender, religion, nationality, physical ability, and so forth. These value structures and other differences between African immigrant teachers and American students complicate classroom interactions (Tatum, 1997; Traore and Lukens, 2006). Often, social conceptions and classroom expectations create friction and misunderstanding in daily interactions. The acknowledgment of cultural diversity within and across nation-states is fundamental to cultural bridging; the obverse is cultural parochialism and xenophobia. Teachers confront issues that reflect social problems. Students exhibit learned behaviors from homes or previous interactions, some of which amount to destructive learning habits. The lack of respect for adults, as well as the denigration of teachers and fellow students inhibits academic progress. For many immigrants these demands amount to an endless waiting game—waiting to settle in a new environment, understand American ways, waiting for the sense of belonging, and finally waiting to find the proper balance between the primary and the new culture. A simple exercise would be to ask students about situations they found alienating. How did it feel? What could they have done to ease the discomfort for all parties? What could the other party have done? Such discussions illustrate the inevitability of cross-cultural exchanges.

Despite the cultural rhetoric within and across nation-states, the reality is more nuanced with individuals embracing structures of meaning in host-country culture or exhibiting behavior patterns that are cosmopolitan in the homeland culture. That cultures are never static, uniform, or homogenous illustrates the dynamic nature of cultural identities. It also highlights the subjectivity of cultural definitions and perceptual locations which are always reductive. Ensconced in a culture, scholars, no less than teachers and students, are ambivalent about the legitimacy of any one structure over the alternatives. Absence from one's country of birth may make the heart grow fonder but it can also expose the blindness of loyalties. Whether in immigrants or natives to the land, claims to essentialist and bucolic cultural appeals border on wishful thinking. The possibility of complicity through assimilation is further heightened by the fact that individuals, in this case, African immigrant teachers, are drawn to various elements in the resident U.S. culture—freedom of expression and social mobility—but also repulsed by particular elements such as disrespectful youth and competitive individualism. This ambivalence is reflected in the teachers' choices and strategies of intervention to classroom breaches; students talk out of turn and yet class participation constitutes an important part of the grade while demonstrating a student's receptivity to learning. Further, students, much like teachers, are an evolving mystery; what works with a student in one particular incident may not be as successful in a different setting regardless of cultural identity; students change with age and through exposure. The center is perpetually redefined by its margins as "foreign" elements become "local." Cultural bridging goes beyond relating to a different other. Most important is the process of coming to terms with one's idiosyncrasies and living with this ambivalence in schools, but also in society.

Notes

Chapter 1   Endemic Racial Hierarchy

1. The system considers biracial children of non-White parents as non-White however light-skinned they may be in complexion.

Chapter 2   Comparative Overview of African and U.S. Society

1. Recent street protests contesting the 2007 presidential elections offer a glimpse of the impact of suppressed dissent among Kenyan youth. It is nothing new, as sporadic accounts of students' riots at the secondary as well as the university level indicate. On July 13, 1991 a mob of male students at St. Kizito Catholic Secondary School in Meru attacked their female classmates in a dormitory. Nineteen girls were killed and more than 70 gang-raped. The school's vice principal claimed that the "boys never meant any harm against the girls. They just wanted to rape." In January 1993, armed men attacked girls at Hawinga Girls' School in Siaya as they slept in their dormitories. Finally, on the night of July 7 1996, male students and villagers attacked and raped a number of girls at the Catholic-sponsored Mareira Secondary school in Muranga District. In the same year, three male teachers were implicated in the pregnancies of 12 students at Keveye Girls' Secondary School (Omale, 2000 cited in Kanga, 2004). These students' embrace of cultural hierarchies, in this case, sexism, and the respect for elders also reflects coercive power over vulnerable members. Across Kenya, evidence of dissenting voices against cultural hierarchies of gender, class and ethnic groups echo calls for more egalitarian structures in schools no less than society at large. Sporadic vandalism and acts of violence reflect years of repressed animosities in cultures that privilege harmony over open contention, tolerance over rebellion, and the value of the group over individual interests.

   A recent spate of school strikes coupled with arson attacks including loss of life led to school closings in the wake of the 2007 post-election violence. At the time some schools were closed for the Christmas holidays. Some schools opened late because of transport problems. A number of schools in the Gikuyu-dominated region of the Rift Valley did not open because most of the students had been displaced. The fracas involved about 254 schools and institutions of learning across the country. Prof. Sam Ongeri, the Minister for Education, attributed the disturbance to "fear of mock examinations; weak institutional management; political and other influences; drugs and substance abuses; misuse of mobile phones; and child abuse." In response, the Ministry developed "manuals for safety and peace" in educational settings. It also stepped up the training of teachers in "guidance and counseling" (Mwaniki, 2008, n.p.). The linear analysis of, and intervention in, social problems ignores the complexity of human behavior. All secondary schools have since established guidance and counseling services albeit with negligible impact. It is a question of overstretched resources.

Notwithstanding the fact that the strikes involved select schools, concern over disgruntled youth goes beyond school settings. Across the country, rogue gangs terrorize individuals and destroy or steal family property. Women's access to economic and political advances destabilizes the traditional gender hierarchy. Dorothy Kweyu (2008) attributes the lack of discipline among youth in homes and schools to parental pampering that idolizes offspring, turning them into "insufferable brats." It is payback time for Kenya, she notes. Social harmony is an ideal that most societies fall short of.

Chapter 4   Respect

1. Among the Bukusu, a Luhia sub-ethnic group in Kenya, communities forbade physical proximity between particular relations-in-law. The avoidance code (*bukhwe*) may have arisen out of a genuine need to avoid sexual intimacy in extremely close-knit families and physical spaces. Ironically, levirate marriages have been the norm, with sons inheriting the father's widow(s).

References

Abebe, T. (2003). "Close Encounters: A Pilgrimage of Penance and Expiation."*African Perspectives in American Higher Education: Invisible Voices*. Ed. F.E. Obiakor and J.U. Gordon. New York: Nova Science Publishers. 11–21.

Achebe, Chinua (2009). *The Education of a British-Protected Child: Essays*. New York: Alfred A. Knopf.

Aman, Mohammed (2002). Foreword. *African Perspectives in American Higher Education: Invisible Voices*. Ed. F.E. Obiakor and J.U. Gordon. New York: Nova Science Publishers. xi–xvii.

American Federation of Teachers (2009). *Importing Educators: Causes and Consequences of International Teacher Recruitment*. Washington, DC: International Affairs Department of the American Federation of Teachers. www.aft.org. Item no. 45–09002.

Amodi, F.A. (2004). "Crossing Borders: Reflections on the Professional Journey of a Teacher Educator in Diaspora." *International Education* 15.2: 166–178.

Appiah, K.A. (1992). *In My Father's House: Africa in the Philosophy of Culture*. New York: Oxford University Press.

——— (2006). "The case for contamination." *New York Times Magazine* 1 Jan. 2006: 30–52.

Apple, Michael W. (1992). *Cultural and Economic Reproduction in Education: Essays on Class, Ideology and the State*. Boston: Routledge & Kegan Paul.

——— (1996). *Cultural Politics and Education*. New York: Teachers College Press.

——— (2006). "Critical Education, Politics, and the Real World." *Ideology, Curriculum, and the New Sociology of Education: Revisiting the Work of Michael Apple*. Ed. Lois Weis, Cameron McCarthy, and Greg Dimitriadis. New York: Routledge. 219–249.

——— (2008). "Patriotism, Pedagogy, and Freedom: On the Educational Meanings of September 11." *The Critical Pedagogy Reader*. Ed. Antonia Darder, Marta P. Baltodano, and Rodolfo D. Torres. 2nd ed. New York: Routledge. 491–500.

Arnot, M. (2006). Retrieving the Ideological Past: Critical Sociology, Gender Theory, and the School Curriculum. *Ideology, Curriculum, and the New Sociology of Education: Revisiting the Work of Michael Apple*. Ed. Lois Weis, Cameron McCarthy, and Greg Dimitriadis. New York: Routledge. 17–37.

Badillo, H. (2006). *One Nation, One Standard: An Ex-liberal on How Hispanics Can Succeed Just Like Other Immigrant Groups.* New York: Sentinel.

Bateson, M.C. (2000). *Full Circles, Overlapping Lives: Culture and Generation in Transition.* New York: Random House.

Benton, Thomas F. (2009). "Hell's Classroom: What Faculty Members Can Learn from Gordon Ramsay." *The Chronicles of Higher Education* 55.32: A39, A41.

Bhabha, H.K. (1996). "Culture's In-Between." *Questions of Cultural Identity.* Ed. H. Stuart and P. Du Gay London: SAGE Publications. 53–60.

Blaut, J.M. (1993). *The Colonizer's Model of the World: Geographical Diffusion and Eurocentric History.* London: The Guilford Press.

Borjas, George J. (1999). *Heaven's Door: Immigration Policy and the American Economy.* Princeton: Princeton University Press.

Breland, Alfiee M. (1998). "A Model for Differential Perceptions of Competence Based on Skin Tone Among African-Americans." *Journal of Multicultural Counseling and Development* 26.4: 294–311.

Brophy, J. (1999). "Perspectives of Classroom Management: Yesterday, Today, and Tomorrow." *Beyond Behaviorism: Changing the Classroom Management Paradigm.* Ed. H. J. Freiberg. Boston: Allyn and Bacon. 43–56.

Bureau of Labor Statistics (2010). "Labor Force Characteristics of Foreign-Born Workers Summary." 19 Mar. 2010. United States Department of Labor. www.bls.gov. Retrieved 21 April 21, 2010.

Butcher, Kristin F. (1994). "Black Immigrants in the United States: A Comparison with Native Blacks and Other Immigrants," *Industrial & Labor Relations Review* 47.2: 265–284.

Carter, R.T., and A.L. Goodwin, eds. (1994). "Racial Identity and Education." *Review of Research in Education* 20: 291–336.

Carlson, D. (2006). "Are We Making Progress? Ideology, and Curriculum in the Age of No Child Left Behind." *Ideology, Curriculum, and the New Sociology of Education: Revisiting the Work of Michael Apple.* Ed. Lois Weis, Cameron McCarthy, and Greg Dimitriadis. New York: Routledge. 91–114.

Casimir, Leslie. "In America, Data Show Nigerians Are the Most Educated Immigrants." *Naijanet.com.* 27 May 2007. http://naijanet.com/news/source/2008/may/27/1000.html. Accessed 11 Sept. 2009.

Clifford, S. (2010). "Scissors, glue, pencils? Check. Cleaning spray?" *New York Times.* 15 August, 2010: 1, 4.

Clignet, Remi P. and Philip J. Foster (1964). "French and British Colonial Education in Africa." *Comparative Education Review* 8.2: 191–198.

Cohen, E.G. (1994). *Designing Groupwork: Strategies for the Heterogeneous Classroom.* New York: Teachers College Press.

Damon, William (2001). "To Not Fade Away: Restoring Civil Identity Among the Young." *Making Good Citizens: Education and Civil Society.* Ed. Diane Ravitch and Joseph P. Vieritti. New Haven: Yale University Press. 122–141.

Daniels, R. (2004). *Guarding the Golden Door: American Immigration Policy and Immigrants Since 1882.* New York: Hill and Wang.

Davis, Thomas J. and Azubike Kalu-Nwiwu. (2001). "Education, Ethnicity and National Integration in the History of Nigeria: Continuity Problems of Colonial Legacy." *The Journal of Negro History*. 86.1: 1–11.
De Oliveira, Ebenezer A., Jennifer L. Braun, Taryn L. Carlson, and Stephanie G. de Oliveira (2009). "Students' Attitudes toward Foreign-Born and Domestic Instructors." *Journal of Diversity in Higher Education* 2.20: 113–125.
Delpit, L.D. (1988). "The Silenced Dialogue: Power and Pedagogy in Educating Other People's Children." *Harvard Educational Review* 58.3: 280–298.
––––––– (1995). "The Silenced Dialogue: Power and Pedagogy in Educating Other People's Children." *Other People's Children: Cultural Conflict in the Classroom*. New York: New Press.
DeVita, P.R. and J.D. Armstrong, eds. (1993). *Distant Mirrors: America as a Foreign Culture*. Belmont, CA: Wadsworth Inc.
Dillon, Sam (2009). "Schools Look Abroad to Hire Teachers." *New York Times* 15 Sept. 2009: A6.
Dodoo, F. Nii-Amoo (1997). "Assimilation Differences among Africans in America." *Social Forces* 76.2: 527–546.
––––––– and Baffour K. Takyi (2006). "Africans in the Diaspora: Black-White Earnings Differences among African-Americans." *The New African Diaspora in North America: Trends, Community Building and Adaptation*. Ed. Kwadwo Konadu Agyemang, Baffour K. Takyi, and John A. Arthur. Lanham, MD: Lexington Books. 168-188.
Drechsel, E.J. (1993). "A European Anthropologist's Personal and Ethnographic Impressions of the United States." *Distant Mirrors: America as a Foreign Culture*. Ed. P.R. DeVita and J.D. Armstrong. Belmont, CA: Wadsworth Inc. 120–145.
Dussart, F. (1993). "First Impressions: Diary of a French Anthropologist in New York City." *Distant Mirrors: America as a Foreign Culture*. Ed. P.R. DeVita and J.D. Armstrong. Belmont, CA: Wadsworth Inc. 66–76.
Duster, Troy (2009). "The Long Path to Higher Education for African-Americans." *Thought & Action* 25: 99–101.
Eckholm, Eric and Katie Zezima (2010). "Questions for School on Bullying and a Suicide." *New York Times* 2 Apr. 2010: A1, A3.
Elbaz-Luwisch, F. (2004). "Immigrant Teachers: Stories of Self and Place." *International Journal of Qualitative Studies in Education* 17.3: 387–414.
Fast, Gerald R. (2000). "'Africa, my Teacher!': An Expatriate's Perspectives on Teaching Mathematics in Zimbabwe." *Anthropology & Education Quarterly* 31.1: 90–102.
Florence, Namulundah (2009). *Multiculturalism 101*. New York: McGraw-Hill.
Fogg, P. (2009). "Losing Sleep Over Tuition: For One Family, Multiple Jobs and Scrimping Pave the Way to Community College." *Chronicles of Higher Education* 27 Mar. 2009: B14–15.
Freud, Sigmund (1918). *Totem and Taboo*. Trans. A.A. Brill (1946). New York: Random House.

Foster, M. (1997). *Black Teachers on Teaching*. New York: The New Press.
Fox, Stuart (2010). "Which U.S. State Has the Most Immigrants?" *Yahoo! News* 28 Apr. 2010. http://news.yahoo.com/s/livescience/20100428/sc_livescience/whichstatehasthemostim.
Freiberg, H. Jerome, ed. (1999). *Beyond Behaviorism: Changing the Classroom Management Paradigm*. Boston: Allyn and Bacon.
Gay, G. (2000). *Culturally Responsive Teaching: Theory, Research, & Practice*. New York: Teacher's College Press.
Genova, James E. (2004). "Conflicted Missionaries: Power and Identity in French West Africa during the 1930s." *Historian Special Issue on Imperialism* 22 Mar. 2004. 26.1: 56–79.
Genor, M., and A.L. Goodwin, eds. (2005). "Confronting Ourselves: Using Autobiographical Analysis in Teacher Education." *New Educator* 1: 311–331.
Gettlemen, Jeffrey (2010). "With Flights Grounded, Kenya's Produce Wilts." *New York Times* 19 Apr. 2010: A1.
Giroux, Henry (2008). "Teacher Education and Democratic Schooling." *The Critical Pedagogy Reader*. Ed. Antonia Darder, Marta P. Baltodano, and Rodolfo D. Torres. 2nd ed. New York: Routledge. 438–459
——— (2005). "Border Crossings: Cultural Workers and the Politics of Education." *The Critical Pedagogy Reader*. Ed. Antonia Darder, Marta P. Baltodano, and Rodolfo D. Torres. 2nd ed. New York: Routledge.
——— (1988). *Schooling and the Struggle for Public Life: Critical Pedagogy in the Modern Age*. Minneapolis: University of Minnesota Press.
Glazer, Nathan (2001). "Some Problems in Acknowledging Diversity." *Making Good Citizens: Education and Civil Society*. Ed. Diane Ravitch and Joseph P. Vieritti. New Haven: Yale University Press. 168–186.
Goodson, Ivor F. and Pat Sikes (2001). *Life History Research in Educational Settings: Learning From Lives*. Philadelphia: Open University Press.
Gottschalk, Peter and Gabriel Greenberg (2008). *Islamophobia: Making Muslims the Enemy*. New York: Rowland & Littlefield Publishers.
Grant, Gerald (2001). "Fluctuations of Social Capital in an Urban Neighborhood." *Making Good Citizens: Education and Civil Society*. Ed. Diane Ravitch and Joseph P. Vieritti. New Haven: Yale University Press. 96–112.
Gross, T. (1994). "Black Africans Now the Most Educated Group in British Society." *The Journal of Blacks in Higher Education* 3: 92–93.
Grossberg, L. (1996). "Identity and Cultural Studies—Is That All There Is?" *Questions of Cultural Identity*. Ed. Stuart, H. and P. Du Gay. London: SAGE Publications. 87–107.
Gwalla-Ogisi, N. (2003). "Surviving the 'Killing Zones' of Higher Education." *African Perspectives in American Higher Education: Invisible Voices*. Ed. Obiakor, F. E., and J.U. Gordon. New York: Nova Science Publishers. 23–34.
Hash (2008). "The $20 Billion African Remittance Market." http://whiteafrican.com/2008/02/08/the-20-billion-african-remittance-market/ 8 Feb. 2008.
Harkau, L., K.M. Losey, and M. Siegal (1999). *Generation 1.5 Meets College Composition: Issues in the Teaching to U.S.-Educated Learners of ESL*. Mahwah, NJ: Lawrence Erlbaum Associates.

Harris, George W. (1997). *Dignity and Vulnerability: Strength and Quality of Character.* Berkeley, CA: University of California Press.

Harris, J.R. (1998). *The Nurture Assumption: Why Children Turn Out the Way They Do.* New York: The Free Press.

Heath, S.B. (1983). *Ways with Words: Language, Life, and Work in Communities and Classrooms.* Cambridge: Cambridge University Press.

Hemmings, A. (2003). "Fighting for Respect in Urban High Schools." *Teachers College Record,* 105.3: 416–437.

Herbert, Bob (2005). "A New Civil Rights Movement." *New York Times* 26 Dec. 2005: A31.

Holmes, Mark (2001). "Education and Citizenship in an Age of Pluralism." *Making Good Citizens: Education and Civil Society.* Ed. Diane Ravitch and Joseph P. Vieritti. New Haven: Yale University Press. 187–212.

hooks, bell (2008). Confronting class. *The Critical Pedagogy Reader.* Ed. Antonia Darder, Marta P. Baltodano, and Rodolfo D. Torres. 2nd ed. New York: Routledge. New York: Routledge. 135–143.

hooks, b. (2003). *Teaching Community: A Pedagogy of Hope.* New York: Routledge.

——— (1994). *Teaching to Transgress: Education as the Practice of Freedom.* New York: Routledge.

hooks, b. and a. mesa-bains (2006). *Homegrown: Engaged Cultural Criticism.* Cambridge, MA: South End Press.

Huntington, Samuel P. (2004). *Who Are We? The Challenges to America's National Identity.* New York: Simon & Schuster.

Hu, W. (2007). "The Original Subprime Crisis." *New York Times* 26 Dec. 2007: A31.

International Association of Universities (2010). *International Handbook of Universities.* London: Palgrave MacMillan.

Jackson, Liz (2010). "Images of Islam in U.S. Media and their Educational Implications." *Educational Studies* 46: 3–24.

Jacobs, Jonathan (1995). *Practical Realism and Moral Psychology.* Washington, DC: Georgetown University Press.

Janofsky, M. (2005). "Some New Help for the Extremely Gifted Students." *New York Times* 26 Oct. 2005: B9.

Jordan, Miriam (2010). "Arizona Grades Teachers on Fluency: State Pushes School Districts to Reassign Instructors with Heavy Accents or Other Shortcomings in Their English." *Wall Street Journal* 30 Apr. 2010: A3.

Judson, G. (1993). "A Pattern of Increasing Student Segregation." *New York Times* 10 Jan. 1993: 30.

The Journal of Blacks in Higher Education (1999–2000). "African Immigrants in the United States Are the Nation's Most Highly Educated Group," *The Journal of Blacks in Higher Education* 26: 60–61. Doc1:10.2307/2999156.

Kaba, Amadu Jacky (2007). "Educational Attainment, Income Levels and Africans in the United States: The Paradox of Nigerian Immigrants." *West Africa Review* 11. http://www.westafricareview.com/issue11/kaba.html)

Kamotho, A.K. (2008). "Reward System for Politicians and Public Servants Flawed." *Sunday Nation* 11 Apr. 2008. http://www.nationmedia.com/dailynation/nmgontententry.asp?category_id=25&newsid=120897.

Kanga, Anne (2004). "Taboo Subject Boldly Bared: A Feminist Analysis of Sexual Harassment as a Major Hindrance to Learning Among High School Girls in Kenya". *Research On Education in Africa, the Caribbean, and the Middle East: An Historical Overview.* Ed. Kagendo Mutua and Cynthia Szmanski Sunal. Greenwich, CT: Information Age Publishing. 33–57.

Kantor, H. and B. Brenzel (1992). "Urban Education and the 'Truly Disadvantaged': The Historical Roots of the Contemporary Crisis, 1945–1990." *Teachers College Record* 94.2: 277–314.

Keith, Verna M. and Cedric Herring (1991). "Skin Tone and Stratification in the Black Community." *American Journal of Sociology* 97.3: 760–778.

Kibui, Rachel (2010). "A Million Kenyan Pupils Out of School: Study." *Nation on the Web* 4 Feb. 2010. http://www.nation.co.ke/News/regional/-/1070/856014/-/8pi7xt/-/index.html.

Kim, J.K. (1993). "American Graffiti: Curious Derivatives of Individualism." *Distant Mirrors: America as a Foreign Culture.* Ed. P.R. DeVita and J.D. Armstrong. Belmont, CA: Wadsworth Inc. 11–20.

Kimmelman, Michael (2010). "Pardon My French: The Globalization of a Language." *New York Times* 25 Apr. 2010: AR 1, 21.

Kincheloe, Joe L. and Weil, Danny (eds.) (2001). Standards and Schooling in the United States: An Encyclopedia. Santa Barbara, California: ABC-CLIO.

Konneh, A. (2003). "My Brother's Teachers: An African at the Vanguard of American Higher Education." *African Perspectives in American Higher Education: Invisible Voices.* Ed. F.E. Obiakor and J.U. Gordon. New York: Nova Science Publishers. 89–95.

Koross, Kibiwott (2009). "Father of Six in High School." *Kenya Nation on the Web* 16 Sept. 2009. http://www.nation.co.ke/News/-/1056/659278/-/umw0q1/-/index.html.

Kozol, Jonathan (1991). *Savage Inequalities: Children in America's Schools.* New York: Crown Publishers.

——— (1995). *Amazing Grace: The Lives of Children and the Conscience of a Nation.* New York: Crown Publishers.

Kreiger, Daniel (2009). "Lives: A Weighty Matter, Coming to Terms with Apparent Insults in Japan." *New Times Magazine* 30 Aug. 2009: 50.

Kweyu, D. (2008). "We Idolised Our Offspring; Now They Are Insufferable Brats." *Daily Nation* 12 Oct. 2008. http://www.nationmedia.com/dailynation.co.ke/oped/Opinion/-/440808/479724/-/31xif5/-/index.html.

Ladson-Billings, G. (1995a). "But That's Just Good Teaching! The Case for Culturally Relevant Pedagogy. *Theory and Practice* 34.3: 159–164

——— (1995b). "Toward a Cuturally Relevant Pedagogy." *American Educational Research Journal* 32.3: 465–491.

——— (2001). *Crossing Over to Canaan: The Journey of New Teachers in Diverse Classrooms.* San Francisco: Jossey-Bass.

Lane, K.L., J. Wheby, and C. Cooley (2006). "Teacher Expectations of Students' Classroom Behavior across the Grade Span: Which Social Skills Are Necessary for Success?" *Exceptional Children* 75.2: 153–167.

Lake, Peter F. (2009). "Student Discipline: The Case against Legalistic Approaches." *Chronicles of Higher Education,* 55.32: A31–A32.
Levin, Elise C. (2000). "Women's Childbearing Decisions in Guinea: Life Course Perspectives and Historical Change." *Africa Today* 47.3/4: 63–81.
Lewin, Tamar (2010). "Citing Individualism, Arizona Tries to Rein in Ethnic Studies in School." *New York Times* May 14, 2010: A13.
Li, G. and G.H. Beckett (2006). *"Strangers" of the Academy: Asian Women Scholars in Higher Education.* Sterling, VA: Stylus.
Lawrence-Lightfoot, Sara (1999). *Respect: An Exploration.* Reading, MA: Perseus Books.
Logan, John and Glenn Black Dean (2003). "Diversity in Metropolitan America." (*2000 Census Data Report,* Lewis Mumford Center for Comparative Urban and Regional Research February 17, 2003. (revised August 15, 2003). http://www.s4.brown.edu/cen2000/BlackWhite/BlackDiversityReport/black-diversity01.htm
LoTiempo, S.M. (2005). "A ticket to bias." *New York Times.* 7 October, 2005: http://query.nytimes.com/gst/fullpage.html?sec=health&res=9802E6D81E30F934A35753C1A9639C8B63&partner=rssnyt&emc=rss
Mathaai, Wangari Matu (2007). *Unbowed.* New York: Anchor Books.
Martin, J.R. (2002). *Cultural Miseducation: In Search of a Democratic Solution.* New York: Teachers College Press.
——— (2007). *Educational Metamorphoses: Philosophical Reflections on Identity and Culture.* New York: Rowan & Little Publishers.
McCarthy, C. (1990). *Race and Curriculum: Social Inequality and the Theories of Difference in Contemporary Research in Schooling.* London: The Falmer Press.
McCarthy, C., and W. Crichlow, eds. (1993). *Race, Identity and Representation in Education.* New York: Routledge.
McCarthy, C., W. Crichlow, G. Dimitriadis, and N. Dolby eds. (2005). *Race, Identity, and Representation in Education.* New York: Routledge.
McCourt, Frank (2005). *Teacher Man: A Memoir.* New York: Scribner.
McEwan, B., P. Gathercoal, and V. Nimmo (1999). "Applications of Judicious Discipline: A Common Language for Classroom Management." *Beyond Behaviorism: Changing the Classroom Management Paradigm.* Ed. H.J. Freiberg. Boston: Allyn and Bacon. 98–118.
McFarland, Daniel A. (2004). "Resistance as a Social Drama: A Study of Change-Oriented Encounters." *American Journal of Sociology 109:* 1249–1319.
McWhorter, J. (2001). *Losing the Race: Self-Sabotage in Black America.* New York: HarperCollings Publishers.
Milner, M. (2004). *Freaks, Geeks, and Cool Kids: American Teenagers, Schools, and the Culture of Consumption.* New York: Routledge.
Miscevic, D.D. (2000). *Chinese Americans: The Immigrant Experience.* Southport, CT: Hugh Lauter Levin Associates.
Moldenhawer, B. (1999). "Turkish and Kurdish Speaking Teachers in the Danish Folkeskole: the Ambiguous Concept of Equality." *Scandinavian Journal of Educational Research* 43.4: 349–369.

Moore, Ami R. and Foster K. Amey (2002). "Earnings Differentials among Male African Immigrants in the United States." *Equal Opportunity International* 21.8: 30–50.

Mori, K. (1997). *Polite Lies: On Being a Woman Caught between Two Cultures*. New York: Henry Holt and Company.

Morrison, T. (1993). *Playing in the Dark: Whiteness and the Literary Imagination*. New York: Vintage Books.

Mucha, J.L. (1993). "An Outsider's View of American Culture." *Distant Mirrors: America as a Foreign Culture*. Ed. P.R. DeVita and J.D. Armstrong. Belmont, CA: Wadsworth Inc. 21–28.

Mufwene, S.S. (1993). "Forms of Addresses: How Their Social Functions May Vary." *Distant Mirrors: America as a Foreign Culture*. Ed. P.R. DeVita and J.D. Armstrong. Belmont, CA: Wadsworth Inc. 60–65.

Mukele, Victor (2009). "Headteacher 'Impregnates' Pupils, Flees." *Nation Media on the Web* 28 July 2009. www.standardmedia.co.ke/InsidePage.php?id=1144020192&cid=5271.

Mukuria, G. (2003). "Adventures in Turbulent Seas." *African Perspectives in American Higher Education: Invisible Voices*. Ed. F.E. Obiakor and J.U. Gordon. In Obiakor, F. E., and Gordon, J.U. (Eds.), *African Perspectives in American Higher Education: Invisible Voices*. (pp. 55–64). New York: Nova Science Publishers.

Mwaniki, M. (2008, September 10). Kenya: School Strikes Blamed on Staff Shortage. http://www.allafrica.com/stories/200809110317.

Mwololo, Millicent (2010). "The Big Show-Off that is School Visiting Day." *daily Nation on the Web* 6 October 2010. "http://mobile.nation.co.ke/The big show off that is school visiting day /-/1017178/1026332/-/uubr2qz/-/index.html" \t "_blank" http://mobile.nation.co.ke/The%20big%20show%20off%20that%20is%20school%20visiting%20day%20%20/-/1017178/1026332/-/uubr2qz/-/index.html

Natadecha-Sponsel, P. (1993). The Young, the Rich, and the Famous: Individualism as an American Cultural Value. *Distant Mirrors: America as a Foreign Culture*. Ed. P.R. DeVita and J.D. Armstrong. Belmont, CA: Wadsworth Inc. 46–53.

Nation Team (2010). "Crisis in Kenyan Schools as Ministry Delays Free Education Funds." http://www.nation.co.ke/New/Crisis%20in%20Kenyan%schools%20. 26 May 2010.

Ndurya, Mazera (2010). "http://www.nation.co.ke/News/500 teachers sent home for impregnating pupils/-/1056/1027034/-/q79fta/-/index.html" \t "_blank" 500 Teachers Sent Home for Impregnating Pupils. 6 October 2010.

Nieto, S. (2004). *Affirming Diversity: The Sociopolitical Context of Multicultural Education*. 4th ed. New York: Pearson.

Nord, Warren A. (2001). "Moral Disagreement, Moral Education, Common Ground." *Making Good Citizens: Education and Civil Society*. Ed. Diane Ravitch and Joseph P. Vieritti. New Haven: Yale University Press. 142–167.

Oberts, Sam (2010). "Census Figures Challenge Views of Race and Ethnicity." *New York Times* 22 Jan. 2010: A13.

Obiakor, F.E. (2003). "Through the Back Door: From Invisibility to Visibility." *African Perspectives in American Higher Education: Invisible Voices.* Ed. F.E. Obiakor and J.U. Gordon. New York: Nova Science Publishers. 1–10.
Obiakor, F.E., and M.O. Afolayan (2007). "African Immigrant Families in the United States: Surviving the Sociocultural Tide." *The Family Journal: Counseling and Therapy for Couples and Families.* 15.3: 265–270.
Obiakor, F.E. and J.U. Gordon, eds. (2003). *African Perspectives in American Higher Education: Invisible Voices.* New York: Nova Science Publishers.
——— and P.A. Grant, eds. (2002). *Foreign-Born African-Americans: Silenced Voices on the Discourse on Race.* New York: Nova Science Publishers.
O'Brien, Donal B. Cruise (1996). "A Lost Generation? Youth Identity and State Decay in West Africa." *Post-Colonial Identities in Africa.* Ed. Richard Werbner and Terence Ranger. London: Zed Books Ltd. 55–74.
Ogbu, J.U. (1992). "Understanding Cultural Diversity and Learning." *Educational Researcher* 21.8: 5–14, 24.
Ogulinck, K., ed. (2000). *Language Crossings: Negotiating the Self in a Multicultural World.* New York: Teachers College, Columbia University.
Ojeda, A.B. (1993). "Growing Up American: Doing the Right Thing." *Distant Mirrors: America as a Foreign Culture.* Ed. P.R. DeVita and J.D. Armstrong. Belmont, CA: Wadsworth Inc. 66–76.
Okome, Mojúbàolú Olúfúnké (forthcoming). "Nigerian Immigrants in the U.S.A." *Multicultural America: An Encyclopedia of the Newest Americans* [tentative title].
Okumu, Wafula (2010). "Our Matatu Mentality and a New Constitution." www.The-African.org 6: 28–30.
Oriang', Lucy (2010). "The Days of Rose-Tinted Glasses Are Truly Over." *Nation on the Web* 11 Feb. 2010. www.nation.co.ke/oped/opinion.
Otieno, Samuel and Ndungu Kangoro (2007). "Kenya: KNEC tough on examination cheating." http://allafrica.com/stories/2007110981.html.
Owolabi, Robert D. (1996). *An African's View of the American Society: An Eyewitness Account of Over 15 Years of Living, Studying and Working in the United States of America.* Chapel Hill, NC: Professional Press.
Patterson, O. (2006). "Poverty of the Mind." *New York Times* 26 Mar. 2006: WK13.
Pixten, R. (1993). "America for Americans." *Distant Mirrors: America as a Foreign Culture.* Ed. P.R. DeVita and J.D. Armstrong. Belmont, CA: Wadsworth Inc. 93–102.
Pogash, C. (2008). "Free School Lunch Isn't Cool, So Some Students Go Hungry." *New York Times* 1 Mar. 2008: A1, 14.
Portes, Alejandro and Rubén G. Rumbaut (2006). "Making it in America." *Immigrant America: A Portrait.* 2nd ed. Ed. Alejandro Portes. CA: University of California Press.
Putnam, Robert D. (2001). "Community-Based Social Capital and Educational Performance." *Making Good Citizens: Education and Civil Society.* Ed. Diane Ravitch and Joseph P. Vieritti. New Haven: Yale University Press. 58–95.

Prazak, Miroslava (2000). "Talking about Sex: Contemporary Construction of Sexuality in Rural Kenya." *Africa Today*. 47.3/4: 82–97.
Preston, Julia (2007). "Survey Points to Tensions Among Chief Minorities." *New York Times* 13 Dec. 2007: A33.
Ramos, F.M. (1993). "My American Glasses." *Distant Mirrors: America as a Foreign Culture*. Ed. P.R. DeVita and J.D. Armstrong. Belmont, CA: Wadsworth Inc. 1–10.
Ravitch, D. (1995). *National Standards in American Education: A Citizen's Guide*. Washington, DC: The Brookings Institute.
Ravitch, D. and J.P. Vieritti (2001). *Making Good Citizens: Education and Civil Society*. New Haven: Yale University Press.
Reitz, Jeffrey G., and Sherrilyn M. Sklar (1997). "Culture, Race, and the Economic Assimilation of Immigrants," *Sociological Forum* 12.2: 233–277.
Rich, Frank (2010). "If Only Arizona Were the Real Problem." *New York Times* 2 May 2010: WK10.
Robinson, G. (2004). "New York Schools: Fifty Years after Brown." *Gotham Gazette* 17 May 2004. http://www.gothamgazette.com/article/20040517/200/981.
Rogoff, Barbara, Ruth Paradise, Rebecca Mejia Arauz, Maricela Correa-Chávez, and Cathy Angelillo, eds. (2003). "Firsthand Learning Through Intent Participation." *Annual Review of Psychology*. 54: 175–203.
Salomone, Rosemary C. (2001). "Common Education and the Democratic Ideal." *Making Good Citizens: Education and Civil Society*. Ed. Diane Ravitch and Joseph P. Vieritti. New Haven: Yale University Press. 213–232.
Schmidt, Peter (2010). "Chief Targets of Student Incivility Are Female and Young Professors." *The Chronicles of Higher Education* 4 May 2010. Online.
Selcuk, Sirin and Michelle Fine (2008). *Muslim American Youth: Understanding Hyphenated Identities through Multiple Methods*. New York: New York University Press.
Sengupta, S. (2006). "Is Public Romance a Right? The Kama Sutra Doesn't Say." *New York Times* 6 Jan. 2006: A4.
Shor, Ira (1996). *When Students Have Power: Negotiating Authority in a Critical Pedagogy*. Chicago: The University of Chicago Press.
Siegel, Jessica (1996). "Pitching In Back Home." *New York Times* 7 Jan. 1996. Education Life Supplement. http://www.nytimes.com/1996/01/07/education/pitching-in-back-home.html.
Singhal, M. (2004). "Academic Writing and Generation 1.5: Pedagogical Goals and Instructional Issues in the College Composition Classroom." *The Reading Matrix* 4.3: 1–13.
Siringi, Samuel (2010). "School Heads Call for Review of Free Learning Programme as Funds Delay." 27 May 2010. http://www.nation.co.ke/-/1148.
Siringi, Samuel (2010). "Publishers and Ministry Wrangle over 8-4-4 Books." *Daily Nation on the Web* 5 May 2010. http://www.nation.co.ke/News/Publishers%20and%20ministry%20wrangle%20over%208444%20books%20/-/1056/924852/-/891qvh/-/index.html.

Siringi, Samuel (2009). "Shocking Details of Sex Abuse in Kenyan Schools." *Daily Nation on the Web* 1 Nov. 2009. http://nation.co.ke/news/-/1056/680450.

Sledge, Matt (2010, July 28). "http://www.huffingtonpost.com/matt-sledge/just-how-far-is-the-groun_b_660585.html" Just How Far Is the "Ground Zero Mosque" From Ground Zero?. http://www.huffingtonpost.com/matt-sledge/just-how-far-is-the-groun_b_660585.html.

Slee, Roger (1999). "Theorizing Discipline—Practical Research Implications for Schools." *Beyond Behaviorism: Changing the Classroom Management Paradigm*. Ed. H.J. Freiberg. Boston: Allyn and Bacon.

Smith, Daniel Jordan (2000). "'These Girls Today Na War-O': Premarital Sexuality and Modern Identity in Southeast Nigeria." *Africa Today*. 47.3/4: 99–120.

Somini, S. (2006). "In The Land of Kama Sutra, a Klamp Down on Romance? Police Beat Couples for Canoodling in Park." *New York Times*. 5 Jan. 2006.: A4.

Starzyk, Edith (2009, November, 21). Ohio Vies for Race to the Top Money for Education Reforms. http://blog.cleveland.com/metro/2009/11/ohio_vies_for_race_to_the_top.html.

Stefan, V. (2000). "Here's Your Change 'n' Enjoy the Show." *Language Crossings: Negotiating the Self in a Multicultural World*. Ed. Karen Ogulinck. New York: Teachers College, Columbia University. 21–29.

Stuart, H. (1996). "Introduction: Who needs 'Identity'?" *Questions of Cultural Identity*. Ed. H. Stuart and P. Du Gay. London: SAGE Publications. 1–17.

Takyi, Baffour K. 2002. "The Making of the Second Diaspora: On the Recent African Immigrant Community in the United States of America," *Western Journal of Black Studies* 26.1: 32–43.

Tatum, B.D. (1997). "Why Are All the Black Kids Sitting Together in the Cafeteria: And Other Conversations about Race." New York: Basic Books.

Thomas, Lynn M. (2000). "'The Politics of the Womb': Kenyan Debates over the Affiliation Act." *Africa Today* 47.3/4: 150–176.

Thornton, Robert (1996). "The Potentials of Boundaries in South Africa: Steps Towards a Theory of Social Change." *Post-Colonial Identities in Africa*. Ed. Richard Werbner and Terence Ranger. London: Zed Books Ltd. 136–162.

Tileston, Donna Walker (2003). *What Every Teacher Should Know about Classroom Management and Discipline*. Thousand Oaks, CA: Corwin Press.

Traore, R. and R.J. Lukens (2006). *"This Isn't the America I Thought I'd Find": African Students in the Urban U.S. High School*. Lanham, MD: University Press of America.

Uwah, G.O. (2003). "A Complex Web of Acceptance and Misgiving: My Journey in American Higher Education." *African Perspectives in American Higher Education: Invisible Voices*. Ed. F.E. Obiakor and J.U. Gordon. New York: Nova Science Publishers. 65–73.

Uwah, G.O. (2002). "Reflections of an African-Born Immigrant: Story of Alienation." Eds.). *Foreign-Born African-Americans: Silenced Voices on the Discourse on Race*. Ed. F.E. Obiakor and P.A. Grant. New York: Nova Science Publishers. 11–19.

Viteritti, Joseph P. (2001). "Risking Choice, Redressing Inequality." *Making Good Citizens: Education and Civil Society.* Ed. Diane Ravitch and Joseph P. Vieritti. New Haven: Yale University Press. 344–346.

Walkerdine, Valerie (1990). *Schoolgirl Fictions.* New York: Verso.

Wasserfall, R. (1993). "Gender Encounters in America: An Outsider's View of Continuity and Ambivalence." *Distant Mirrors: America as a Foreign Culture.* Ed. P.R. DeVita and J.D. Armstrong. Belmont, CA: Wadsworth Inc. 103–111.

Index

Abebe, T. 50, 53, 76, 145
academic excellence 31, 52, 57, 75, 78, 101, 118, 164
academic performance 15, 30–31, 61, 79, 85, 93, 113, 117, 153, 165
accents 6, 16, 20–22, 47, 50, 62–67, 71, 73, 75, 115, 141
accountability ix, 12, 21, 67, 100, 123, 140, 147, 163, 157
Achebe, Chinua 1, 2–3, 7, 10, 18–19, 24, 26, 27, 35, 39, 46–48, 55–56, 82, 157, 172, 176
adolescence 68, 108, 155, 165
African-American x, 5–6, 13, 17–18, 44, 48–49, 51–55, 58, 62–63, 65, 67–68, 70, 91, 97, 101, 104, 113, 117, 132, 139, 170, 178
African immigrants x, 4–6, 11–13, 16, 19, 21–24, 40, 48, 50–52, 54, 58–59, 61, 66, 68–70, 84, 89, 109, 113, 118, 121, 126, 134–135, 157, 162, 168–169, 174, 176
   teachers 10–11, 16, 18, 20, 24, 29, 30, 41, 51, 68, 71–72, 75, 77, 84, 88, 92, 94, 97–98, 100–101, 107, 110, 114, 123, 126, 130, 157, 159–160, 173, 175–180
alienation 10, 11, 15, 16, 21, 23, 28, 45, 114, 156, 157
Aman, Mohammed 12–13, 35, 52, 94
American Federation of Teachers 16, 71–73

Amobi, F. A. x, 23, 67, 85, 145, 156, 177
Appiah, K. A. 1, 3–4, 7, 10–11, 18–19, 23, 47–51, 55–56, 63, 65, 70–71, 88, 104, 107–108, 112, 118, 143, 147, 151, 156, 167, 170, 174–175, 177
Apple, Michael W. 15–17, 58, 68, 77–78, 80, 82, 95, 170
Armstrong, J. D. x, 10, 16, 84, 110
Asian/Chinese Americans 7–8, 20, 57–59, 65, 79, 81–83, 110, 117–118, 164, 167, 169
Assimilation 3, 15, 24, 26–28, 62, 65, 71, 103, 112–113, 180

Badillo, H. 18, 79, 100, 128, 145, 163, 167
Blackness 1–2, 4, 18, 27, 76, 156
Blacks 4, 6, 8, 12–13, 16–17, 45, 51–55, 58–59, 62, 68, 76, 82, 117, 164, 173
Borjas, George J. 3–4, 13, 15–16, 19, 48, 63, 65, 79, 128, 154, 167–168
British 2, 8–9, 24, 26–28, 38, 64, 66, 177

classrooms 17, 35, 41, 57, 66–67, 76, 80, 85, 101, 106, 121, 130, 134, 157, 162–163, 167, 172, 178
cliques 39, 43, 118, 122, 128, 136, 137, 142, 151
colonial 1–2, 12, 18–20, 24, 26–28, 38, 49, 56, 64, 97, 157, 167, 175–176
consumerism 4, 50, 125–126, 128, 135
cross cultural exchanges 70–71, 124, 149, 179

Index

cultural
　accommodation 102, 118, 123, 156, 168
　adaptation 16, 19, 50, 78, 88, 118–119, 169, 173–175
　differences ix, 12, 16–18, 20–24, 38, 41, 105, 108, 121, 159
　identities 1, 18, 52, 55, 58, 62–63, 136, 167, 174, 179–180
　insider 48, 63, 68, 118
　outsider 10, 45, 63, 71, 79, 112, 118, 157, 168
cultural relevant pedagogy 15, 18, 53, 156, 161, 167, 169
culture 3, 8–12, 17–20, 22, 25–26, 32, 34, 45, 49, 54–56, 58, 62, 69–70, 72–73, 80, 87, 95, 100–101, 104, 108, 109–112, 115, 118–119, 122, 125, 127, 129, 132, 141–143, 147, 150–151, 160, 162–164, 167, 169, 172–173, 179–181

Damon, William 87, 100–101, 109, 145
Delpit, L. D. 1, 10, 18, 31, 63, 156, 160
DeVita, P. R. x, 10, 16, 84, 110
Discipline 19, 21, 29, 32, 44, 69, 71, 85, 87, 95, 97–98, 101, 103–104, 107–110, 112, 142, 150, 160, 162, 177–178, 182
Disparities 20–25, 33, 39, 41, 62, 66, 72, 75, 79–81, 84, 86, 106, 117, 121–123, 127, 148, 162, 168–171
Diversity 12, 20–21, 41, 59, 62, 65, 71, 74, 81, 83, 96, 106, 109, 137, 178–179
Dodoo, F. Nii-Amoo 49, 59, 62, 66–68, 85
Duster, Troy 13, 17, 29, 160

Examinations 21, 25, 28–31, 33–35, 38, 76, 159, 182

Fast, Gerald R. 31, 56, 92, 108, 111, 175–176

Foreign-borns 7, 16, 22, 54, 61, 73–74, 87, 133
Foster, M. 15, 26, 62–63, 161–162, 178
French 22, 24, 26, 27, 54, 56, 64, 70, 77, 174

Gay, G. 10, 15, 117, 161
Giroux, Henry 10, 12, 17, 21, 75, 78, 82, 94–95, 102, 106, 112, 115, 117, 122, 149, 153–154, 156, 160, 169–170, 176
Glazer, Nathan 68, 113, 145, 170
Globalization 10, 124–125, 127, 169
Gottschalk, Peter 26, 58, 67, 171–172
Grades 17–18, 21, 25, 29, 31, 46, 76, 78, 83, 91, 98, 138, 145, 153, 157–158, 161, 163, 166
Greenberg, Gabriel Gross, T. 26, 58, 67, 171–172

Hemmings, A. 45, 87–88, 105–107, 112–113, 115–116, 118, 155–156, 168, 178
Holmes, Mark 68, 87, 101, 106, 112–113, 145, 160, 165
hooks, bell 3, 6, 10, 12, 18, 21–22, 37, 52, 58, 62–63, 65, 82, 95, 121, 126, 128–129, 132, 154, 160–161, 170, 173, 175, 178
Huntington, Samuel P. 6, 8, 12, 17, 65, 116, 173

imperialism 2, 10, 170–172
individualism 111, 125, 147, 151, 165, 173, 180

Kenya ix, 2–3, 18, 20–22, 24–41, 43, 47–49, 53, 55–56, 63–67, 68, 76, 79, 83–86, 91, 97, 99, 109, 111, 123–125, 127–128, 130, 135, 138, 141, 143–144, 147, 150, 152, 158, 173–174, 181–182
Kim, J. K. 16, 110–111, 139, 147

Lane, K. L. 17, 45, 107, 113, 115, 153
languages 3, 12, 21–22, 27–29, 56, 65, 70, 94, 156, 173
liberties 40, 91, 99, 111, 131, 143, 156

Martin, J. R. 10, 12, 16, 45, 66, 75, 82, 140, 149, 156, 175
McCarthy, Cameron 1, 10, 15, 18, 117, 164
McFarland, Daniel A. 44, 112, 115, 153–156
McWhorter, J. 11, 18, 53, 58, 62, 79, 101, 128, 163–164, 167
Milner, M. 17–18, 44, 96, 101, 104, 115, 128–129, 132, 136–137, 139–142, 150–151, 155, 165, 178
minorities 15, 20, 49, 52–53, 82, 117, 164, 167, 172
Mori, K. 55, 62, 81, 84, 89, 96, 98–100, 110, 115, 145, 150, 156–157, 162, 168, 170
Morrison, T. 1–2, 7, 10–11, 13, 18, 63, 117, 173
Motivation 29, 57, 73, 102, 105, 147

Nieto, Sonia 1, 11, 15, 22, 63, 161
Nord, Warren A. 78, 100–101, 170

obedience 9, 72, 77, 106, 109
Obiakor, F. E. X. 1, 16, 23, 44, 49–50, 52, 54, 64, 66, 76, 84, 89, 108–110, 135
Ogbu, J. U. 1, 11, 17, 53, 82, 96–97, 164, 168
Okumu, Wafula 39, 48, 125, 135
Owolabi, Robert D. 3–4, 7, 16, 22–23, 47, 49–50, 53, 63, 65, 67, 89, 92, 110, 126, 134, 156

parents xi, 5, 7, 25, 29, 32–34, 36–39, 41, 43, 48, 51, 53, 58, 61, 68, 72, 77, 79–80, 86–87, 96–99, 109, 112, 114–115, 121, 125, 128, 130–131, 137, 139, 144–147, 152, 156–157, 177, 179
peers 17, 39, 66, 68, 97, 106–107, 115, 126, 128, 132, 136, 138, 142, 159, 178–179
see also cliques
personal space 129–130, 150, 165, 168

racism 13, 18, 39, 48, 51, 82, 91, 100, 102, 163, 178
Ravitch, Diane ix, 15, 18, 21, 68, 75–81, 84, 98, 145, 160
religion 9, 39, 48, 54, 101, 167, 172–173, 179
responsibility 55, 62, 84, 89, 93, 100, 102, 106, 109, 118, 134, 140–141, 149, 169–170, 175, 177
role models 61, 74, 79, 161

Shor, Ira 12, 17–18, 43, 82, 112, 115, 149, 154, 170
social hierarchies 2–4, 6, 9–10, 81, 103, 172, 177
social interactions 10, 16, 19–20, 22–23, 41, 52, 53–55, 58, 103–107, 111, 118, 136–137, 153–154, 168, 175, 178
social status 57, 66, 75, 86, 97, 116, 121–122, 151
socialization xi, 12, 21, 24, 44, 121, 145, 148–149
standard English 22, 63, 65, 160, 163
standards ix, x, 3, 5, 15, 20–21, 25, 30–31, 33, 42–44, 53, 55, 66, 72, 75–79, 82–85, 89–90, 101–102, 114, 121, 127, 150, 153–154, 157, 160–163, 176
stereotypes 4, 20, 49, 54, 58, 62, 64, 70, 73–74, 139, 167, 170, 176

Tatum, B. D. 1, 3, 18, 52, 57–58, 64, 68, 82, 97, 169, 174, 178–179
testing 1, 25, 34, 44, 80, 98, 115, 155
see also Examinations

Traore and Lukens, R. 1, 3, 6, 13, 32, 45, 47, 49–50, 54, 66–68, 76, 84, 98, 108–111, 135, 179

Uwah, G. O. 6, 10, 52, 53, 65, 76–77, 111, 173–174

Violence 29, 47, 99, 116, 124, 181
Viteritti, Joseph P. 15, 75–76, 78, 80, 113, 145

Walkerdine, Valerie 10, 12, 106, 156
Whiteness 1, 3–4, 6, 10, 13, 18, 172, 176
Whites 1, 5, 7, 9, 13, 27–28, 58–59, 62, 68, 82, 169, 175
Willis, Paul 11, 82, 99, 101, 115, 151
Women 12, 45, 49–50, 57, 82, 97, 103–104, 106, 131, 133, 138, 143–144, 172–173, 182

GPSR Compliance

The European Union's (EU) General Product Safety Regulation (GPSR) is a set of rules that requires consumer products to be safe and our obligations to ensure this.

If you have any concerns about our products, you can contact us on

ProductSafety@springernature.com

In case Publisher is established outside the EU, the EU authorized representative is:

Springer Nature Customer Service Center GmbH
Europaplatz 3
69115 Heidelberg, Germany

www.ingramcontent.com/pod-product-compliance
Lightning Source LLC
LaVergne TN
LVHW011822060526
838200LV00053B/3873